1 MONTH OF
FREE
READING

at

www.ForgottenBooks.com

By purchasing this book you are
eligible for one month membership to
ForgottenBooks.com, giving you
unlimited access to our entire
collection of over 700,000 titles via
our web site and mobile apps.

To claim your free month visit:

www.forgottenbooks.com/free435530

ISBN 978-0-428-67783-1
PIBN 10435530

0

PRACTICAL ECONOMY;

OR, THE

APPLICATION

OF

MODERN DISCOVERIES

TO THE

PURPOSES

OF

DOMESTIC LIFE.

Second Edition.

LONDON:

HENRY COLBURN & CO.

CONDUIT STREET, HANOVER SQUARE.

1822.

LONDON:

SHACKELL AND ARROWSMITH, JOHNSON'S COURT, FLEET STREET.

PREFACE.

THERE is, perhaps, no subject so much talked of, or so little understood, as that of DOMESTIC ECONOMY.

When FRANKLIN wrote "To Save is to Gain," he left a text for future writers capable of much expansion. To SAVE, is one thing, TO ECONOMIZE is another. Absolutely to avoid expense, is to preclude enjoyment; but to economize expenditure, is to unite enjoyment with prudence.

The ultimate point of saving money, is often best attained by a route not, apparently, the most direct; nay, sometimes by an expenditure which, at first sight, may seem superfluous. A man, to save time, may begin building a house, without plan or preparation; but how much time will be afterwards wasted, and temper expended, in the endeavour to render it comfortable and convenient?

TRUE ECONOMY consists not in saving, merely; but in adapting every thing to its specific use; by which much is enjoyed at a small expense.

b 3

It is in this that the real secret of Economy is to be found. Any man may retrench his house expenses, if he please, by dispensing with a necessary meal; but will the saving recompense the deprivation? May not that very attempt at economy produce other and far greater expenses? And will not he be the true Economist, who seeks to preserve appearances, yet contrives to save, even whilst he enjoys?

Again, as to the situation most favorable to Economy: some may think it better practised in France than at home. But instead of going to an enemy's country, (for such it always must be) to live cheap, is it not better to practice the art of living cheap in our own?

Who need go to France to avoid observation whilst aiming at economy, when they can avail themselves of much more retirement in their native country? But " *house rent* is cheap in France," and so it is in Devonshire, or in Cumberland— but " *wine* also is cheap in France!" and so may the retired economist in England drink wine of his own making, from the foreign imported grape or raisin, much better, and equally cheap, with the *vin ordinaire* of the restaurateur, or the ill-prepared refuse of the ordinary vintage.

But education is cheaper in France than at home!—this we doubt; provided the parent can suppress his vanity, and abstain from sending his boys to RUGBY or ETON—and why should we be more ashamed of a cheap school in England than in France, especially when we recollect that one country affords an *English*, the other a *French* education? If a parent educates his offspring from infancy to boyhood in a French provincial town, how can he at a future day expect from them either patriotic exertion or self-devotion for a country with which they are not connected by a single idea of juvenile recollection? But if the subject is so serious in regard to boys, how much more so to females? Will the whiffling, sibilant Parisian pronunciation be a counterbalance for the want of those mild virtues that spring up round an English fire-side? We put the question pointedly; let our fair countrywomen answer it to themselves candidly.

It is chiefly for THEM that we have undertaken our task, to unite elegance with economy, not only in the highest, but in the middle walks of life; and to shew that good old English housewifery is still a good old English virtue.

But we confine not ourselves to the old family receipt book. We are aware that one great object of *philosophy* is to improve our condition in this world, as religion is to fit us for the next: we therefore feel the propriety of bringing it forward in the most popular shape. In fact, there is not a single point in DOMESTIC ECONOMY that does not depend, more or less, upon philosophical principles. But the gay world is terrified at the name of philosophy in a didactic work, though pleased with it in a lecture room ; and why so?—simply because that, like freemasonry, it has too long been the fashion to make it both incomprehensible and alarming.

Let it be our task, then, to produce a familiar application of philosophy; or rather to display the art of making philosophy useful : and, in order to do so, it has been our object to avail ourselves of all those modern discoveries that can be applied to the improvement of human life. If it requires the power of nature to produce a feather, we should not be ashamed to apply even the greatest of her forces, if necessary, in arranging that feather, and in making it useful or ornamental, as may be required.

———

₊ Any hints or communications connected with the objects of this work, addressed to the Publishers, will be thankfully received, and duly attended to in a future edition.

CONTENTS.

SECTION I.

RESIDENCES.

SECTION II.

PRINCIPAL APARTMENTS.

SECTION III.

AUXILIARY APARTMENTS.

SECTION IV.

DOMESTIC OFFICES.

SECTION V.

STORE OFFICES.

SECTION VI.

EXTERNAL CONVENIENCES.

SECTION VII.

GENERAL OBSERVATIONS.

PRACTICAL ECONOMY.

—◆—

SECTION I.

—

RESIDENCES.

—

The DWELLING-HOUSE—*Preliminary Considerations—Style — Safety— Architecture — Situation — Soil— Water — Materials — Chimnies — Roofing —Floors.* CLEANLINESS—*Dry Rot —Inside Walls — Papers —Carpets—Furniture.* VENTILATION—*Air Funnels — Smokey Chimnies.* HEAT —*Stoves—Firelamps.* ILLUMINATION—*Gas-lights— Reflectors— Lamps—Chemical Ignition, &c.*

To ensure the certain and convenient practice of Domestic Economy, much depends not only on the style and situation of our family residence, but also on the arrangement of the building; its capability of judicious alteration or extension when required, the actual state of its materials, and its facility of repair when such may become necessary.

These are objects of the first consideration to all who may be either about to build or to rent a

B

habitation; and though we sit not down to compose a treatise on architecture or on leaseholds, yet we may help our readers to economize, if the following hints should induce them to pause and consider before they adopt a plan or hire a house; and to reflect that a little time, spent in careful investigation at the outset, may ultimately produce a considerable saving both in time and money : whilst a hasty choice might have forced them to increased cost in correcting a faulty plan; or, to the trouble and vexatious expenditure connected with the removal from an inconvenient residence, after, perhaps, months of labour and dissatisfaction in fruitless attempts at a more comfortable arrangement.

That these considerations are seldom totally neglected must be allowed; but they are too often coupled solely with the query, " will the house suit me?" forgetting another necessary inquiry, " shall I suit the house?"

This, however, is not so much a matter of fact, as a matter of *taste*—a word which has caused more useless expense in London and its vicinity, than would have formed a handsome sinking-fund for the payment of the national debt.— Nor would even this be a subject of actual complaint; provided such extra expenditure, however injudiciously incurred, had tended to the encouragement of laborious industry, which, in a populous country, must always depend for its reward in a great measure upon the luxuries of the more opulent. But, instead of this, whilst the positive quantity of labour has been scarcely, if at all, increased, a non-descript class of buildings has been run up, neither ornamental in the exterior, nor convenient within, yet much more expensive to preserve in order than larger houses, whose absolute taxes seldom exceed, and sometimes do not equal those of the gaudy, ill-arranged, insignificant villas, with lawns of ten feet in front, and shrubberies which afford not covering even to a duck-pond.

In short, as has been well observed upon this subject, taste consists neither in the flimsy, expensive style so much in vogue, nor in the absurd saving of expense in roofing, which has produced so many cottages four stories high, between Holloway and Dulwich. Good taste will always be careful that the house and grounds, whether upon a large or small scale, shall be in due proportion with each other; that, as the mansion ought to harmonize in exterior and interior, both in regard to the arrangement and size of its apartments, so ought the out-of-door conveniences and ornaments, such as gates, paling, walls, rails, &c. to harmonize with the size and distribution of the grounds. Ornaments, ill-placed, lose their effect; and, if too numerous, become a nuisance. Here then is a sure basis for present and future savings; if it shall be recollected, in preparing plans, that the great art required for a building of moderate dimensions is to proportion the decorations to the space they are destined to fill, so that they may not by their multiplicity, or disproportionable size, disfigure and encumber that which they were intended to adorn.

Whilst on this part of the subject, let us not forget the absurdity of applying the same species of ornament to all kinds of edifices, whether public offices, churches, buildings, or *mausolea*. As an idle boy at school acquires the bad trick of writing only from one copy, so an architect may become bigotted to his favourite ornament, and all this he may think in taste; but the world must judge whe. ther or not it is a good taste.

If we look for the origin of the choice and distribution of ornament, as directed by true taste, we shall find it to arise from a judicious idea of the rich and simple beauties of nature. But if we look for it around the metropolis, we might be tempted to suppose that expense, not taste, is the parent of beauty; were it not that the ugliness of the offspring, so misnamed, speedily calls us back to her real pedigree.

Too much expense has also been often incurred, both in town and country, in sacrificing to the ambition of producing novelty: without reflecting that a happy imitation is of more real value than a defective original, which, like an usurious bond, speedily doubles the principal, by annual charges. This is a useful hint for the *builder*, whilst even the *architect* may console himself with the reflection, " that to copy excellence in spirit and in character is at all times a test of no mean ability." Let *both* consider *what* it is, and for *whom*, they are going to build; let them consider that it will be an important saving in time and in expense, if, when the plan, as a plan for a good house, be perfect, they also reflect, whether the intended resident will suit the house. To produce illustrations of this, is not easy, without running the risk of being thought invidious, whilst only striving to be intelligible; but our readers may recollect many instances where the uncomfortableness of a mansion has depended more upon its tenant than upon the house itself.

If taste is, as has been well defined, a just relation of parts in forming a whole accordant with the use and purpose of the building; so may it be added, that it is also a just relation between the habitation and the occupant. Bad taste will, however, sometimes forget, in its fondness for ornaments, the original and obvious intentions of buildings, by affected imitations of something incongruous, or by the paltry attempts at disguising particular objects, which, in fact, only render them more conspicuous, making the disgust counterbalance the convenience. Hence arise steeples upon stables, and Gothic battlements upon summer-houses, with Rialtos thrown across puddles which a lively frog would hop over.

There is also another very important point that ought to be sedulously attended to in the erection of buildings, whether in town or country, and in the examination of premises which it may be intended to rent—the saving of lives in case of fire.

A correspondent of a weekly journal recently observed, with reference to the many fatal accidents which have lately happened, that the present mode of building adopted by gentlemen in their country residences, is the best that could possibly be invented to give success to a fire: story raised over story, timber piled upon timber, and the kitchen underneath, bonfire fashion. He animadverts on the absurdity of having the nursery at the top of the house, while the parents themselves sleep one or two stories underneath. " What is the consequence," he continues, " in case of fire in the night? Why this—the children in the nursery have no chance of escape, the parents have very little, and that little is of course lost by their anxiously rushing up stairs for their children. Now, it appears to me, the sensible way to erect a house is, to make it only one story high, and let the children sleep on the ground-floor, and the parents in an adjoining room ;

let the kitchen be detached from the house, so that they may sleep in safety; and thus have a prospect of raising up a family with straight legs and bodies, for more than half the children we see crooked and deformed have been made so by accidents on staircases."

This, however, is, generally speaking, impracticable from want of space, and would be an unnecessary increase of expense, when the simple plan of dividing a house by party-walls in its centre, with double staircases, where there is room, and a clear communication between each, might be found equally efficacious, at least in all ordinary cases. But this part of the subject shall be noticed more fully under the head of *Domestic Accidents:* at present let us proceed to the great point of economy, which depends upon the judicious selection of style in regard to the conveniences it may afford, without any palpable necessity for an absolute departure from it in the making a house habitable: for many a mansion may be striking to the view, whilst to the resident it is a constant and never-failing source of expense and distress.

If we really wish to imitate the ancients, we ought to adopt not only their classic style, but also their shrewdness and common sense, and not forget, that what we often introduce solely as ornamental, was with the Greeks and Romans a useful thing ornamented.

Porticos and piazzas are useful for shade and air in the warm climates of Greece or Italy; but are little wanted in front of a mansion where half the year is passed by the fire-side. In palaces, indeed, even in this cold climate, they may be allowable; or where ornament is really and appropriately the first consideration: but in houses designed chiefly for domestic purposes, they are worse than useless. How often does this rage for architectural ornament strike at the root of that income which would otherwise have been expended under its shelter ? How many have been involuntarily led into frivolous, yet devouring expenditure, solely by taking a house unfit for them, doubling their taxes and their necessity for servants, whilst their inconveniences and expences increase in a mutual ratio.

It ought to be remembered, whilst we endeavour to keep the love of ornament within the limits of economy, that it is not quite impossible to combine the advantages of an English arrangement with all the beauty and grace of a Palladian or Vitruvian plan. Pure Grecian architecture, even as exhibited in its native soil, transcendently chaste and beautiful as it may be, is yet somewhat liable to the imputation of a monotonous correctness; consequently deviations from it, where their use is apparent, may produce beauty instead of incongruous deformity. But these deviations must be solely useful and not ornamental; for though in Greece and Italy it is only necessary to keep off the direct rays of the sun, or the tempestuous shower, whilst the surrounding air is rather grateful than otherwise, whence came the high raised roof, the open portico, and the lengthened colonnade, yet was there no absolute incongruity on the introduction of that mode into colder countries, in attending to the necessity of filling up the interstices with solid work, so that the side walls actually support the roofs, rendering pillars, pilasters, and columns totally unnecessary for any purpose but that of ornament. But in preserving unnecessary ornament, it must be considered, that real beauty in architecture, from the palace to the cottage, will always be most judiciously and most cheaply produced by discarding all that is superfluous, and bestowing decoration on that only which is really useful.

But if *Classic Architecture* has been misunderstood in its character and application, thereby causing much unnecessary expense, the *Gothic* has been, and is likely to be much more so. Perhaps the shortest mode of keeping it within rational bounds, by lessening the number of its imitators, would be to render it at once unfashionable by investigating the origin of the term. Yet it is a term which minds of taste and feeling will admire, and consider as possessing a secret charm: we wish not then to shock their feelings, though puny imitators may thence shrink from it, when we record that the term " Gothic," though sanctioned by habit, and though having now acquired a value from the idea being combined with all those sentiments which arise in the breast on contemplating the castles of our ancestors, and the religious piles where devotion and superstition went hand in hand, and where a warm imagination may even suppose it sees the spirit of departed times glide solemnly through the gloomy aisles, was originally nothing more than a word of contempt, applied by the Italians on the revival of classic architecture, to express what we do by the term " barbarous:" the one being metaphorically drawn from the Goths of ancient Europe, the other from the savage inhabitants of the northern districts of Africa.

Whilst endeavouring then to save money that might have been uselessly expended upon Gothic brewhouses and Saracenic pigsties, we may also encourage the beautifying the face of the country, in general, by investigating the most judicious adoption of situation, and the most economic modes of procedure, if taste, or fashion shall propel to the erection of a Gothic mansion, or to the remodelling of one already built, on the sheer principles of economy in pounds, shillings and pence; inasmuch as money injudiciously laid out in an improper place, and needlessly expended in misapplied ornament, is money thrown away, or worse: since what is only lost may be forgotten, but the same sum raised into a monument of folly, is certain to expose the individual to the derision even of his most ignorant neighbours in addition to his own vexation. Well has it been observed by a modern writer, that the Gothic shows how the rules of classic architecture may be violated or forgotten, whilst in itself it has a character of originality, which, in its general and complete effects, surprises until we become enchanted with its influence. This, at once, points out that situations in which the Grecian style would be appropriate, are by no means fitted for the Gothic: nor must we combine the one with the other in the same building, since the regularity of Grecian architecture would be incongruous with the wild sublimity of Gothic vastness.

The Gothic often receives the most absurd misapplication from our forgetting that nothing ought to be Gothic but what existed, or had a counterpart in feudal times. For instance, we may have a Gothic library, but a Gothic hothouse would be an anachronism. Gothic walls with modern casements are also absurd, independent of their admitting too much light into the interior; but when the casements are pointed, and filled with lozenged glass, particularly if of a green tinge, then the sombre tints modify the general light, and blend the ornaments of the interior,

if due keeping be preserved, into a mass of exquisite richness. But the grand features of the Gothic
are vastness, irregularity and sublimity, especially
in the castellar mode, which ought not to be blend-
ed with the cathedral, or ecclesiastical order.
The grand features of Gothic sublimity are the
height and extent of the edifice, and the vast masses of wall, unbroken either by cornice or window
frame, or else so broken by buttresses and turrets,
as to give those masses an appearance of much
greater extent than they really possess. Where windows do occur in the castellar Gothic, they are
always distant from the ground, always distant from
each other, and always irregular in their disposition; but, with this impression on the mind, who
can forbear laughing at those things called Gothic
villas, and Gothic summer-houses, surrounded by
the trim nicety of civic, or suburban gardens and
flower-plats, which line the roads in all' directions
within the limits of the short stages round the
metropolis !

But having thus pointed out how to save money,
by avoiding absolute expenditure upon the absurd
and the incongruous, it may be expected that we
shall also point out how money is to be saved where
it may be fairly expended: and we must confess,
that, if science can really contribute to the happiness
of mankind, it can never be better applied than in
this department, since our real comforts are pro-
verbially and very properly sought for at our own
firesides: and we have, therefore, every inducement to direct all the means of philosophy to the
increase of domestic happiness.

But it is much to be regretted that our habitations in general, from the lowly cottage to the
superb palace, have hitherto been constructed with-

out any apparent regard to those principles that may afford the greatest comfort to the occupants; for whilst in the exterior the architect seldom aims at more than the perfection of just proportion in outline, the disposition of the interior is entrusted to artists who, in furniture and decorations, seem only anxious about the taste and fashion of their labours, rendering their proceedings to be rather in the style of incumbrances than of convenience or utility: inasmuch as that, which was at first solely tolerated because it was fashionable, retains all its imperfections when that charm is gone, and the unfortunate possessor must either put up with want of comfort and want of fashion, or else incur a new expense in procuring that whose day of glory will in like manner fade away, prompting to new expense, or subjecting to renewed inconvenience.

We wish not, however, to stop the hand of luxury even in this. Where a superabundance of wealth prompts to an expenditure that gives support to industry, we hail it as a blessing to a community so populous as our own—as a saving, a material saving in fact to the public at large, since sums thus expended, if withdrawn from circulation, would consign thousands of families, especially in the metropolis, to idleness, beggary, and the poor's rates. Consequently this individual expense becomes a general saving, and leaves us no cause of regret for the sums expended, but only for the absolutely improper and immoral use to which they may sometimes be applied.

The first object to be considered, either in building or renting a habitation, must be its site. It must be remembered, that however well cleared and cultivated a country may be, yet the current of air passing over a large tract of land, is never so pure, or at least so healthy, as that which passes over the ocean.

Altitude, so long considered as securing the purest air, is now proved by chemical experience, to be of no importance in itself; the quantity of oxygen and azote being pretty equal in the centre of the largest towns, and even at a mile above their surface. With respect to moisture or dryness, indeed, altitude is an object of importance; as even in the dryest soils, though the valley is warmer than the hills, yet there the transitions from heat to cold are greater, and there will always be the greatest portion of moisture in the air, unless there be a thorough vent in the quarter of the most customary winds. Gentle rising grounds, not the highest, are then the best situations upon the whole; for in moist vallies we inhale more hydrogen with the atmospheric air, and if elevated above all, the house is exposed to every blast, and must be colder than is always agreeable: though even there, great melioration may be expected from planting for shelter, and from active cultivation in the immediate vicinity, which always has a more extensive effect than would readily be imagined.

If the neighbourhood of the metropolis be the field of the builder's wishes, it will be proper not only to consider what the place is, but what it may become. If a man retires a short distance from town for fresh air and cheerful meditations, he will not choose the immediate vicinity of a burying-ground; but how often does it happen that, although the man does not go to the burying-ground, the burying-ground comes to him; and that the pleasing cheerfulness of his retirement is thus broken in upon by an unwelcome visitant—but this is a grave subject: we quit it therefore for other, grievances, such as the dye-vats, glue-frames, founderies, tan-yards, patriotic tea-manufactories, chemical laboratories, and other nuisances, which often tend to the manifest deterioration of those places towards which we are looking for an increase of our domestic comforts.

As every one who retires into the country, though but for a few months in the year, may wish to hold some land in useful occupation, he will naturally be solicitous to know the quality of the soil, before he either purchases, builds, or rents. To ascertain the exact quality of land, requires, indeed, considerable practice and experience: but a general idea may be formed by the simple experiment of turning up a turf, pouring some soft water on it, and kneading it with the fingers, when a kind of adhesiveness will be perceived in proportion to its fertility. It will be proper also to ascertain the depth of good soil, by digging small trenches in different places, when this simple rule will suffice for general judgment. If the soil dug from any trench, does not refill it, then the land is bad: if it fills up the space exactly, then the land is middling. But if the trench shall be not only filled, but heaped, then the soil may be considered as rich and excellent. It must be added, however, that this rule is not strictly applicable to stiff clay or marl.

On such a soil, and on a slight elevation to guard against dampness, a man may fix without danger of inconvenience; provided he pays some attention to a proper supply of water, so that it shall neither be too much nor too little, and at all times under his own control.

Of all adventitious circumstances, indeed, perhaps the first is water, not only in regard to quantity, but to its chemical qualities. In building a house, therefore, in a new situation, it may be well first to chuse the spot, and then to dig for a well; by which means the expense may often be saved of trying the foundation for that purpose merely.

To impress the importance of this consideration upon our readers, we may throw out a few chemical reasons for the necessity of examination, as well as a few of the simplest chemical tests for ascertaining the question, on which depends so much of the health and comfort of our household, and of domestic convenience and domestic economy. Persons unacquainted with the chemical powers of water, as a solvent, may suppose that the effects produced by foreign matters, with which it may be impregnated, cannot be of any great importance. But a moment's reflection on what they feel after drinking hard water, or on the difficulty they experience even in washing their hands with it, will serve to convince the most incredulous that even a pint of water may contain that which is injurious to the human system. These hard waters always contain saline and earthy substances, and are invariably hurtful in diseases of the kidney; besides their being inapplicable to culinary purposes in many instances, and particularly so, where the beer-cellar is to be stocked with home-brewed. Even at the tea-table they fail to extract the high flavour of the fragrant Chinese leaf; and in the wash-house they require the additional expence of vegetable alkalies to counteract their rigidity, and to neutralize their salts for the convenience of ablution.

For the kitchen, soft water is indeed invaluable, whilst hard water only spoils the produce of the garden. Spring-water in some counties is much harder than in others, dependent upon the soil from whence it flows. How easily water may be rendered hard by the soil through which it percolates, may be drawn from the chemical fact that distilled rain-water can be made as hard as the hardest spring-water, by the addition only of one two-thousandth part of its quantity.

To judge of water it may be observed that it is purest when flowing over granite or gravel, or those rocky soils which geologists call primitive. When first taken up, good water will be transparent; and the examiner is not to be content with looking through a drinking glass filled with the element, but ought to have the deepest ale-glass into which he may look downwards, when the slightest tinge from extraneous substances will infallibly appear. Rain-water requires only mechanical care in its collection; and river water, except in some few instances, will be always found sufficiently soft for any domestic purpose. In general it may be added, though chemical processes on water never fail of success, that the cheapest, and perhaps the readiest method of softening hard water, or of purifying river-water, is to boil it, and then leave it to atmospherical exposure; especially when the hardness arises from the solution of sub-carbonate of lime: but not so with sulphate of lime.

To ascertain this, there is an easy, yet perfectly chemical experiment. Dissolve some soap in strong spirits of wine, and pour a few drops into a wine-glass full of distilled water, for the test of which, a few drops are to be poured into a glass-full of the water to be tried. If the water be not quite pure, a turbidness will instantly shew itself, and the surface of the water, if left undisturbed, will soon be covered with a portion of flocculent matter, manifesting the absolute degree of impurity, proceeding from the solution of earthy salts. Take another glass of water and pour into it half a teaspoonful of a solution of oxalate of ammonia; then, if the water is unboiled, and a precipitate takes place, the impregnation is with carbonate of lime; and if it has been boiled and a precipitate ensues, then it may be considered that the sulphate of lime is present, and that the water will never be generally convenient for domestic purposes, without the trouble and expense of chemical purifications, which will render it useless also for culinary application. The absolute hardness of water may also be often ascertained by cattle or pigeons refusing to drink it.

Situation and the supply of water being thus ascertained, a judicious selection of which, in regard not only to country, but also to town residences, will be found in the course of a life-time to ensure a great saving in health, in family anxiety, and in medical expenses; we may now examine the economy of the materials with which we mean to build, and even of the house which we may mean to rent, especially if on a repairing lease; a little attention to which will often save both money and patience. To investigate the nature of such materials to the best effect, we must do it not only with reference to the convenience of procuring them, but also as to the chemical qualities of those which present themselves in reference to the action of the atmosphere upon them, not forgetting their fitness for architectural beauty.

Upon a general principle then we may lay it down as a maxim, that the outside walls should be formed of the worst conductors of heat; besides which their thickness must depend upon the durability of the material and its power of supporting the incumbent weight. Generally speaking, the materials should not be susceptible of the action of air or moisture; and, above all, they ought to be incombustible.

Well-burnt bricks, made of good components, are the best materials in this country; not only for their durability, as manifested in the remains of Roman architecture, but for other advantages of considerable importance. They are worse conductors of heat than stone, and therefore brick houses are warmest. Mortar adheres more strongly to them than to stone. They absorb moisture readily, when it is applied to their surface, and therefore seldom present the appearance of damp walls, as in stone buildings, except where the mortar has been injudiciously mixed with sea-sand. We speak not, however, of the modern London bricks. They are of most perishable materials, like many others which may be seen to decay rapidly when exposed to the air, covered with a white efflorescence which chemistry shews to be a sulphat of magnesia, arising from some species of clay abounding in their composition, and very susceptible of atmospheric influence.

Some persons consider stone as the only ornamental material, and where first expense is no object, there will certainly be an ultimate saving by its use; but then whenever it is employed, it ought to be well ascertained to be capable of resisting both air and water. It is true, indeed, that stone in England is not so permeable to water as in other countries. In Bermuda, for instance, where the stone is a species of filter, a new house bears no proportionate value to an old one of the same size, whose walls have been saturated with repeated white washings for a number of years, so as to have acquired an artificial impermeability. With us, however, several species of stone, exposed to the air, are rapidly destructible, sometimes crumbling to powder, although extremely hard when first dug from the quarry. In this class are all those stones which abound with clay, or alumine, which has so great an affinity for water as to absorb moisture from the air to the extent of destroying its own aggregation. Other species again lose their aggregation by an opposite cause; such as marbles of particular kinds, also crystallized carbonates of lime, or stones composed of an acid and earth combined with water, called the water of crystallization. Chalk only differs from marble in having lost that water, advancing thereby more rapidly to decay: which is also the case with several species of lime-stone after aerial exposure, particularly when the air is frequently saturated with water in the presence of carbonic acid. Such are the Derbyshire caverns, which yield petrifactions and stalactite. Gypsum also, though durable when dry, is so easily soluble in a quantity of water, that even if it were plentiful, it would be imprudent to use it. But the granite, the basalt, or whin-stone, and all stones consisting principally of silex or flint like the mill-stone grit, may be used with every prospect of permanence. In other countries, indeed, with a drier atmosphere, many of these rejected species will last for ages, though so destructible with us, as may be seen here in our edifices built with Portland stone; but even the worst of these may now be rendered more durable by the application of casing with the new invented cements.

Mr. Randolph, of Richmond, in the United States, has recently announced the discovery of a cement which resists the action of water and fire, and which contracts additional hardness with time.

The composition consists of two fossils of a mineral or volcanic substance. Two bricks joined together by this cement, were laid in water on the 1st of June, 1817; they were taken out in August 1818, and then formed a solid compact mass; the cement having grown as hard as the bricks. Another experiment was afterwards made by applying the cement to the surface of a piece of brick-work exposed to the air, and the result proved equally creditable to the value of the invention.

It must not be forgotten, that several very economical inventions have recently been recorded at the Patent Office, and in the philosophical journals of the day, by means of which all the beauty of stone may be imparted to a brick building.

That valuable property which the Roman cement is known to possess, of becoming in a short time as hard as stone, points out its peculiar eligibility for the employment of it in buildings; and by combining it with other durable materials, in the form of bricks, and laying them in the cement instead of common mortar, a building may be rendered literally a stone edifice; for the cement (when deprived of its water with which it is mixed to render it plastic, which is the case after a short exposure to the atmosphere) does actually become stone. By their being produced without artificial heat they retain the exact form of the moulds in which they are made, so that accuracy is preserved in laying them without much trouble, and much less cement or mortar is required than with any other kind of bricks. Pointing is not necessary either for use or beauty; and as water cannot penetrate them, they are an effectual preventive of damp walls. When laid in putty, or fine mortar, of which but little is required, they make excellent work, the joints being hardly perceptible. The expense of a front of these bricks will not be more than one of fine malm stocks when pointed; as, in consequence of their uniformity in size and shape, they will be laid in much less time than any other kind of bricks. Closers and arches are furnished at prices proportioned to the rest, so that no loss is occasioned by waste in cutting, which in other bricks is considerable.

Another plan has been proposed for forming blocks with bricks and cement, in the form of ashlar stone, and with all the appearance of that material.

This invention consists in uniting bricks together with Roman cement, or with any other mortar or cement that will set sufficiently hard, in the form of ashlar stones, which the patentee calls ashlar blocks. These blocks he coats, or stuccoes, on the external surface, with Roman cement, or any other cement proper for that purpose, in a mould or case so as to imitate any kind of stone ashlar, and afterwards builds in walls in the same manner as stone ashlar is built. These ashlar blocks form the outward surface or surfaces of the walls; the inside may be built in common brick-work. The patentee recommends that the blocks be formed with a tail for bonding them with common brick-work; but their size and form may be varied to suit the nature of the edifice, or the fancy of the builder. By this method of building, when properly executed, the walls will be free from those unsightly cracks so common in stuccoed buildings; and less pervious to moisture; they will look more like stone-work, and the building may be finished as the walls are carried up.

Another very ingenious invention has been brought forward, for fronting houses with a thin caseing of real stone, at a rate not much more expensive than the imitative substitute.

The plan is first to prepare thin pieces, plates, or slabs of stone, of sizes to fit the sides and ends of the bricks, blocks, masses or lumps, intended to be used in the fronts of buildings. These pieces, plates, or slabs, being previously cleaned and wetted, are then placed in moulds; and Parker's cement, or what is more commonly known by the name of Roman cement, or any other proper cement, in a fit state of moisture, is laid upon them, and is to remain till the cement be sufficiently indurated and united to the stone; or the cement may first be put into the moulds, and the pieces, plates, or slabs of stone laid upon it, and remain till the cement be sufficiently indurated and united to the stone. They are then to be taken out of the moulds, and piled up, or placed in a proper situation for drying; the longer they are exposed to the atmosphere the harder they will become; and in a few days, they will be hard enough for use, without the application of artificial heat. The pieces, plates, or slabs of stone, need not be more than half an inch thick, but may be thicker or thinner according to the discretion of those interested in the work. The quality of the stone is best if somewhat bibulous or porous; and for this reason the patentee prefers Bath stone, but Portland or even marble may be applied if the cement be such as will cohere to the stone or marble. It is not necessary to use Parker's or any other cement without the admixture of any other materials; on the contrary, it will be advantageous in many cases to mix with it clean rough sand, small gravel, or even round pebbles.

We may also mention that a patént has been very recently obtained for certain improvements in the facing of exterior and interior walls of Gothic or other structure, built of brick or other material, with strong milled or sawn slates, bound and secured by mouldings, grooves, and tyes of cast iron, in such a manner as to have the appearance when sanded, of finely wrought stone-work in ornamental pannels or otherwise; with ceilings of correspondent tracery, form, and character, of the same materials, which may be supported by pointed arches, rising from single or clustered columns of cast iron.

This patentee likewise recommends plans for capping buttresses of Gothic architecture with highly enriched pinnacles of cast-iron only, which being connected by metal with the spouts also of metal, and carried down to the ground, form conductors for the protection of lofty buildings from the effect of lightning; also for a spiral stair, of cast-iron, of a light and simple construction, which may be carried up, or inserted within the corner of a buttressed tower wall, or in the cylinder of a small turret; by which mode of facing, adorning, and constructing, churches, or other buildings of pure Gothic design, may be erected of brick, and finished with light ornamental carved work, of appropriate taste and elegance, at less expense than if wrought in stone, and in materials that will endure.

In forming the walls, due attention must be paid to the windows, so as to afford sufficient light and air—two things essentially necessary for the health and eye-sight; and though, to lessen the window-tax, may be a very proper part of domestic economy, still it ought not to be forgotten that although the deterioration of the general atmosphere by the breathing of all living creatures is not of a moment's consideration, yet the effect of human respiration on those atmospheres which we inhale in our habitations, and particularly in crowded apartments, is not to be overlooked. The vitiated condition of the air, in this way, being at least one of the causes of that *pallor* observable on the cheeks of people subjected to its influence.

This, however, shall be more particularly noticed under the head of Ventilation; and we shall only remark, at present, that provided the diminution of windows is not carried beyond healthful propriety, it may be rendered particularly conducive to the beauty of Gothic buildings where irregular casements in vast masses of wall form a prominent feature.

Our ancestors were profuse of *Timber* in the erection of their houses, whilst we now find it the most expensive article in regard to price, to say nothing of the enormous loss occasioned by the purchase of timber badly seasoned, rendering sumptuous palaces and more lowly residences alike uninhabitable from the dry rot.

To save in timber, we must therefore say, that the *best* will be found the cheapest; and, as an assistant in that economy, we may record a preparation extracted from a foreign publication, where it is said to be more advantageous than soaking the wood in a solution of salt. Take three parts of slaked lime, two of wood-ashes, and one of fine sand: sift the whole; add as much linseed oil as is necessary to reduce the composition when well mixed to such a consistence that it may be applied with a brush. The wood requires only two coats; the first may be thin, but the second as thick as the brush can lay it on. This coating, when well prepared, is represented as impermeable to water, and to resist the influence of the weather and the action of the sun, which harden and render it more durable.

Under the head of Ventilation we shall notice the various modes of curing smoky chimnies in habitations already built; but it will be appropriate here to record some of the cheapest methods of guarding against such inconvenience whilst a house is in the progress of erection or repair. The common causes of smoky chimnies are either that the wind is too much let in above at the mouth of the shaft, or else that the smoke is stifled below; also they may proceed from there being too little room in the vent, particularly where several open into the same funnel. The situation of the house may also affect them, especially if backed by higher ground or higher buildings.

Several artificial modes of regulating these apertures, according to circumstances, have recently been proposed and patented: one of these plans, as described, consists of two sides, or parts, to form the back coverings of a fire-place, fixed on the top of the hobs of the grate or stove, at the back part of the same, extending from about the back of the stove or grate each way, till they reach the chimney jambs. "The covings are connected at bottom and top, behind the back of the grate or stove, with either a fixed or a moveable bar, in order to admit the sweeper to pass freely into the chimney, or for any other purpose. In the covings, about straight with the under side of the top fixed or moveable bar, is a register, blower, or door, to serve as a ventilator, if required; and on the covings are placed flutes, astragals or beads, or both, to receive the second part, consisting of a register, blower, door, or shutter, on both sides, shutting when closed, against the top and bottom fixed or moveable bar. On the top of the covings, and to the top bar, hang one or more register or blower, extending from wing to wing of the chimney, against the breast of the chimney, and from the breast of the chimney, to be raised or elevated by degrees, as may be required by a screw or other wise.

" The register thus hung, will, when shut up, square with the front of the jambs; and intersecting with, or meeting, or folding against the back covings, form a right angle, and a square hob, and will, when moved forward towards the fire, or centre of the fire-place, into the grooves, or against the astragals, and in and on the back covings, contract the opening of the fire-place, and constitute a variety of bevel hobs. The front register being brought forward from its bevel situation nearly flush with the stone or other jambs and mantle, to which it may be attached, will close or shut up, and thereby constitute a register, blower, or fire screen in the front of the fire-place, from which it may be affixed or hung to, in front and on each side also."

Another mode has been proposed for the cure of chimnies already built; but it is so cheap, and so easily put up whilst building, that we insert it here, as a proper safeguard to be adopted either then, or when repairing. The apparatus is strong and simple, all of cast iron, and may be used with any grate. It consists of a long upright back, as high as the mantle-piece, with open perpendicular ribs behind the fire-place, the height of the grate. This back divides the vent into two branches, which are opened or shut at pleasure, by means of a damper in the throat of the chimney. The damper is inclosed in an iron case, or box, of an oblong square form, and is half the breadth of the box, having ends the whole height of it, so as to continue the contraction to the top of the box, whichever branch of the vent may be open. The box is supported by arms from the back of the grate, and the damper is worked by a handle, which has a knee to it, to let it come out under the breast of the chimney, with a brass nob on the end of it, and has a neat appearance. The sides of the chimney are finished in the usual manner, with cast iron, brass, or steel plates; and the corners are neatly built up, so as to leave no access to the air, unless through the branch of the vent. The back of the chimney, opposite to the fire, is lined with fire-brick, or fire-tile, to resist and throw back the heat; and there is a sliding shutter at the bottom of the branch of the vent behind the grate, which may be drawn out when the grate is cleaned, to allow any ashes which may have got into it through the open ribs to fall down, and be taken away.

In the article of Roofing much may be saved, it is true, by diminishing the extent of the ground-plot, and raising the house one or two stories higher; but the amount even of that saving will scarcely counterbalance the increased inconvenience, to say nothing of the greater danger to human life from fire and other accidents. Where ground then is not an object, the mere saving in roofing, for it will be nothing more, is scarcely worth attending to, especially as due attention to the materials used will serve to guard against frequent repairs. The difference of price between tiles and slates will ultimately be far from economy, when we consider the more frequent repairs required in tiles; but then the slates must be judiciously selected, otherwise they prove a source of ruin to the strongest roof frames. When slates are only so far porous as to admit of moisture, without absolute percolation, a bed is formed for vegetation; and moss and lichens, with other parasitical plants, soon make their appearance. In summer this may not be considered as an inconvenience, but, in some instances, as a picturesque ornament; in winter, however, the case will be different, for where moisture has been absorbed, a sudden frost will infallibly split the slates into shivers Again, when slates are so porous as to allow the rain to percolate, even a child must know that the wood-work must become rotten, and the entire roof soon useless.

On these considerations, a few hints on the choice of slates will not be unacceptable. The first criterion may be judged of at a glance; for all that is required is that the slates shall be thin and of a smooth surface, such being most impervious to the weather. If a more accurate test be wanted—lay a slate in an oven until perfectly dry; weigh it, and then immerse in water, where it must lay for some time; let it then be taken out, wiped carefully with a dry cloth, and weighed—it will be evident then that those slates which thus acquire the least additional weight, must be the fittest for domestic purposes.

The absolute strength of a slate, in regard to brittleness, may be tried various ways: perhaps the best and easiest is to balance it on the finger, and strike it with a hammer. If the tone is clear and sonorous, the slate may be considered firm and elastic; if dull, then it ought to be rejected. Where slates are very full of pyrites, it may prove a fair objection to them; for it often happens that the decomposition of the pyrites, by the atmosphere, leaves holes in the slates, the wet proceeding from which being attributed to other causes, repeated repairs are had recourse to without effect; as the damaged slates, being sound in appearance, are again unconsciously applied by the workmen. Generally speaking the Welsh slates, especially those from the Penryn slate quarry, are good; but the blueish green slate from the Westmoreland quarries is considered better; with this difference, however, that being of a smaller size, there is some slight additional expence in preparing and laying them on.

A plan has lately been proposed, and a patent granted, for covering roofs with iron. The mode is simple. After the framing of the roof has been constructed of the usual materials, it is covered with plates of sheet iron, or other fit metal or material, having the borders turned back so as to form hitches or laps. These hitches, on the upper parts, or edges, should be made to turn outwards; and such as are on the lower parts, or edges, inwards; so that the inward hitches of the one drop into, and hold in the outward hitches of the other.

Where ornamental or even useful buildings are wanted in haste, or for temporary purposes, a quick and cheap, as well as durable mode of forming a roof may be adopted by dipping sheets of coarse paper in boiling tar and nailing them on boards or laths in the same manner as slates. The whole is then painted over with a mixture of pitch and powdered coal, chalk, or brick-dust. This forms a texture, which completely resists all kinds of weather, for a great length of time, without requiring repairs. As the roof is made to rise not more than two inches in a foot, the quantity of timber required is much smaller than for any other mode.

In regard to Flooring, the use of plank is so congenial to our habits of comfort and cleanliness, that we shall be unwilling to recommend any attempt at economy in that article, except in the offices, where floors, not combustible, though laid on combustible materials, might often tend to check the progress of flame. But whenever taste or convenience leads to the turning of arches in an under story, the floor immediately over it may always be laid with some incombustible material; the best and readiest of which is the composition called plaster of Paris, the materials for which are abundant in England. Large bricks well burnt, might often be adopted with propriety, even if laid upon wooden joists; or the process mentioned for fronting houses might be applied for making paving blocks or slabs, in the same manner as the faced bricks, by laying the thin pieces, plates, or slabs, of stone or marble, at the bottom of the mould, and applying the cement or composition upon them.

In addition to the purposes for which Roman cement is commonly employed, it has been found in many instances to be highly serviceable in another respect. A portion of it mixed with an equal quantity of coarse sand and water, and applied to walls or floors, forms an effectual barrier against rats.

A cheap flooring material has long been used in Italy, which might be applied with great propriety to many domestic purposes, especially in the erection of cottages, or porter's lodges, instead of the earthen floors sometimes used. This composition consists of nothing more than fine clay tempered with ox-blood, which, if well laid on, soon becomes hard, smooth, and glistening enough to be even ornamental, if applied to walls. It has also been proposed to form floors of small clean rubble, or pebbles, in the following manner: To any quantity, of recently calcinated lime, add bullock's blood (that of any other fresh killed animal will do equally as well,) in the proportion of two parts blood to ten parts lime; the mass should then be beaten up, as mortar is made, adding water in small quantities from time to time, till the whole assumes the consistency of thick paste, when it should be poured upon the rubble. The lime should be exposed to the action of the atmospheric air as little as possible before it is saturated with the blood; it may, however, then be kept some time, and when wanted for use it must undergo the operation of beating up and watering.

A word only remains to be said on the ornamental materials required, a great variety of which may be found, the produce of our own country.

The exquisite beauty of the Devonshire marble, of which new varieties are daily discovered, is fast gaining ground on the admiration and taste of the discerning and munificent.

From the Isle of Anglesea also, the most beautiful specimens of serpentine, now known by the name of Mona marble, may be readily and cheaply procured. It is in some respects superior to Italian marble, being more durable, and less liable to be injured by scratches. The colour is believed to be permanent; and the polish is very fine; besides which it may be had in slabs or blocks of any required dimensions.

The Kilkenny marble may also be adopted, though

of a sombre grey or deep black, in preference for cheapness, nay, perhaps for beauty, to many of the Italian marbles. These are important considerations, when we reflect that the chance of warfare may sometimes render a fashionable foreign marble unattainable, except at a price which bids defiance to all ideas of economy. During the force of the Berlin and Milan decrees, the price of foreign marbles rose to an unprecedented extent; that of pure statuary marble being as high as seven pounds per cubic foot, and the others in proportion. But such extravagance is absurd, whilst we have the beautiful Petworth marble from Sussex; the Purbeck and Babbicombe marbles from the West of England; and a very fine species of Scottish marble, equal in beauty and goodness to the famed Pentelic marbles of antiquity, considered as yielding only to the Parian. This marble comes from the vicinity of Perth, and is known by the name of Glen Tilt.

Any of those marbles may be cheaply imitated by means of a mixture of burnt gypsum, or alabaster and quick-lime well powdered, and tempered with glue or isinglass.

The different imitations of foreign woods, which have within a few years been introduced with much success into our houses, will be found to make a cheap and beautiful variety, in the decorations of our doors, mouldings, and furniture. The plane-tree wood is the best for this purpose, as it is beautifully veined, and easily polished. The surface must be rendered perfectly smooth, and then be rubbed with diluted nitrous acid; after this, take one ounce and a half of dragon's blood, dissolved in a pint of spirits of wine, and one third of that quantity of carbonate of soda, all properly mixed together and filtered; lay it on the wood with a soft brush, repeat the operation a few times, and the wood will assume the colour and polish of fine mahogany, and should the surface occasionally become dull, a little cold drawn linseed oil, will restore it to its brilliancy. Elm and maple for the boards of apartments may be easily made to resemble mahogany, by washing their surfaces with aquafortis diluted in water, and when dry rubbing them with a mixture consisting of one dram of dragon's blood, half a dram of alkanet, and a quarter of a dram of aloes, dissolved in four ounces of proof-spirit; the quantity made, must of course, be determined by the extent of the surface, which is to be covered, taking care only to observe the proportions as here given.

Having thus prepared the house for habitation, the next point of general direction is in regard to

CLEANLINESS.

When, however, we compare the domestic nicety of English mansions with those of other countries, it may at first sight appear superfluous to enter upon a subject already so well understood; it is not our intention, therefore, to urge advice, but merely to offer a few hints which may produce a saving both of time and expence in operations of such constant recurrence.

In order to proceed methodically, we shall begin literally, at the foundation, and first notice the most important enemy to cleanliness that we have to contend with, and which ought, therefore, to be sedulously guarded against, even if it did not affect the very duration of our residences as well as their comfort and cleanliness—we allude to the *Dry Rot*, on which we have already slightly touched in our remarks on buildings.

This destructive visitant, in dwelling-houses, generally grows, or originates in the cellar. If persons *white*-washing cellars will mix as much copperas with the wash as may give it a clear yellow hue, and repeat this every year, they may prevent the dry-rot, or stop its progress if it has already begun. This is so easy and so cheap an experiment, that, being well assured of its efficacy, we trust it may be generally adopted.

At the same time we particularly recommend the investigation of the principle to our indefatigable chemists; as the saturation of wood in a weak solution of copperas, for joists, beams, rafters, and floorings, might be resorted to with propriety, in the erection of new buildings, and secure them from a secret, and far more destructive enemy than any of those against which we are guaranteed by the insurance offices.

The prevalence of the dry rot in the timber used in this country, whether it be from the changeable nature of the climate, or from the carelessness of builders in exposing it, without proper seasoning or preparation, to the influence of an unequal temperature on different parts of the same beam, is the greatest possible obstacle to the magnificence of our public edifices, or even the durability of our private ones. In America, the trees are barked a year or two before they are cut down; this process is supposed to season the wood effectually, and it is certain that the American timber is by no means so liable to dry-rot as the timber in our own country, which is not barked until after it is cut down.

It is calculated on an average, that every ship in his Majesty's navy, and every merchantman trad-

ing to the East or West Indies, or any other hot
climate, is in consequence of repairs made from
time to time, by taking out decayed planks and
replacing them with new, nearly re-built in the
course of fourteen years; and with respect to the
navy alone, it is computed that a saving of twenty
millions would accrue to the government, in that
period of time, during a season of warfare, could
a remedy for the disease which causes the expenditure of the sum, be found.   In the magnificent
edifices of our nobility and gentry, a discovery of
the dry-rot has often, a very short time after their
erection, nearly doubled the calculation of their
original cost; and whilst the palace of the Alhambra
in Spain, has proudly stood a thousand years,
though chiefly constructed of timber, our noblest
structures are frequently threatened with irretriev-
able decay, in less than half a century from their
being raised. As, however, we are not in this
little work, going to enter upon the best method of
erecting palaces, or building fleets, we will confine
ourselves to a much humbler view of the subject of the dry-rot, and consider it as affecting in
particular the flooring of kitchens, or sitting rooms
on the basement story.

No piece of timber, however sound in its original
constitution, can stand in a difference of temperature in the same instant; that is to say, one part
wet and another dry; any more than it can, for
any length of time, support the variations of being
throughout alternately wet and dry.

Now in boarding kitchens, and other rooms on
the basement story, three sides of the joists, and
the lower face of the flooring, are generally bedded
in earth, so moist as to amount to absolute wetness;
whilst the upper sides of the joists and the outer

surface of the flooring are perfectly dry, and exposed to all the heat of a large fire, and a temperature proportionally high. The consequence is, that joists and floorings, however sound when they are laid down, generally become rotten in a few months; and that there is scarcely a house to be found in which a tenant has not, in the course of ten years, to lay down a new floor in his kitchen, and sometimes even to do it twice in that period. It follows then that there cannot be too much pains taken in preparing the earth on which the floor is to be laid, with gravel, chippings of stone, refuse of lime-kilns, and other dry substances, which should be also well beaten down before the planks are laid; the planks themselves should be steeped in a strong solution of vitriol or alum, and when they are dried, the side next to the earth should receive a coat of tar, or common paint; thus prepared, they will resist every species of damp so effectually, that the person who lays down a floor according to these directions, in a cellar or kitchen, will have the satisfaction to think that in all probability he will not be ever called upon to do it again in the same house.

When *Walls* are so damp as hitherto to have been considered incorrigible, we must not despair. An ingenious patentee has recently invented a remedy, which, if it does not remove the absolute inconvenience of general dampness, will yet produce a considerable saving in regard to paint and stucco where repeated repairs have formerly been found necessary. The mode proposed, is to line the walls with sheet lead, rolled to extreme fineness, and worked into breadths, so as to be fixed up like paper hangings; and thereby to check the passage of moisture either to stucco, or to common plaster intended for papering or wainscot.

If this be thought too expensive, a cheap mixture may be adopted, consisting of one gallon of tar, and a quarter of a pound of common kitchen-stuff, or other offal fat, boiled together carefully for about twenty minutes, until intimately amalgamated. Whilst hot, add to it a powder consisting of one third of finely pounded glass, and two thirds well dried and sifted slack lime, working up the whole until of the consistence of common plaster, which must be laid upon the walls in dry weather, giving two or three coats, according to circumstances. When thoroughly dry, it forms a basis for stucco, or for the usual coat of plaster to receive either paper or distemper painting.

We can also recommend, as an improvement in refitting apartments, even where dampness has not manifested itself, a very useful water cement or stucco, the method of preparing which, is as follows : take fifty-six pounds of pure coarse sand, forty-two pounds of pure fine sand, mix them together, and moisten them thoroughly with lime water; to the wetted sand, add fourteen pounds of pure fresh burnt lime, and while beating them up together, add, in successive portions, fourteen pounds of bone-ash; the quicker and more perfectly these materials are beaten together, and the sooner they are used, the better, as their induration is extremely rapid.

When well dried, this stucco may be very cheaply coloured in distemper by the following preparation. Take a quart of skimmed milk, half a pound of burnt chalk, or very fine quick-lime, a quarter of a pound of painter's oil, adding a pound of Spanish white, or finely powdered ochre of any colour wished for; proceeding in their mixture in the ensuing manner. Dip the lime in water, leaving it when drawn out to the action of the atmosphere,

which will speedily reduce it to a fine powder.
Put the lime into a clean well burnt earthen vessel,
pour on it a little milk, until it becomes fluid, then
add a little oil, stirring the whole up with a wooden
spoon or spatula; add the remainder of the milk
and oil alternately, concluding with the colouring
matter previously amalgamated with a portion of
the milk.

If the mixture is intended to be white, the
purest and most colourless oil must be used; but
if red, blue, brown, or yellow are wanted, then
the common linseed oil will answer the purpose,
as it seems to disappear as soon as mixed with the
milk and lime. In adding the colouring matter
great care must be taken not to pour it into one
spot, but to spread it over the surface of the liquid,
and to mix the whole as rapidly as possible; otherwise it will be rather difficult to bring the whole
mixture to an equality of colour.

Ten minutes will be sufficient to mix as much as
will paint all the inside walls of a moderately sized
mansion; but the quantity here mentioned will
not serve for more than one coat to about twenty
four square yards.

Where the plaster is previously in good order and
not partially discoloured, one coat will be found
sufficient for halls, staircases, or ceilings; but when
used for wainscotting, instead of paints, two coats
will be necessary, and which may be laid on almost
immediately, as it is perfectly set and dry in the
course of an hour; becoming not only more solid,
but also much handsomer than any other modes
in common use, requiring less labour, and no fire
in the preparation.

When the walls upon which this colouring is to
be applied are not in a very perfect state, and appear to require the assistance of the plasterer, a

cheap substitute may be found in laying on a common kind of wrapping-paper, which will receive the mixture with great facility.

Another point of saving may be found in the adoption of the newly invented washable paper-hangings; and it must not be forgotten that old furniture paper may be very readily cleansed by the application of stale bread, taking care to rub the paper down in one direction: a half quartern loaf should be cut into about four pieces, and the soft side of the bread applied.

An important point in domestic cleanliness is to guard against the filth produced by chimnies which are not often and thoroughly divested of the soot which lodges near the fire-place, even when the chimney itself is not absolutely foul, especially in the country, where the attendance of a chimney-sweeper cannot always be commanded: an ingenious gentleman has recently offered a plan for that purpose, and has also called the attention of the Society for abolishing the practice of sweeping chimneys by means of climbing-boys, to an idea which seems capable of being made subservient to that benevolent design. He proposes that the top of each chimney shall be furnished with a pot somewhat in the shape of a bell, underneath the centre of which shall be fixed a pulley with a chain of sufficient length for both ends to be fastened when not in use to nails or pins in the chimney, out of sight, but within reach from below. One or both of these ends should be adapted to the reception of a brush of an appropriate construction; and thus by this simple contrivance, masters and mistresses might have their chimneys swept as often as they pleased by their own servants, with very little additional trouble to the latter.

Where painted wainscot, or other wood work

requires cleansing, fuller's earth will be found cheap and useful; and, on wood not painted, it forms an excellent substitute for soap. Where extreme nicety is required, use a mixture of one pound of soft soap, two ounces of pearlash, one pint of sand, and one pint of table-beer. Simmer these substances in a pipkin over a slow fire, and let them be well mixed. The mode of application is to put a small quantity in flannel, rubbed on the wainscot; wash it off with warm water, and dry thoroughly with a linen cloth.

Oil cloths are a great improvement in modern furnishing; but they are so expensive that they demand considerable care to preserve them in their beauty and freshness. They ought never to be wetted, if it can possibly be avoided — but merely to be rubbed with a flannel, and polished with a brush of moderate hardness, exactly like a mahogany table; and by this simple means, the fading of the colours, and the rotting of the canvas, which are inevitably attendant upon the oil-cloth's being left in a state of moisture or dampness, are entirely avoided.

Fuller's earth may also be applied with great success to the cleansing of Carpets, even the finest Turkey or Brussels, according to the following mode. Beat the carpet well, then stretch it out and cleanse it with a pretty hard brush, dipped in soft water, in which bran has been boiled for some time. Whilst wet, rub the carpet over with fuller's earth, laying it in the sun to dry, and repeating the process two or three times. The carpet must then be beaten until the fuller's earth be wholly expunged, next well rubbed with a soft brush dipped in alum water, and suffered to dry in the shade; when the whole surface, if not too much worn, will have all the appearance of newness, and the colours be nearly as bright as when first purchased.

The Cleaning of Furniture forms an important part of domestic economy, not only in regard to neatness but also in point of expense.

The readiest mode indeed consists in good manual rubbing, or the essence of elbows, as it is whimsically termed; but our finest cabinet work requires something more, where brilliancy of polish is of importance.—The Italian cabinet work in this respect excels that of any other country. To produce this effect, the workmen first saturate the surface with olive-oil, and then apply a solution of gum arabic in boiling alcohol. This mode of varnishing is equally brilliant, if not superior, to that employed by the French in their most elaborate works.

But another mode may be substituted, which has less the appearance of a hard varnish, and may always be applied so as to restore the pristine beauty of the furniture by a little manual labour.

Heat a gallon of water, in which dissolve one pound and a half of potash; add a pound of virgin wax, boiling the whole for half an hour, then suffering it to cool, when the wax will float on the surface. Put the wax into a mortar, and triturate it with a marble pestle, adding soft water to it until it forms a soft paste, which laid neatly on furniture, or even on paintings, and carefully rubbed when dry, with a woollen rag, gives a polish of great brilliancy without the harshness of the drier varnishes. *Marble chimney-pieces* may also be rubbed with it, after cleaning with diluted muriatic acid, or warm soap and vinegar; but the iron or brass work connected with them requires other processes.

Polished iron work may be preserved from rust by a mixture not very expensive, consisting of copal varnish intimately mixed with as much olive oil as will give it a degree of greasiness, adding thereto nearly as much spirit of turpentine as of varnish. The cast iron work is best preserved by rubbing with black lead.

But where rust has begun to make its appearance on grates or fire irons, apply a mixture of tripoli with half its quantity of sulphur, intimately mingled on a marble slab, and laid on with a piece of soft leather. Or emery and oil may be applied with excellent effect; not laid on in the usual slovenly way, but with a spungy piece of the fig-tree fully saturated with the mixture. This will not only clean but polish, and render the use of whiting unnecessary.

Brass ornaments, when not gilt or lackered, may be cleaned the same way, and a fine colour given to them by two simple processes. The first is to beat sal ammoniac into a fine powder, then to moisten it with soft water, rubbing it on the ornaments, which must be heated over charcoal, and rubbed dry with bran and whiting. The second is to wash the brass work with roche alum boiled in strong ley, in the proportion of an ounce to a pint; when dry it must be rubbed with fine tripoli. Either of these processess will give to brass the brilliancy of gold.

As the greatest domestic cleanliness will not always preserve a house from Vermin, it is of the utmost consequence to be able to get rid of them by artificial means.

Bugs in particular, may readily be destroyed by dissolving half a dram of corrosive sublimate in a quarter of an ounce of spirits of salts, mixing it with one quart of spirits of turpentine. Let these be shaken well together, dip a brush in it, and wash those places where bugs are supposed to

resort, which will remove them to a greater certainty than the usual modes of laying gunpowder
in crevices and setting fire to it; or sprigs of fern,
or wormwood and hellebore, or the decoction of lime
and salt: or the more unpleasant mode of burning
brimstone.

A decoction of bitter apple also, about sixpenny-
worth in a pint of water, is an easy and simple
preventative to the increase of these insects; crevices in walls, and the joinings between the boards
in floors, ought to be rubbed over three or four
times with a small brush dipped in the decoction.

Their number in beds also, may be much de-
creased by the use of what is vulgarly called a
bug-basket, which can be had of any basket-ma-
ker for about two shillings, and which is placed at
the head of the bed, behind the bolster. The basket should be well washed twice a week, and the
joints of the bedsteads cleaned with soft soap.

There is one species of vermin, which cannot be
expelled too soon from a residence, when once they
take post near the kitchen fire; for they will soon
swarm thence, all over the house, to the utter destruction of clothes, hats, pictures, &c. It is pleasant,
indeed, to hear the cricket ' chirping on the hearth,'
but the cock-roach ought to be expelled. The remedy is short, and infallible. Take a small quantity of white arsenic finely pulverized, strew it on
crumbs of bread, and lay it near the haunts of
these insects; a few nights will suffice; but dogs,
cats, and other pets must be kept out of the way
of partaking of the fare.

It is a well ascertained fact, that hedge-hogs
suffered to roam about a house infested with beetles,
cock-roaches, or crickets, will soon destroy them;
or a more artificial mode may be adopted by taking
a large bason, or deep pie-dish, well glazed and

smooth within side, and putting some sweet liquor, such as beer and sugar, or the grounds of wine into it, about half full; then placing it at bed-time wherever they most frequent; putting pieces of wood on every side from the ground to the edge of the bason, or dish, to serve as ladders. These they run up, attracted by the sweet liquid, and drop into it; the smooth surface within allowing no hold for their feet, it becomes a complete trap, and in a short time the house will be cleared.

It has been said, that the smoke of burnt fern will destroy flies, and that the leaves of the ash-tree hung up in a room will attract them; but, perhaps, a more certain and equally humane method may be adopted, and that too without the use of poison: take half a tea-spoonful of black pepper in powder, one tea-spoonful of brown sugar, and one table spoonful of cream, mix them well together, and place them in the room on a plate where the flies are troublesome, and they will soon disappear.

Indeed, we recommend not the domestic use of poison in any instance, where it can be avoided, not even for the destruction of rats and mice; for which, however, a safe, but not a very humane method is sometimes used, by mixing ground glass with oatmeal: but this is much more cruel, and not more efficacious than a method recently found to answer, of cutting sponge in small pieces, and dipping them in melted dripping, to be laid where those vermin resort. If scented with a little anniseed it will attract the rats the more readily.

The last subject to mention, is the cheapest and readiest mode of getting rid of unpleasant Vapours.

The drains in London are often extremely offensive, particularly to the inhabitants of cellar kitchens, to whose lot it seldom falls to breathe an air any way resembling "gales of Araby;" but the almost putrid effluvia that arises occasionally from these drains, may often be carried off with very little expense, simply by the adoption of what the bricklayers expressively term a stink-trap, and which even the clumsiest of the fraternity can set in half an hour.

The unpleasant smell of new paint is best removed by time and atmospheric ventilation: but tubs of water placed in the apartment, will act more rapidly; with this inconvenience, however, that the gloss of the paint will be completely destroyed by them. Unpleasant smells from water-closets, or all articles of furniture connected with them, may be modified by the application of lime-water, to which may be added the soap-suds that have been used in washing, which neutralize the pungently offensive salts; a little quick-lime put into a night-chair, will destroy all disagreeable effluvia, and aromatic pastiles of the following composition may be burned with great success: take of camphor, flowers benzoin, powdered charcoal, powdered cascarilla bark, powdered Turkey myrrh, powdered nitre, of each equal quantities; beat them with sirup sufficient to form a mass, and divide into pastiles of a conical shape.

They may be mixed up with spirit of turpentine (the rect. oil) or any thing that is inflammable. Sirup does best, as it is most adhesive.

But if the disagreeable odour arises from causes connected with infection, a more efficacious fumigation may be produced by means of equal quantities of powdered nitre and sulphuric acid, or spirit of vitriol, adding the nitre gradually to the oil, placing the earthen vessel on a plate of hot iron, or a shovel, stirring the mixture with a tobacco-pipe, and carrying it to the various corners and crevices of the apartment; the operator must however be careful not to inhale any of the fumes which are extremely unpleasant.

We cannot dismiss the subject of cleanliness without briefly noticing, that nothing gives an air of neatness and respectability to a house, more than the cleanliness and brightness of the windows, which immediately excite the admiration, as well of the passer by, as of the visitor; and certainly contribute very much to the comfort of the family by the additional light and distinctness which they afford; and in London, in some situations in the city particularly, this is a matter of more importance than persons living in the country, in the full enjoyment of " garish day," can easily imagine. Nevertheless, this comfort in London can scarcely be commanded without an almost weekly expense in paying persons who are accustomed to the employment, for cleaning our windows, unless we chuse to save our money at the risk of our servants' necks. We, therefore, strongly recommend to all persons who are building, or repairing houses, or to whom the cost of alteration is no object, to adopt the window frames which have lately been advertised by an ingenious patentee, and which are made upon a principle that allows them to be turned, or taken out, with the utmost ease. The next important consideration is

VENTILATION,

without which even cleanliness would be of little use.

It is totally unnecessary, however, to expatiate upon the propriety of strict attention to this subject, further than to observe that the noxious qualities of an exhausted or impure atmosphere have long been known, and the importance of furnishing a continued supply of oxygen or vital air, frequently pointed out by some of the most learned chemists in ancient and modern times; yet it unfortunately happens that there is scarcely a branch of our domestic economy less attended to. Dr. Hales was the first person to point out an effectual mode of supplying prisons, and other public buildings, with pure air in large quantities. The method of drawing off mephitic vapours by means of fire-pipes was, we believe, suggested by Sir Robert Moray, in 1665. These were formed of metal, about two inches and a half in diameter, reaching from the fire-place to the lower part of the house, and the ash-hole being closed up, the fire was supplied by the air intended to be drawn off.

The Marquis de Chabannes has also applied the principle of a forced ventilation to several of our public buildings, which has been attended with considerable service: a plan, however, has lately been adopted by Mr. Tyer, in the ventilation of Hackney workhouse, which appears to combine nearly all the desiderata essential for this purpose; and it possesses the additional advantage of being applicable to almost every species of building, at a comparatively small expense.

In the ceiling of the room intended to be ventilated, is formed an aperture of from six to nine inches in diameter, into which is introduced a hopper or funnel, having its mouth level with the ceiling, and connected by a branch-pipe to the nearest stove. It is there made to enter a cast iron box, behind the back of the grate, from whence the ascending vapour is carried some distance up the chimney, the pipe terminating in a situation where it is least likely for the soot to fall into it. The air being thus rarified by its passage through the cast-iron box, will readily ascend the chimney, while that in the lower part of the pipe will pass on with a rapid current to restore the equilibrium.

The power of this species of ventilation may readily be ascertained by placing a lighted candle near the opening of the ceiling, when the flame will dart towards the aperture with the greatest rapidity.

Or a simpler process may be adopted, in making holes in the upper part of the walls, with sloping cases of paste board or tin, to throw the current of air along the ceiling; and the aperture may easily be concealed by a picture judiciously placed. These processes are completely applicable to houses already built; but there is another and a more powerful mode recently adopted; yet with this drawback, that the ventilation of houses on the new principles must be provided for previous to erection, as well as the warming of them with a due equality of heat at all seasons. At present we talk of the comforts of our fire-sides, when, in fact, in one respect, the fire-side is the most uncomfortable place in the house, arising from the usual construction of our chimnies, which favour the escape of smoke and vapour, of which a great part ought to be consumed, whilst the warm air is also carried off, and only replaced by the cold air, which finds an entrance through accidental crevices in doors or windows. The results of this it is needless to enumerate. It is needless to expatiate on the comfort of sitting before a good fire, scorched on one side and chilled by the cold air on the other; whilst the current of cold air entering into the wide-mouthed chimney, without passing through the fire, destroys its draught, and renders the combustion of the fuel so imperfect, that a considerable portion passes away unburned, or comes down again into the room in the form of smoke; producing one of the most annoying of our domestic evils. That which does escape from the top of the chimney forms an annoyance out of doors; but a great proportion adheres to the sides, and is one of the principal causes of the present necessity for climbing boys, which might entirely be avoided upon the new principle.

This new mode has also one great advantage, that its principles may be most usefully extended to water-closets, so that the person who enters them, by the mere action of the door, and without any particular attention on his part, expels all the foul air; which may be at the same time replaced by atmospheric air, or by the warm fresh air from the house. The action of shutting the door in returning supplies a fresh quantity of air, and produces also all the necessary action of the cisterns.

For these purposes a variety of tunnels and cavities will be required to be made in the foundation; which, unfortunately, cannot be conveniently done with houses already erected. When this is attended to, a proper temperature may always be preserved with less expense than the common method of warming rooms; independent of the advantages of health, and general convenience.

Though certainly expensive at first, yet ultimately this becomes economical, for one pound of coal, in the new stoves, will raise 5085 cubic feet of air through 59 degrees; and the purity of the air is always greater than when heated by steam, besides a considerable diminution in expense. Even in old houses this plan may be adopted in halls and staircases by means of flues, drawing the cold air to the stove and sending it back again by the flues, whilst the due degree of ventilation is kept up by local circumstances.

In regard to Smokey Chimnies, a few facts and cautions may be useful; and a very simple remedy may often render the calling in of masons and bricklayers unnecessary.

Observe that a northern aspect often produces a smoky chimney.

A single chimney is apter to smoke, than when it forms part of a stack.

Straight funnels seldom draw well.

Large fire places are apt to smoke, particularly when the aperture does not correspond in size; for that, a temporary remedy may be found in opening a door or window; a permanent cure by diminishing the lower aperture.

When a smoky chimney is so incorrigible as to require a constant admission of fresh air into the room, the best mode is to introduce a pipe, one of whose apertures shall be in the open air, and the other under the grate; or openings may be made near the top of the apartment, if lofty, without any inconvenience even to persons sitting close by the fire.

This species of artificial ventilation, will always be found necessary for comfort, where gas is used internally, whether a fire is lighted or not.

Where a chimney only smokes when a fire is first lighted, this may be guarded against by allowing the fire to kindle gradually; or more promptly by laying any inflammable substance, such as shavings, on the top of the grate; the rapid combustion of which will warm the air in the chimney, and give it a tendency upwards, before any smoke is produced from the fire itself. If old stove grates are apt to smoke, it may be stopped by setting the stove further back. If that fails, contract the lower orifice.

In cottages, the shortness of the funnel or chimney may produce smoke; in which case the lower orifice must be contracted as small as possible by means of an upright register.

If a kitchen chimney overpowers that of the parlour, as is often the case in small houses, apply to each chimney a free admission of air, until the evil ceases.

When a chimney is filled with smoke, not of its own formation, but from the funnel next to it, an easy remedy offers in covering each funnel with a conical top, or earthen crock, not cylindrical but a frustum of a cone; by means of which the two openings are separated a few inches, and the cold air, or the gusts of wind no longer force the smoke down with them.

If these remedies fail, it will generally be found that the chimney only smokes when the wind is in a particular quarter, connected with the position of some higher building, or a hill, or grove of trees. In such cases the common turncap, as made by tinmen, and ironmongers, will generally be found fully adequate to the end proposed. A case has occurred of curing a smoky chimney exposed to the N. W. wind, and commanded by a lofty building on the S. E. by the following contrivance.

A painted tin cap of a conical form was suspended by a ring and swivel, so as to swing over the mouth of the chimney-pot by means of an arched strap or bar of iron nailed on each side of the chimney. When a gust of wind laid this cap (which from its resemblance in form and use to an umbrella, is called a paravent or wind-guard,) close to the pot on one side, it opened a wider passage for the escape of the smoke on the opposite side, whichever way the wind came; while rain, hail, &c. were effectually prevented from descending the flue.

A patent has recently been granted for an apparatus to be fitted to chamber doors, and applicable, indeed, to every kind of door, for the purpose of stopping out cold currents of air from parlours, drawing-rooms, dining-rooms, halls, passages, bed-rooms, &c. &c. and likewise for stopping out sound, smoke, steam, dust, foul air, and floating vapours from without; so contrived as to admit, when required, any quantity of air in an instant by a simple move-ment with the thumb and finger. Rooms having this invention, will be more equally heated through-out with a saving of nearly half the fuel. On the lower part of the door is fixed the patent slider, made of thin wood or iron japanned. When the door is shut against the jamb, it presses against the end of an iron rod, and causes the slider to move down to the floor or carpet, and when the door is opening, this rod is forced back again by means of springs, which causes the slider to run upwards, and ride over the carpet.

It is urged by the inventor that, with this inven-tion applied to door-ways, nearly half the fuel may be saved, the room much more equally warmed throughout, and the most tender persons may safely sit near the door without fear of catching cold or rheumatism; there will be no further oc-casion for screens or baize doors. It will stop out sound, smoke, and dust, foul air and floating va-pours from without, and the whole, when fixed, will be found to be extremely simple, and elegantly neat.

Although ventilation depends in a great degree upon the internal temperature of our mansions, and is, therefore, strictly connected with the subject of

ARTIFICIAL HEAT,

yet, hitherto, sufficient care and attention have not been paid to that fact. It is, therefore, important to consider, that as great part of our domestic inconveniencies are produced by air, so are they

to be cured by the same substance, properly adapted and supplied; for it has been proved that the
most effectual means of applying external heat to
animals and vegetables, for the purpose of keeping
up the natural temperature, is by making the air
the vehicle of heat.   When we are surrounded with
air which is not in motion, its little tendency to
conduct heat keeps us warm, by our natural heat
being accumulated.   But when exposed to air in
motion, it becomes the means of carrying off our
heat, as we experience by the refreshing breezes in
summer. The pleasurable feeling we are conscious of,
in a temperature of about 60 degrees, with a moderate breeze of fresh air, is during that uniform ab-
straction of native heat which leaves no sensation
of heat or cold.   But this temperature will vary
with different people; and, in 'all, in proportion
with the quantity and nature of their clothing.
To preserve this equality of temperature is the object of the new domestic economic philosophy so
happily broached, and so successfully pursued by
our chemical philosophers, our philosophical architects, and ingenious mechanics.

From various useful inventions which may be
seen every day in the warehouses of the metropolis,
convenient specimens might here be selected.   But
as each inventor takes care to bring his improvement sufficiently before the public eye, we shall
content ourselves with one which we have not yet
seen exhibited, although a patent was obtained for
it some years ago.

This economical invention consists of a fire-pan,
or fire-lamp, and a fire-grate, or fire-stove, in
which small or inferior coals may be consumed for
all the same purposes as large or round coals.

The fire-pan or lamp may be made of any convenient shape, with a bottom formed into one or

more vertical tubes, or such tubes should be fixed in the bottom, and provided with valves or dampers to regulate the admission of air. A funnel, or funnels, should be placed on the side of the firelamp from which the wind may happen to blow, to be used as occasions may require.

The fire-grate is made with a pervious back, between which and the wall, at the back of the fireplace, a space must be left for the admission of air, for the regulation of which this aperture is provided with a damper.

By this invention, much of the waste is prevented which arises from the indiscriminate and injudicious use of the bellows, elsewhere noticed at some length; to which observations we will here add a useful hint, that a saving will be found if, instead of applying the bellows to a doubtful fire, in some instances, a very small quantity of nitre should be dropped in. The effect is generally instantaneous, and, without any unpleasant odour.

Let it be observed also in the economy of artificial heat, that every part of a fire-place which receives the radiant warmth ought to be white, in order to reflect, instead of absorbing it. The rationale of this will be further noticed; and is, in fact, well known to every tyro in optical philosophy.

From Heat we naturally proceed to

ILLUMINATION,

respecting which it must be acknowledged that there is no part of domestic economy for which, of late years, philosophy and mechanics have done more than for the production of artificial light. To particularize all that has been done, is needless; but it may be useful to select and record some of the

most economical of recent discoveries, as hints
for domestic practice.

We believe it may now be considered as an established fact, that gas light, even for domestic purposes, is the cheapest and best, with the exception
of the first cost for an apparatus, which can only
be covered by savings on extensive illuminations;
but is hardly within the compass of domestic expenditure, where required only by one family. Even
in the metropolis, and in large provincial towns,
where gas pipes can be led into every apartment,
there still exists another difficulty, in the way of its
becoming an entire substitute for oil or candles;
which is, that it has not yet, with any success, been
adapted to portable lamps, though such improvement may yet take place, as a candlestick, or lamp
in the shape of one, may be formed with a reservoir sufficiently large for casual purposes, without
being of a very inconvenient size; though, even
then, a ready supply would be difficult, unless we
produce our own gas, or can send off to the gas
shop for a cubic foot of gas, as readily as for a
pound of candles, or a farthing rush-light.

That the burning of gas, however, generally
speaking, is an important saving, is clear from repeated experiments, by which it appears, that one
gas lamp gives as much light in the street as four
lighted with oil. In shops, it has been found that
three gas lights, at 25s. each, per year, will illumi-
nate the windows and the whole apartment in a
much superior style to what could be done by five
or six mould candles. The estimated difference
of cost per annum, is 3l. 15s. for gas, fully equal to
12l. for candles. This saving may also be much increased by improvements in the lamps, particularly
those on the argand construction. It has been
proved by experiment that an argand gas burner,

seven-eights of an inch in diameter, perforated with
18 holes one thirty-second of an inch in diameter,
consumes, when the flame of the gas is three inches
high, four cubic feet of gas in an hour, and produces a light equal in intensity to six tallow candles,
eight in the pound. It ought also to be observed,
and this part of gas management is of more importance than is generally supposed, that when the
flame obtained by these kind of burners, rises to a
greater height than from two to three inches, the
combustion of the gas is imperfect; and the same
holds good with regard to the size of the holes
from which the gas issues. A simple and sufficiently
accurate test for ascertaining whether any portion
of the gas escapes unburned, may readily be procured. For this purpose, it is merely necessary to
hold a piece of clean writing paper a short distance
from the apex of the flame, and if the combustion
is not perfect, the paper will be discoloured, and
immediately imbibe a very fœtid smell. But even
the power of the argand lamp may be increased by
parabolic reflectors; which also, where oil is burned,
produce a double saving, it being now ascertained
as a curious fact in the theory of artificial light,
that, when reflected by a parabolic mirror, this reflected light is greater in proportion to the diminution of the wick. This has been ascertained by
the experiments of the French academy, when it
appeared that an argand lamp of six lines diameter
gave a better light than one of sixteen, consuming
at the same time only half the quantity of oil.
This improvement may be applied with great success to carriage lamps, particularly in travelling;
and is not unworthy the notice of those metropolitan districts where gas illumination has not yet
taken place.

They have already begun to apply this principle

to public use in France, and M. Bordier Marcet,
the relation and successor of M. Ami Argand Marcet, the inventor of the lamps called after him, has
made considerable improvements in regard to the
lighting of public streets. The mayor of Valogne
has certified that his lamps, with parabolic reflectors,
give so good a light that a person may see to read
with ease at the distance of 120 yards; that they
are very little affected either by rain or wind, and
that the quantity of oil consumed by them is only
one ounce and one-fifteenth per hour. Thus the
whole town is now better lighted by eighteen of
M. Bordier's lamps, than it was formerly by forty
on the old plan.

This is certainly highly deserving notice, both
in domestic economy, and in parochial vestries,
considering the very indifferent light in our streets,
where the gas has not yet been introduced.

Another great saving may result from the philosophical inventions of the ingenious Mr. Lester,
who, we understand has recently brought his new
discovery in optics to perfection, and from its simplicity and utility, it promises to be of great importance. Two cones of light produced from the lumi-
nary being placed near to their respective apexes, and
in opposite directions, base to base, form a parallelo-
gram of indefinite dimensions, that would fill the
room with an equal light of the same tensity in
every part of its space; and as the fountain of light
would be in opposite directions, the bodies equally
divided, would have but two sides as opposed to
the lines of vision; no shadows can be produced
by the application. Rooms of all descriptions may
be lighted by the flame being placed on the outside of the wall, and its reflection thrown through
an aperture, by which means the smoke arising
from the combustion will pass off into the atmo-

sphere without entering the room, and the light will have the most beautiful effect, by illuminating a space void of smoke, which is far from being the case with rooms lighted in the common way. It has been clearly ascertained that one of Mr. Lester's Mirrors, 13½ inches diameter, placed before one of the lamps commonly used to light stages, and fixed to the foot-board of the driver, will render the smallest print legible at the distance of 100 yards before the leaders heads.

We should not wish to see coal-gas become entirely a substitute for oil; as our Greenland trade is of too much importance to the country, especially as a nursery for seamen, to be sported with rashly: but as oil may be applied to the production of gas, though by a different process from coal, the trade is not in much danger. Indeed, it may even be expedient to find a substitute for whale-oil, and we see with pleasure that an Irish chemist, desirous of introducing the patent lamp into general use in that part of the United Kingdom, has found means to improve rape oil by a simple process, which renders it equal to spermaceti for the purposes of illumination. He began by washing the oil with spring water, by shaking the former violently with a sixth part of the latter. By this operation the two substances are intimately commixed; if left at rest they separate completely again in less than 48 hours, the oil swimming at top, and the water with all the feculent and extraneous particles, subsiding to the bottom. Upon this method he improved much by substituting sea-water for fresh; the latter impregnated with salt is less fit for the purpose than sea-water, as the light is not so bright and of a reddish cast. Rape oil thus treated does not give out any bad smell, and is not to be distinguished from spermaceti. By this process of washing, the oil loses less than $\frac{1}{1000}$.—Mr. Roche intends to perform it in a churn, with a cock towards the bottom, the water to come up very near to the cock, by which all the oil can be drawn off after it has deposited its impurities.

Whenever oil is used for the purpose of artificial light, it should be kept free from all exposure to atmospheric air; as it is apt to absorb considerable quantities of oxygen, which renders it more tenacious and less adapted to use, by capillary attraction through the common lamp wicks.

If oil is very coarse and tenacious, a very small portion of oil of turpentine may be added.

Family clocks ought only to be oiled with the very purest oil, purified by a quart of lime-water to a gallon of oil, in which it has been well shaken, and suffered to stand for three or four days, when it may be drawn off.

There are some recent economical discoveries in regard to gas, which are highly deserving of notice. It has been found by experiment at Manchester, that oil of bitumen, or coal tar, which is considered as waste by those who make and burn gas, if mixed with dry saw-dust, exhausted logwood, or fustic, to the consistence of paste, and allowed to remain until the water has drained off—two cwt. of the mass being put into the retort, instead of coal, will produce more gas, and be less offensive than the same quantity of canal-coal; and the process may be repeated until the whole of the tar is consumed.

If oil is preferred to pit coal, a great saving is now opened to our view; for, by a new discovery, combustible gas is procured by causing oil to fall drop by drop into a tube heated red hot, and which is kept in that state. The gas passes immediately from the tube to the lamp, and produces a beautiful flame, without any smell.

Nor are these the only cheap materials; for we understand that an American chemist has invented a lamp in which tar is burnt instead of oil. It consists of a fountain reservoir to supply and preserve a constant level, and a lamp which receives the fountain-pipe at one end, and at the other a burner for the tar: this is merely a small cup placed on the axis of the lamp, and supplied with tar from the fountain. A draught tube is fixed in the lanthorn, or external part of the lamp, and air is admitted by a hole at the bottom. The current of air, in passing through the lamp, envelopes the burner, and urges the flame, and the draught-tube conveys off the smoke. Nor must it be forgotten, that our great and indefatigable chemist, Sir H. Davy, has, in the course of his important researches, improved our modes of domestic illumination, by guarding against accidental fire, he having very recently found means to procure permanent light without flame: he has taught us that a platina wire of sufficient fineness, and an inch, or an inch and a half long, which has been heated red hot, may be long preserved in this state over a vessel in which there is sulphuric ether or alcohol, in a state of evaporation. Thus this incandescent wire may be employed as a cheap night-lamp, or instead of a steel to light tinder.

Since this discovery the principle has been applied to practical uses by another very ingenious individual, who has ascertained that if a cylindrical coil of thin platina wire be placed, part of it round the cotton wick of a spirit lamp, and part of it above the wick, and the lamp be lighted so as to heat the wire to redness; on the flame being blown out, the vapour of the alcohol will keep the upper part of the wire red hot for any length of time, according to the supply of alcohol, and with little expenditure of it, so as to be in constant readiness to kindle German fungus, or paper prepared with nitre, and thus to light a sulphur match or any other, at pleasure. The proper size of the platina wire is the 1-100th part of an inch; a larger size will yield only a dull red light, and a smaller is difficult to use. About twelve turns of the wire will be sufficient, coiled round any cylindrical body, suited to the size of the lamp; and four or five coils should be placed on the wick, and the remainder of the wire above it; the latter will be the part ignited. When the wire has become oxyded, it will be necessary to uncoil and rub it bright with fine glass-paper, which will cause it to act again with increased effect. This lamp while it affords a sufficient light to show the hour of the night by a watch, and to perform many other useful services, does not disturb persons unaccustomed to keep a light burning in their bed-rooms. From its constantly keeping up an uniform heat, and not requiring to be snuffed, like other lamps, it may prove a valuable acquisition to the chemist, for experiments on a small scale, where a long continuance of a gentle heat is desirable. Its peculiar safety, as not a spark can fall from it, and its being totally free from the unpleasant smoke and smell common to oil lamps, are additional recommendations.

But discovery on discovery is rushing into light, for Professor Meinacke, of Halle, has just succeeded in producing a brilliant illumination by means of electric light, and with the aid of an artificial air inclosed in glass tubes. As the electric sparks propagate themselves to infinity, the Professor thinks it will be possible to light up a whole city with a single electrifying machine, and at a very trifling expense, by the adoption and probable improvement of the apparatus he has already invented.

Nor is it Heaven and Earth alone that are ransacked to enlighten the world—water has also been pressed into the service, as we find that an apparatus called the American Water Burner, has lately been invented by Mr. Morcy, of New-Hampshire. It is a rough blow-pipe; but is applicable in many cases in place of a furnace. Tar is intimately mixed with steam, and made to issue from a small jet, in the manner of an eolipile; and the stream of matter, being ignited, produces a flame of great size and intensity. It appears that the water is partly decomposed towards the middle of the jet, and that the heat is thus increased, by increasing the quantity of active agents. But whatever the exact effect, the water is found to be useful in preventing the formation of smoke, and increasing the combustion.

This is a hint which may become highly useful upon the plan of constructing furnaces so as to become the consumers of their own smoke.

Even the tricks of chemistry may be applied with success in many cases to Domestic Economy, and in none more advantageously, upon a small scale, than in safe means for instantaneous ignition. One of the readiest, but most dangerous of these, was founded on the experience that hyper-oxymuriate of soda, brought into contact with a combustible body (wood for instance), which has been plunged into sulphuric acid, sets fire to this combustible. Latterly this apparatus has been rendered more convenient and less dangerous, by putting into the phial, instead of liquid sulphureous acid, very fine sand, asbestos, gypsum, or some other body, which the acid does not destroy, and which is moistened with it. Several thousand matches may be lighted in this manner before it is necessary to renew this kind of indissoluble sponge, which is to produce the inflammation.

A method nearly similar, but rather more simple, has recently been proposed; and matches for the purpose are prepared by mingling two parts of the oxymuriate of potash and one of sulphur, which, by means of a little gum, is attached to a common sulphur match. This match on being dipped into, or rather slightly wet with oil of vitriol, immediately catches fire. The sulphur and salt should be pulverized separately; if rubbed together in a mortar, they form a dangerous explosive mixture.

Having thus far endeavoured to illumine the world, we shall proceed to another subject.

SECTION II.

PRINCIPAL APARTMENTS.

BED-ROOMS— *Ventilation*— *Air-bath*— *Bedding*—*Air-beds.* DRESSING-ROOMS — *Home Manufactures* — *Odours* — *Ornaments* — *Flowers*— *Teeth*—*Hair* — *Razors* — *Cosmetics* —*Dress* — *Dying* —*Choice of Colours*—*Diamonds, &c.*—*Trinkets*—*Pearls.* BREAK-FAST AND TEA-TABLES—*Utensils*—*Tea, Coffee, &c.* HUNTING-PARLOUR — *Fowling-pieces* — *Powder* — *Veterinary Art.* LIBRARY—*Comfort*—*Convenience* — *Arrangements*—*Light*—*Collecting*—*Selection*— *Care of Books and Prints*—*Fine Arts*—*Sculpture*— *Paintings*—*Cabinets of Natural History*—*Medals* —*Gems*—*Antiques*—*Chemical Experiments, &c. &c.* DINNER-TABLE—DRAWING-ROOM.

BED ROOMS.

WHETHER in the palace or the cottage, whether reclining on the state bed or stretched on the humble pallet, the reader will find more real economy, as well as pleasure and comfort, in attending to his dormitory than to his larder. Sleep is the food of half our life, the regenerator and regulator of all our faculties both bodily and mental—in short, as Sancho says, " it covers a man all over like a cloak :" but to render it salubrious, indeed to prevent its being morbific, it is absolutely necessary that the time when, the manner how, and the *place where*, ought to be sedulously regulated.

Our poet of the Avon justly describes a sleepless monarch as envying the repose enjoyed by the " wet sea-boy" in the rude hour of midnight tempest, even whilst exposed to the inclemency of the season in the fore or main-top; but, notwithstanding the beauty of the passage, every one practically acquainted with such occurrences well knows that the thoughtless sailor ought to have postponed his nap, until he could turn into a dry hammock.

Our readers will therefore do well not to indulge in sleep, in every place where it may offer itself, and they will also do well to attend to the regulation of those places where repose is proper.

Air and exercise during the day are most essential to man; and though at night he is quiescent, yet his air must still be attended to, as the privation of salubrious air always produces disease. For this purpose whenever the air is dry, it ought to be freely admitted during the day; nor ought it, unless damp or locally insalubrious, to be excluded totally during the night. It is true, that where a current of air falls upon the bed, it ought to be prevented from direct influence by means of the usual curtains; but these curtains, even in the best aired apartments, should never be closely drawn, not even round the couch of the invalid, any more than round that of the most robust son of health and strength. A very simple experiment, though one which humanity will not wish to be often repeated, may be tried by hanging up a small bird in a cage, at the head of a bed of which the curtains are kept closed during the night; where the experiment has been tried, the result was that the unfortunate bird appeared to be expiring, when morning dawned upon the face of nature; and was only recovered, and that with difficulty, by immediate exposure to the atmosphere.

Upon this principle, too, we ought to be particularly careful of all fires in bed-rooms; from the quantity of carbonic acid gas which developes itself from fires, whether of coal or wood, and may be dangerous if persons retire to sleep, without attending to the freedom of ventilation.

Under the head of *Ventilation*—some of the readiest and cheapest modes of producing a free current of air in all apartments, have been duly noticed; but here we must particularly caution our readers not only against the use of charcoal fires upon any account whatsoever, but also against the use of charcoal in warming-pans, or even of common coals until they have been burnt to a cinder. To the healthy, the vapours thence arising and left in the bed, where they remain on account of their density, are often troublesome; but to the sick, they are palpably injurious, and frequently prompt to that cough which annoys the phthisicky and asthmatic, the moment they lie down for repose. Where circumstances require a bed to be heated at a moment's notice, a little salt thrown into the warming-pan, and suffered to burn for a minute previous to use, will generally be beneficial; and as chambermaids are seldom either philosophers or chemists, it may be better to make this a standing order than to trust to their judgment on gaseous combustion. Those who wish to ascertain whether their bed be properly aired, will do well to introduce a glass goblet between the sheets for a minute or two, just when the warming-pan is taken out; if the bed be dry there will only be a slight cloudy appearance on the glass, but if not, the damp of the bed will assume the more formidable appearance of drops, which will act as a sufficient

warning to drop the idea of sleeping in a situation
so fraught with danger.

As the utmost attention to cleanliness will not
always prevent the intrusion of certain little insects,
too indelicate to name, but which take longer leaps
in proportion to their size than any other known
animal in existence, it has been customary to scatter fresh leaves of penny-royal in bedchambers as
an antidote against their appearance; but fresh
vegetables in a dormitory have been found prejudicial to health, and growing ones much more so.
Hence flowers and shrubs, whether in bowpots or
vases, though highly ornamental and not injurious
in a dressing-room, ought to be excluded from the
bed-chamber.

Even the honey-suckle and jessamine, so beautiful when embowering a cottage window, ought to
be excluded, by a shut casement, at the hour of
repose; nay, the branches of flowering hawthorn,
so frequently introduced into fire places in the
spring, may prove injurious to weak lungs at night,
however grateful during the day.

These things often produce an inaptitude to
sleep, even in the healthy, without the cause being
suspected; but to the sick they are invariably
hurtful. The dead hour of night, however, is
seldom a convenient time to get rid of such nuisances;
but they may be corrected in part by the temporary
opening of a window, and that too without any
danger of catching cold, if proper precautions are
taken. In fact, a current of air in the night, for
a short time upon the body, is by no means insalubrious if accompanied with due care.

Dr. Franklin, in one of his letters, declares that
he preferred the *air-bath* to the use of cold water,
finding it much more analogous to his constitution,
as well as more agreeable. He adds that he has

even got up in the night, and remained undressed for half an hour or longer, according to the season, either walking up and down his apartment, or occupying himself with a book: after which, on returning to his bed, he was certain of enjoying sound repose.

Where the invalid thinks this too violent an exposure, a partial bath, free from any absolute current of air, will not be hurtful. This species of exercise, for such it really is, may be easily accomplished by means of simple machinery, which will forego the trouble and anxiety of depending upon assistance, and in many cases will save the expence of a nocturnal attendant. Several inventions have been offered for this purpose; but perhaps the best may be found in a recent patent machine, or wind-up bedstead for sick or lame persons, by which their position can be easily altered without occasioning pain or fatigue. It works smoothly without any jerks, and by one rack only, which enables a single attendant to raise, or depress the bed at pleasure. The patentee* can furnish bedsteads on this construction at the rate of 36s. each, and an old bed may be easily altered to this plan. He can also, if necessary, lower the foot part of the bed by the same movement, so as to make the bed answer the purposes of a chair.

In all these cases, however, the moment the use of this species of bath is over, the person applying it ought to return to his accustomed temperature by laying down under the bed-clothes: and here it may not be improper to remark that these should in all cases be apportioned to the season or to the prevailing temperature, regulated by the bodily health of the individual, so as just to preserve the insensible perspiration, and no more.

* Mr. Woodall.

It will, amongst other things connected with the dormitory, be found a great saving eventually of time, and trouble, and accomplished at a small expence, to have all beds and mattresses opened out at intervals not very distant, so as to have the feathers or other internal materials beaten, cleaned, and dried, and the cases washed. The bedsteads ought also to be taken down three or four times a year, the screws rubbed with pure oil, and a good manual cleaning given to all parts. This plan, which has been slightly noticed under the general head of cleanliness, will render all poisonous mixtures unnecessary; besides saving all the trouble, filth, and expence consequent upon the use of those medicaments so much recommended by quacks, bug-destroyers, &c.

One word in regard to materials may here be introduced. The very high price of feathers of late years has completely done away the practice of having one well filled feather-bed laid upon the bottom sacking; and the substitutes of straw mattresses, with bed-cases half filled with indifferent feathers, are poor indeed. Instead of these it will be found not only cheaper, but more comfortable and healthful to use hair-mattresses, with straw palliasses if you please, but with sedulous attention to have the latter renewed at intervals not longer than a year each.

In this age of adulteration, duck's feathers are frequently substituted for those of the goose; but these are highly pernicious, being often covered with small insects, which destroy the substance of the feathers, and produce the most disagreeable results. Where the absolute expence is not a first object of consideration, and even there the difference is but trifling, it may not be injudicious to adopt beds upon the new patent principle of an ingenious mechanist in Somersetshire, which consists in rendering the case of the bed, pillow, &c. impervious to air, and filling it, by means of an air-pump, with common atmospheric air, instead of down or feathers. The air is introduced through an aperture, or tube, into the case, and prevented from returning by means of an air-tight stop-cock or valve. The case may be rendered impervious to air by various methods; but that recommended by the patentee, is a composition of India rubber, spirits of turpentine, and linseed oil, which when dry, is extremely pliable, and so elastic, that if the cloth be folded in sharp corners, it will not crack, or peel off.

The advantages of this method of construction for beds and pillows, are their superior degree of elasticity, affording the most refreshing and easy repose either in this or even in the warmest climates; that they may when required, be changed from the greatest degree of softness to the hardness of a mattress, by moving the handle of the air-pump, which is placed commodiously within reach; or may be rendered soft to any required degree, by the exhausting pump, also within reach.

In addition to these conveniences, they may at any time be rendered perfectly fresh and cool, by merely changing the air, by the alternate use of the air-pumps; this may be effected in a few minutes, without the person sleeping on the beds being moved: hence their great advantage to invalids, and their generally refreshing and salubrious effects.

Such machinery may at first sight appear too philosophical for common use, and too cumbrous for a sleeping-apartment; but as to the first point, only a very small portion of ingenuity is required to become conversant with their application; and as to the second it is merely necessary to say, that the air-pumps, together with all the machinery for filling and exhausting the beds, being inclosed under the bedsteads, and communicating with cords and tassels (resembling bell-pulls) suspended immediately above the pillows, any alteration in the state or temperature of the beds is thus easily effected, at any time required.

The fact is, that they save much manual labour, as they require no making up; for by their elasticity, they rise immediately when left, and are then in the state of other beds after being shaken and made up, the counterpane, &c. being returned as usual: hence they occasion no dust or film in the rooms, or on the furniture, which is always the case where feather or down beds are used.

For medical purposes also, they may be filled with air at any required temperature; or with water, steam, or other fluids, wet or dry, elastic or non-elastic, to which the case is equally impermeable. In addition to which they have several other advantages. They are not subject to be sloping on one side, nor to those hard clumps or knots which feathers or down gradually acquire in the course of a few years.

They are likewise extremely light, the largest weighing only a few ounces, and portable also, being easily folded or rolled, after being previously exhausted.

Under such advantages, a night's good repose can scarcely be doubted—but day breaks, and we therefore proceed to the

DRESSING ROOM,

which may be considered with reference to both sexes.

To the ladies, however, we now more particularly address ourselves; and we cannot couch our address in more forcible terms than in the words of a fair-writer, a real Englishwoman, who has recently offered a sensible and well-written appeal to her countrywomen in general, exhorting them, in these times of general distress, to discourage, by their conduct and influence, the importation, both legal and illegal, of foreign manufactures.—" I allow," observes the writer, " there are some temptations to be resisted—the gaily coloured silks and hand-kerchiefs of French manufacture—the gloves which set off the forms of our hands and arms, are cer-tainly far superior to our own; but if there were no temptation, there would be no merit in the for-bearance. And if we look down on our dresses, unadorned by handsome laces, because from prin-ciple we abstain from purchasing them, and use our arms clothed in less elegant or becoming attire than we have been accustomed to, let us reflect with pleasure that we have, by these little sacrifices, contributed, as far as we can, to the employment of our industrious countrymen. What, therefore, can be more desirable, than that Englishwomen of all ranks should combine in determining to purchase only the manufactures of their own country, and resist the temptation of adorning their persons, at the expence not only of the comforts, but the morals of their countrymen ?"

After this spirited and patriotic address, we shall at once proceed to the most economic mode of orna-menting the apartment itself; and then offer some remarks on the ornamenting the persons of our fair readers, which may lead, not only to the saving, but also to the gain of beauty.

The first point of consideration must be that which first strikes the sense on entering this apart-ment of sweets, and which the most gallant ad-mirer must acknowledge is dependent upon the smell, even before the sight. Cleanliness and ventilation are indeed preferable to all factitious odours; but as these are generally adopted, not, however, we hope to the neglect of the former, it may be consistent with our plan to offer a cheap substitute for the Otto of Roses, so difficult to procure in a genuine state. The recipe is very simple, being nothing more than to dip the finest cotton wool in clear olive oil, which must be spread in thin layers, in a tall glass vessel, with alternate layers of jessamine flowers which, in a few days, will impart the whole of their perfume to the cotton. The oil may then be pressed out for use: and the cotton itself may be laid in drawers or band-boxes, where its perfume is wished for.

Beyond this we advocate not artificial odours, unless, indeed, that musk should be introduced for the purpose of removing destructive insects. This drug is expensive, and therefore seldom to be had genuine; which, however, is not an object of great importance, as a very small quantity will suffice for a life-time. If, however, our fair readers should wish to ascertain its genuineness, that may easily be done by steeping a silken thread in garlic-juice, or drawing it two or three times through a clove of moist garlic, and then through the musk, which, if genuine, will instantly so overcome the odour of the garlic as to render it imperceptible to the most acute olfactory feeling.

It is not unfrequent to ornament dressing-rooms with artificial flowers; yet these, however beautiful, have no odour: but a cheap and elegant substitution may be found by taking natural flowers in bloom and dipping them in alcohol, or strong spirits of wine, for about a quarter of an hour; after which the colour will appear to have entirely faded: as they become dry, however, they may be arranged for the beaupots, when it will be found that their colours will revive and their odour will be much prolonged beyond the usual time.

Most flowers begin to droop and fade after being kept during twenty-four hours in water; a few may be revived by substituting fresh water; but all (the most fugacious, such as the poppy, and perhaps one or two others excepted) may be completely restored by the use of *hot* water. For this purpose, place the flowers in scalding water, deep enough to cover about one-third of the length of the stem; by the time the water has become cold, the flowers will have become erect and fresh: then cut off the end of the stems, and put them into cold water.

We have seen another ingenious method of preserving flowers throughout the winter, which may serve as a cheap and pleasing mode of decoration. The plan is to pluck the flowers when half blown, and to put them in an earthen vessel with a close cover, immersing them, with the stalks downwards, in a mixture of water and verjuice, of each equal parts, sprinkled with a small portion of bay salt. The vessel must be well closed up and kept in a warm place, safe from the action of frost; and then on the coldest day in winter, nothing more is necessary than to take them out, wash them in fair water, and hold them before a gentle fire, when they will open as if in all their vernal bloom.

As the flowering of bulbous roots is always an agreeable decoration of the dressing-room in winter, it may be amusing to state an easy method of encouraging it rapidly, even in the coldest weather. Take three ounces of nitre, one ounce of common salt, half an ounce of potash, half an ounce of sugar, and dissolve them in a pint of rain water. Keep your glasses near the fire. Change the water every ten or twelve days; and each time put in about half a tea spoonful of this mixture.

E

It must not be forgotten that the perfumes of ornamental flowers, when growing, will be increased, as well as their beauty, by affording as much sun and air as possible, and also by being careful always to set them out under genial showers. It is literally sending them to a watering-place.

An elegant mode of combining the odours of different flowers is, by preserving the leaves in vases, or china jars, in the form of a *pot pourri*, as the French term it; for which fine perfume, the following is a genuine receipt. Take one pound of orange flowers and common rose leaves, half a pound each of the leaves of red pinks, marjoram and myrtle; the leaves of musk roses, thyme, lavender, rosemary, sage, camomile, melilot, hyssop, sweet basil, and balm, two ounces of each; two or three handfuls of jessamine flowers, a large handful of lemon rinds, cut as thin as possible; the same quantity of those of small green oranges, and fifteen or twenty laurel leaves; put them all into a well leaded earthen jar, with half a pound of bay salt, and stir the whole carefully with a wooden spatula, or spoon, twice a day for a month; then add florentine white iris and benzoin, of each twelve ounces; powdered cloves and cinnamon, two ounces of each; mace, storax, calamus aromaticus, and cypress, of each one ounce; lemon-coloured sandal, and long sweet cypress, of each six drachms: stir all together; and if the proportions be carefully attended to, according to the above directions, a most delightful compound of fine odours will be obtained, in which no one scent will predominate, whilst the fragrance of the whole will remain unimpaired for a great number of years.

It is needless to expatiate upon the utility of these odours in correcting all acquired unwholsomeness of

the air in our dwellings, or rather in correcting the
effects of that unwholsomeness. To understand the
principles of action in this case, may be of some
import. Wholesome air is that which affords the
due stimulus to the lungs, and to the blood: un-
wholesome air, generally speaking, is that which,
although not possessing qualities absolutely noxious, is yet destitute of the proper quantity of oxygen required by the system, in the proportion of
about seventeen parts in an hundred of atmospheric
air; as for those species of noxious airs which are
positively deleterious, they come under a medical
head, and need no reference here. But, as to that
air which is hurtful to the constitution from want of
due stimulus, we may usefully correct its deficiency
by the stimulus of artificial odours. It will happen
sometimes, however, that, even in our wardrobes
most carefully kept, clothes long laid up, will acquire
a very unpleasant smell; to counteract which, perfumes may be used; but the readiest method is
to neutralize or destroy it, which may at once be
done, by placing pieces of new burnt charcoal
amongst the clothes, when the whole of the unpleasant fumes or odour will be absorbed in a day or
two.

Charcoal is also a very useful tooth powder; but,
although extremely efficacious when used alone, it
may, perhaps, be more actively employed along with
the following ingredients. Take half a drachm of
tartar of vitriol, same quantity of myrrh, also of
dragon's blood; to which add one drachm of gum
lac, and four grains of ambergrise, with two grains
of musk, and fine powdered charcoal equal to the
whole. Beat them into a fine powder, and keep
in a phial close stopped. To use it, take a fine linen
cloth, wetted on the end of your finger; dip it in

the powder, and apply it well once a day; after which twice a week will be sufficient to preserve the beauty of the teeth, and to correct any unpleasant savour from the breath, even where there is a carious tooth.

Amongst the various cosmetics recommended for the dressing-room, there are none, perhaps, that seem more harmless than those which profess to give a fine curl to the hair. Now, to assert that the application of any liquid will, of itself, give a permanent or temporary curl, is absurd in the extreme; but it is very true that the application of a weak soap lye, or a solution of caustic potash, will render the hair more susceptible of adopting the artificial curl given by putting it in papers. But let it be remembered that this effect is only produced by a complete alteration of the organic structure, super-inducing a slow but certain destruction of the hair itself. This may not be immediately observed, either in youth or advanced life; in the former case, indeed, the loss is easily renewed, as if the hair had been merely cut: but in age there is no renewal; if the hair be destroyed, baldness must ensue.

Equally destructive are the various liquid dyes so loudly boasted of by quacks for colouring the hair; some of them, indeed, do produce the effect proposed, especially the black dyes; but these latter are most injurious, as their basis consists always of nitrate of silver, or lunar caustic when in a dry state, the colour from which certainly is indelible as long as the hair lasts; but surely no person who is aware of the effect of the caustic on warts, or on the skin, can for a moment suppose that its operation on the hair can be less destructive.

--- If we wish then to *save our hair*, we must *save our money* first, by abstaining from the whole list of those puffed recipes that stare us in the face in every newspaper, and in almost every shop window!

Equally destructive are the advertised Depilatories, the general basis of which is yellow orpiment, a certain poison if taken inwardly. It is true that the Turks, with whom bald-heads are in fashion, and also the Chinese, do use this as an unguent, to save the trouble of frequent shaving; but those cosmetics which may be harmless on the head of a robust Janisary, of a Bashaw of three tails, or a fat Mandarin, do not necessarily become fit adjuncts for the toilette of a British belle!

As a point then of domestic economy we recommend the disuse of all these quackeries. Those who are very anxious to restore hair, when ill-health or the rapid approach of age has removed it, may try the stimulating powers of onions, rubbed frequently on the part requiring it. In some instances this application has restored the tone of the skin, and assisted the capillary vessels in sending forth new hair; but it is not infallible. Should it succeed, however, the growth of those new hairs may be assisted by the oil of myrtle-berries, the repute of which, perhaps, is greater than its real efficacy. But these applications are cheap and harmless, even where they do no good—a character which, we fear, by no means belongs to the trash puffed in advertisements by fellows who seem themselves in need of the essence of Lindley Murray, or some other writer for grown-up children—to teach them a little plain English.

Connected with this part of the subject, is a hint which we beg leave to offer for the Gentlemen's dressing-room. We do not expect them, indeed, upon an economic principle, to turn razor-grinders; but if they chuse to be their own *tonseurs,* in preference

to being taken by the nose by a Frenchman, they will
save much time, much patience, and considerable
pain, by keeping their *hones* in a proper state. This
can only be done by frequently moistening them with
oil, and laying them up in a place where they will
not readily become dry.

' If we disapprove of cosmetics for the hair, our
objections are much stronger in regard to the complexion. The greatest part of those are formed
from metallic oxydes, which are known to be highly
deleterious. Their effects, indeed, may not at first
be very apparent; but it will be too late when
nervous affections, perhaps palsy, come on—to regret that a silly desire to obtain, or retain brilliancy
of complexion should have led to their use, to obviate the effects of late hours and of careless, nay
unwarrantable, personal exposure.

On this part of the subject we shall offer a hint
to the male sex, which the Ladies may, perhaps,
find worth attending to. We have already recorded
chemical tests on various subjects, and we now propose an infallible one to be tried by any gentle
Philander who may be anxious to ascertain whether
his fair one's lillies and roses are really her own or
not! Let him persuade her to take a trip to Harrowgate, the waters of which fashionable place of resort are strongly impregnated with hydrogen, a gas
that acts powerfully upon all the metallic oxydes.
When safely arrived at this new lecture-room of
nature, he may then try whether the bloom and
brilliancy that withstood the test of hot rooms in
Grosvenor-square, or Argyll-street, will likewise stand the test of those genial springs. If the
fair one's face retains its pristine beauty after half
a dozen ablutions, he may consider the article as
genuine and unadulterated, and free from all the

terrors of "Death in the Pot"—but if the dame or damsel begin to look blue, or turn black, he will at once perceive that beauty, like London porter, may be doctored for the market.

At the head of the list of those destroyers of beauty, is the "pearl white," a precipitate of the oxyde of bismuth dissolved in aqua-fortis, and separated from it by the addition of water, for which the aqua-fortis has a stronger affinity than for the bismuth, and, of course, permits it to fall to the bottom of the glass in a white powder. If our fair readers are, however, dissatisfied with the faces which God has given them, or which they may have made for themselves, let them throw away all their washes and lotions, and, if they must have artificial cosmetics, let them infuse horse-radish in cold milk, as a stimulant to the pores of the skin, or powder the roots of the cuckoo plant, sometimes called "lords and ladies," but botanically known as the *arum*; yet this latter must first be well dried and deprived of its acrid juice. It may be had in the shops under the name of cypress powder, but is seldom to be got genuine.

After all, perhaps, the best and safest cosmetic, next to plain soap and water, is a little good butter-milk, fresh or stale. It speedily removes freckles, and acts generally as a stimulant of the mildest nature.

In the economy of the dressing-room, the economy of Dress must not be neglected: we shall here confine ourselves, however, to two points strictly applicable to the costume of the present day, velvets and straw hats; other points of considerable importance will come with more propriety under the head of the LAUNDRY. With respect to the first of these articles, it is perhaps not generally known, that velvet pelisses are readily restored, by passing the under side of the velvet over a warm smoothing iron: the best way of doing this is for one person to hold the velvet tight, and another to pass the iron over it on the wrong side; after which the garment must be spread out, and a brush, or very fine whisk, like those now sold about the streets by Dutch women, passed gently yet briskly over the pile. The good effect of this, even upon the most worn out dresses, will scarcely be credited, until tried; and it is equally applicable to dresses that are but little worn. The customary mode of whitening straw for ornamental use, has been to stove it in a cask with burning brimstone; but there is a readier method, if judiciously applied: take a solution of muriatic acid, and saturate it with pot-ash until the effervescence subsides. Dip the straw in the solution. Again, the oxygenated muriate of lime, which may be had at any chemist's shop, dissolved in water, will bleach straw without the least diminution of its flexibility.

Recently in Germany fashion has introduced a new application of cork, which is now used for making ladies' hats. They differ from straw hats in this particular, that the material is put together in the manner of fish scales.

When laying up muffs and tippets for the winter, if a tallow candle be placed on or near them, all danger of moths will be obviated.

To renovate feathers, it is necessary first to wash them carefully in soap and water; but as the original pure white can never be restored in its true brilliancy, it may be useful to know the simplest methods of giving a tinge of artificial colour agreeable to the fancy of the wearer.

The first and simplest is, a *grey*, which may be produced by sprinkling common ink judiciously upon the feather, reduced by water to any shade; or the feathers may be dipped in ink, reduced at pleasure.

Tincture of turmeric, to any depth of tint, will give a fine *yellow*. The spirituous tincture is best; and the colour may be brightened by means of lemon juice, either added to the tincture itself, or applied to the feather afterwards.

Liquid blue, added to the tincture of turmeric, affords a *green*, which may be given of any tint, by altering the proportions of the dying materials.

Where yellow is thought too gaudy, a fine *buff* may be produced by adding a little pearl-ash to annatto boiled in water.

Liquid *blue*, applied solely, will yield a fine tint of the same colour; or the sulphate of indigo may be adopted for the same purpose.

If *purple* is wished for, add to the liquid blue a little of the red sold in saucers; or dissolve a few grains of carmine in a little spirits of hartshorn, which mix with a solution of orchil.

To produce a *red* colour, nothing more is necessary than to dip the feather in lemon juice until thoroughly wetted, and then into the saucer red, or solution of carthamus.

Whilst on this part of the subject, we may offer a few hints to our fair readers on the philosophical economy of *Colour* in all parts of their dress; nay, even in regard to the hangings and carpets of their apartments, where they receive visitors, and when they may wish to look particularly lovely.

We must first premise, that white reflects all rays of light, and that black absorbs them all; but this, though optically and philosophically true, has certain exceptions, as white dresses, from peculiar circumstances of position, have been observed to reflect only particular tints. All coloured dresses, or coloured objects, indeed, between the extremes of white and black, absorb the rays of light in certain proportion and quality; the particular rays *reflected* by each object, being the basis of its colour. Thus brown substances reflect the red rays in a very small degree; purple reflects the red and blue rays; green the blue and yellow rays; orange the red and yellow, &c.

Again, it must be observed, that reflections from any particular object become confused and intermingled, from partaking of the luminous rays from other surrounding bodies; and it is known, that the rays from white dresses will actually enlighten and whiten shadows upon white substances. In like manner, whenever dresses of different colours are grouped together, the reflected rays from each fall upon the others, and consequently produce a temporary discolouration wherever they fall.

Thus, in a group of ladies, principally in coloured dresses, it will be observed, that the white dresses, whether of silk or muslin, not only receive a confused tinge from the others, but actually alter the tints of the other colours.

This shews clearly, that however judicious a lady may be in the adapting her own colours to her own complexion, yet she must still be very careful with whom she associates, not only in regard to character but colour. Nay, an envious fair one, though she may not wish to stab her rival to the heart with a dagger, may yet give as deep a wound by ascertaining what colour that rival is to wear upon any particular occasion, and then forming a conspiracy amongst her friends to disregard their own charms for one day, and attack her at the important moment under false colours!

Ladies also, who are particularly susceptible upon the score of good looks, must not only select colours for their own carpets and hangings, compatible with their complexion and their mode of dressing, but must also ascertain the colours of their friends' apartments, before they dress for dinner or a rout, and be prepared for a change of colour, for each change scene.

At public places also, this is not unimportant. A lady may look irresistible in white or blue at Covent Garden or the Opera, and appear an old woman in the same costume at Drury Lane.

Again, some ladies look best in a glare of light; others will study their own interest by keeping in the shade. The different effect produced by a seat in the centre box of the Opera House, and a stage box in the glare of the lights, is, we believe, well known to many of our fair readers. However, where choice between these two is impossible, much may still be done by a judicious attention to the colour of the costume.

The *Opera House*, of course, leads us to the consideration of diamonds and jewellery. With a few economical observations on that important part of female ornament, we shall close this subject.

It is of great importance to lapidaries, and purchasers of precious stones, to possess some means of ascertaining their soundness, or freedom from flaws, when in the rough state. Till lately, artists had no rule to direct their judgment in this respect, and in consequence were frequently exposed to considerable loss; but Dr. Brewster has now constructed an instrument for distinguishing the precious stones from each other, and from artificial imitations, even when set in such a manner that no light can be transmitted through any of their surfaces. The same instrument may be employed to distinguish all minerals that have a small portion of their surface polished either naturally or artificially. Its application is so simple that any person, however ignorant, is capable of using it.

Another method has also been proposed by the same indefatigable philosopher, which has this advantage, that it may at any time be tried, where the more accurate instrument is not readily to be procured. It is thus:—Immerse the rough unwrought stone in Canada balsam, oil of sassafras, or any other fluid of nearly the same refractive density, as oil of anise seeds, and turn it round with the hand, so that the rays of light may pass through it in every direction. The slightest flaws or cracks may be immediately perceived, in consequence of the changes which they produce on the transmitted light. If the stone be examined in water, the flaws become more perceptible than when viewed in the air; and the distinctness with which they are seen increases as the refractive power of the fluid approaches that of the solid. Thus diamond jargon, and the spinelle ruby, which exceed any fluid in refractive power, have their imperfections detected when immersed in oil of cassia, or muriate of ammonia. Natural and artificial stones may likewise be discriminated by oil of cassia, as the refractive powers of diamond, jargon, ruby, garnet, pyrope, sapphire, tourmaline, rubellite, pistazite, axinite, cinnamon stone, chrysoberyl, and chrysolite exceed it. If an object be viewed through two polished and inclined surfaces of any substance supposed to be one of those minerals, when plunged in oil of cassia, the substance is a paste or artificial stone if the refraction is *from* the point to which the surfaces are inclined, and a real mineral when the refraction is made *towards* that point. The soundness and purity of glass for lenses may be ascertained in a similar manner.

But as those for whom these pages are principally designed, seldom have occasion to purchase jewellery, except in a cut state, a still more simple method may be pointed out:—it is to rub the precious stone, of whatever species, upon lead; when it will change colour if counterfeit, but preserve its lustre if genuine.

But if the uninitiated are liable to deception in the jewels themselves, so may they be also even in the gold setting of their ornaments.

Jewellers' gold is, indeed, well known to be, legally, of inferior value to the mint standard; and necessarily so, because pure gold is too soft to retain the precious stones within its grasp. The difference is, that the jewellers' gold has six parts copper alloy in twenty-four, whilst the mint gold has but two.

Observe that the real jewellers' gold is always stamped; but the gold commonly used in trinkets, toys, seals, rings, &c. contains much more alloy; though that is generally of silver instead of copper. The common test of aquafortis is not always applicable to wrought ornaments; but those who chuse may use the touchstone, which, however, though formerly in high repute as a test, is now almost obsolete. The best of these is the Lydian stone, now found in the hills around the Scottish capital. The mode of experiment is to rub lightly, or rather to draw the gold along its surface, not hard enough to rub off the metal, but just to leave a streak behind it, the colour of which is the test of purity. Gold alloyed with silver, beyond the due proportion, leaves a pale whitish mark; if alloyed with copper, the mark is brownish.

But in numberless instances, where the ornaments are so wrought as to be inconvenient for any kind of test, even by weighing, a careless purchaser may often be deceived with a base metal, merely covered with a very thin plate, or coat of real gold. As the manner of doing this may be useful to our fair readers themselves, in various ornamental processes in their own dressing-rooms, we may state that the method is to dissolve gold in aqua regia, in which linen rags must be deposited, until the whole solution is absorbed. The rags, as soon as dry, must be carefully burnt in a china cup so as to preserve the ashes, which form the golden powder; then take the article to be gilded, silver is always the best, clean it very bright; then cut a close grained cork into a convenient shape and size, dip it first into clear water, then into the golden ashes, and rub them on the polished surface until it assumes a brilliant appearance, like the best gold. When ornaments or trinkets, in daily use, lose their colour and golden appearance, these may be very easily restored by this process, looking as well, and lasting as long as if sent to the gilder, without the necessity of taking the article to pieces.

These general directions will be found of beneficial use in every day purchases; but still it may not be amiss to enter upon some short specifications of the various articles of ornamental jewellery.

The *Diamond*, of course claims the preference, and consists of several varieties; the black species are so scarce as to be seldom found, except in mineralogical collections, they are, therefore, the most valuable; whilst the cheapest are those whose tints incline to brown or grey. For ornament, however, the most valuable are those whose transparency is perfect, and their colour of the purest white. Next to these are the specimens with a greenish tint; after these come the yellow; and next the blue varieties. But all of these, to command their full value, must be without flaw, and free from all intermingled tints. The hardness of the diamond is well known, and is one of its tests, especially in cutting glass; but there are other stones which will perform the same office. The real diamond will resist the hardest blow, or merely split into leaves; but that is a test which, in jewellery, cannot conveniently be tried. In the rough state they may, however, be rubbed together, when, if both real, a harsh grating sound is distinctly heard; and, whether rough or polished, a good judge will be able to ascertain their genuineness by the brilliant light which is seen to play with great lustre when in motion.

Substitutes for diamonds are sometimes made by exposing sapphires to a strong heat, which destroys their colour, but improves their hardness and transparency. Against such a deception a casual purchaser has no guard, except in the honesty and good character of his jeweller; and it will always be better to pay an apparent high price to a respectable dealer, than to risk being cheated by those who have no character to lose.

When diamonds, however, are purchased from a good house, it will be proper to observe that the table-cut diamonds ought always to be the cheapest, as they are the thinnest; next to them are the rose cut, which require a whitish coloured foil; but the real brilliant is always upon a black ground, and produces even a finer effect if set round a good emerald.

Of the more valuable of the other precious stones, the real *Amethyst* will be known by its purple tinge; but rock chrystals of a violet tinge are often substituted for them. The *Emerald* ought to be of a fine green, and of a hard texture, though not so hard as most of the more valuable kinds of stones. The *Ruby* ought to be of a fine brilliant purple; but the inferior species are often met with in rings. Since we have got possession of Ceylon, many of these have found their way into the market. The real ruby is nearly of equal value with the diamond, especially when of the larger sizes. The beautiful celestial blue of the *Sapphire* renders it a becoming ornament to fair complexions; but the real stone is of high value, increased, perhaps, by the trick of substituting it for the diamond, as already mentioned. The bright golden yellow of the *Topax* makes it fitter for rings than for situations near the face of the fair. The Saxon topazes are the palest, though most transparent; they are even more brilliant, though less valuable, than those of Brazil, some of which are naturally of a bluish colour, or may be made so by the application of a powerful heat.

It is almost needless to enumerate the various ornaments in which the different precious stones may be arranged.

Bracelets, of course, may be formed of every species; but for general, and not very expensive use, the violet coloured amethyst may be adopted.

Ear-drops, like the bracelets, admit of all kinds of stones that may suit the complexion. When formed of emeralds, the most valuable are seldom selected. Some very handsome ones have lately been made of the Chrysoberyl, which may be obtained in considerable quantity from the Brazils, where they are in much repute.

Necklaces of aqua marine, when of a pale colour, look very handsome; but when of a deep green there are few complexions that will stand the foil: and even so with regard to the high crimson coloured *Garnet,*

Rings generally have the most valuable emeralds; but where expence is an object to be avoided, the chalcedony forms a very handsome ornament, as does the hyacinth, of a beautiful blood red; likewise the onyx, a clouded or veined stone, and the opal which displays a greater variety of colours than any other precious stone.

Of the cheaper kinds of ornamental stones we may enumerate the *Jet*, especially in mourning ; for which use the *Jargon* was once in great repute, though not of a black, but dark brownish colour. The *Malachite* is of a fine green, and forms handsome necklaces ; but is not considered as very valuable. The last we shall mention is the *Tourmaline*, which our fair readers may chuse as being, literally, the most attractive. It is purely electrical when heated, and exhibits the varieties of positive and negative electricity, or of galvanism. A tourmaline ring, when rubbed, will attract straws ; but whether it will, or will not, attract lovers, we must leave for female experiment.

With a brief notice of PEARLS we shall close the subject. As these will sometimes become discoloured, they may be readily restored to their original purity by a simple process. Soak them in hot water in which bran has been boiled with a little tartar and alum, rubbing them gently between the hands, when the heat will admit of it ; when the water is cold renew the application until the object is attained, when the pearls may be rinsed in luke warm water, and laid on white paper in a convenient dark place to cool.

Due attention thus paid to outward appearance, we may join our friends at the

BREAKFAST TABLE ;

the various circumstances connected with which being equally applicable to the

TEA TABLE,

we shall so far venture on an anachronism

in the disposition of the day as to notice them together.

Respecting the economy of the tea-kettle we shall offer one hint to our fair readers, which is, that however cleanly their hand-maidens may be, and however careful they themselves may be to procure the best water, yet almost every kind of water in use, except rain water, will speedily cover the inside of the kettle with an unpleasant crust. This may be easily guarded against by placing a clean oyster-shell in the tea-kettle, which will always keep it in good order, by attracting the particles of earth, or of stone, or of such peculiar salts as the water may be impregnated with. To those who may wish for something of a more solid nature than tea at this meal, and who may yet be unwilling to pollute the fragrance of it with the grossness of animal food, we beg leave to recommend chocolate, as it contains a fine vegetable oil, which lubricates the coats of the stomach as well as, if not better than, animal oils; and is much fitter for a delicate stomach than rancid ham, with its pyroligneous odour; especially if care be taken to procure it genuine, as it has been suspected that much of the chocolate sold here is adulterated with flour and Castile soap.

Perhaps the best mode of guarding against these tricks of home manufacture, for the nuts only can be imported into this country, is for the family to purchase the nuts, which, by a very slight species of manual labour, may be pounded sufficiently small for all domestic purposes. If pounded until perfectly oily, then a considerable saving may be made in regard to the quantity used; but they must be well dried in an oven previous to the operation.

We are not radical enough to recommend substitutes for tea or coffee; but we may state that

the inhabitants of Irkutzk are in the habit of drinking different infusions in the place of tea, prepared
from the leaves of the following plants:—Saxifraga
crassifolia, clematis alba, pyrola uniflora, spiræa
coronata, polypodium fragrans, pyrola rotundifolia
(winter green), prunus padus (bird cherry), ulmus
campestris (common elm), and rosa canina (common dog-rose) ; the last four of which are natives
of Great Britain, and the last two, especially, abundant all over our island.

The universal use of tea as an article of diet si-
lences any observations which might have been
made with respect to its medicinal or deleterious
effects on the animal economy. It is, however,
somewhat remarkable that this powerful plant has
seldom been used medicinally ; and still more so
that other vegetables, possessing similar properties,
should prove offensive, while this is highly grateful.

Before we enter further, however, upon its
medicinal qualities, let us shortly analyze its properties in regard to domestic economy.

The best way to chuse gunpowder tea is to try
it by infusion, as it is too often adulterated with a
mixture of common hyson, dyed a deeper green
with verdigrease, and rolled up like it in small
round grains.

Hyson tea is larger in grain, and not so tenacious,
as it will fall to dust with a slight pressure of the
finger ; yet its leaf is large after infusion. Its infusion is deeper coloured than the Singlo, which
may be known by the flatness of its leaf, whilst
that of the Hyson is round.

These are green teas.—The best of the black is the
Pekoe, yet it is little used here, in comparison with
the northern parts of Europe, where it is a great
favourite. Next is the Souchong; but very little

of the real sort ever comes to this country, that which goes by its name being merely the best Congo, which has a much larger leaf, and is allowed to come to greater maturity before pulling.

As a test in general to distinguish genuine tea from the sloe-leaf, let it be infused, and some of the largest leaves spread out to dry: when the real tea leaf will be found narrow in proportion to its length, and deeply notched at the edges with a sharp point; whilst the sloe leaf is notched very slightly, darker in colour, rounder at the point, and of a coarser texture.

In regard to medicinal qualities, tea very generally restores regularity to a pulse which is habitually or frequently irregular; the reverse of this however is sometimes, though rarely observed. Green tea may prove very beneficial in the higher degrees of fever, especially pulmonary consumption, where, as the quantity of fluid daily drunk is considerable, the tea may be diluted to that state which is found most palatable. In some cases its good properties are much increased by the addition of a little juniper; with this fact drunkards are acquainted, who make use of green tea punch to obviate the plethora attendant on their excesses.

In other cases it acts as an antidote. A very delicate lady once took, in a mistake, two ounces of camphorated tincture of opium; the effects were soon apparent, and a physician was sent for. With great difficulty she swallowed a cup of strong green tea, which soon proved a complete emetic. She drank some more in a weaker state, and was soon perfectly recovered. Not having swallowed more than four grains of opium no permanent ill effects could be expected.

In preparing the fragrant infusion for the tea table, a good economist will be careful to have the best water, that is the softest and freest from foreign mixture. If tea be infused in hard and in soft water, the latter will always yield the greatest quantity of the tanning matter, and will strike the deepest black with sulphate of iron in solution; consequently, according to the technical term, it will always be found " to draw best."

. In the management of the tea urn, it may be observed, that a polished urn may be kept boiling with a much smaller quantity of spirits of wine, than when a varnished or bronzed one is used, so that a silver urn is actually an object of economy. Whatever may have been said against tea, in itself, we must confess that we are by no means friendly to the substitutes that have been offered for it: because we are confident that neither naturally nor individually will they eventually be found cheap or economical. If substitutes were universally to be adopted, our China trade and shipping, and a considerable portion of export trade must be annihilated. If tea be left off entirely, we know of no saving that would ensue, except, perhaps, in the article of scandal.

But, whilst professing to disapprove, in toto, of those attempted substitutes, we may, without injury either to the health or to the revenue, record that vine leaves, dried in the shade, make a most excellent beverage.

That we shall ever be able to raise tea for our own consumption, or in a hot-house, so cheap as we can import it is by no means likely, yet it is certainly true that M. Deschamps, an agriculturist and botanist of Lausanne, has communicated some interesting experiments on the culture of the tea-tree of

Japan, which have convinced him that it will succeed perfectly well in Europe, if the seed be sown in a proper soil and climate. He accompanied his paper with directions how to gather and prepare the leaves for use. Having analysed tea of his own raising, he found that it contained neither tanning nor gallic acid, which common tea contains, and to which is ascribed the property of affecting the nerves, and producing trembling.

COFFEE has been so much talked of, so much written about, and so much drank, that it may appear superfluous even to offer a hint respecting it. We shall, however, record a few particulars not undeserving of notice. The best coffee is always the cheapest. Burn it at home in small quantities; taking care, if using a close roaster, never to fill it more than half. Turn the roaster slowly at first, more rapidly as the process advances, and keep up a lively fire by the repeated addition of chips or other inflammable materials, in small quantities. Burn it until of a light chesnut colour. Keep it in close canisters or bottles. Grind it as wanted. Boil it, in a vessel only half full, to prevent boiling over, in the proportion of one ounce and a half to a pint of water. Put in a few hartshorn shavings, or isinglass if you will; but if the coffee is taken off the fire whilst boiling, and set on again alternately, until nothing remains on the top but a clear bubble, and then some poured out to clean the pipe, and poured back again, it will be as fine as if cleared artificially.

We may add further that the Dutch, so noted for making good coffee, never boil it, but infuse merely in hot water, in a close vessel. They roast it until uniformly brown and clear, and with butter or sugar to prevent its burning.

The French, however, roast it to a coal, and produce a high coloured decoction.

Observe that long boiling does not make coffee stronger, but has the certain effect of destroying its colour, and rendering it more turbid, with the unpleasant effect that, if cleared by isinglass or white of egg, the oily matter is precipitated, and the flavour almost totally destroyed.

In making coffee, observe that the broader the bottom and the smaller the top of the vessel, the better it will be.

The Mocha coffee, or Turkey coffee has generally been esteemed the best; but it is now understood that the Java coffee is superior, as it contains a considerably greater proportion of oil. This oily, or extractive matter, however, is easily dissipated by exposure to air.

It is well known, that on the introduction of coffee into western Europe, a great outcry was raised against that beverage, which was pronounced to be an absolute poison. It was with reference to this opinion that Fontenelle, whose favourite drink was coffee, and whose life was prolonged to very near a century, observed :—". If coffee is a poison, it must be a very slow one, for it has been above eighty years killing me."

We do not, however, recommend its use generally. At breakfast it is unnecessary as a stimulant, though very agreeable and useful after dinner, particularly after a frugal one, when milk coffee is best, yet still to be used in moderation.

Coffee may be made from turnips, parsnips, or beet root; but best from the blue succory, or cichorium intybus of Linnæus. Even in making real coffee, a small portion of the latter is a pleasant addition; or else a very small quantity of common table salt.

But we recommend not any of these substitutes. We wish to improve the revenue, and to encourage our own West Indian Colonies. The slight saving to individuals would be nothing, but disuse in the aggregate would be ruin to thousands.

Though recommending infusion of coffee only, or at least nothing more than rapid and short boiling, we should do injustice to our readers, if we did not present them with another and an economical mode proposed by an intelligent correspondent to a periodical work of celebrity. He says :—

" My process, is that of *simmering* over the small but steady flame of a lamp—a process at once simple, easy, and (without watching or attendance) uniformly productive of an extract so grateful to the palate and the stomach, as to leave me neither the want nor the desire of any stronger liquor.

" But, to accomplish this, a vessel of peculiar construction is requisite.—Mine is a straight-sided pot, as wide at top as at bottom, and inclosed in a case of similar shape, to which it is soldered air-tight at the top. The case is above an inch wider than the pot—descends somewhat less than an inch below it—and is entirely open at the bottom—thus admitting and confining a body of hot air all round and underneath the pot.—The lid is double ; and the vessel is, of course, furnished with a convenient handle and spout.

" In this *simmerer*, the extract may be made either with hot water or with cold. If intended for speedy use, hot water will be proper, but *not actually boiling* ; and the powdered coffee being added, nothing remains but to close the lid tight, to stop the spout with a cork, and place the vessel over the lamp ; where it may remain unnoticed and unattended, until the coffee is wanted for immediate use.

It may then be strained through a bag of stout, close linen, which will transmit the liquor so perfectly clear, as not to contain the smallest particle of the powder.

"The strainer is tied round the mouth of an open cylinder, or tube, which is fitted into the mouth of the coffee-pot that is to receive the fluid, as a steamer is fitted into the mouth of a saucepan; and, if the coffee-pot have a cock near the bottom, the liquid may be drawn out as fast, and as hot as it flows from the strainer.

"If the coffee be not intended for speedy use, as is the case with me, who have my simmerer placed over my night-lamp at bed-time, to produce the beverage which is to serve me the next day at dinner and supper; in such case cold water may be used, with equal, or perhaps superior advantage; though I have never found any perceptible difference in the result, whether the water employed was hot or cold. In either case it soon begins to simmer, and continues simmering all night, without ever boiling over, and without any sensible diminution of quantity by evaporation.

"With respect to the *lamp*—although a fountain-lamp is undoubtedly preferable, any of the common small lamps, which are seen in every tin-shop, will answer the purpose, provided that it contain a sufficiency of oil to continue burning bright during the requisite length of time.—The tube, or burner of *my* lamp, is little more than one eighth of an inch in diameter; and this, at the distance of one inch and three quarters below the bottom of the pot—with the wick little more than one eighth of an inch high—and with *pure spermaceti* oil—has invariably performed, as above described, without requiring any trimming, or other attention—and without producing any smoke; whereas, if the wick were too high, or the oil not good, the certain consequences would be—smoke, soot, and extinction.

"One material advantage, attending this mode of coffee-making, is, that a smaller quantity of the powdered berry is requisite to give the desired strength to the liquor.—The common methods require that the powder be coarse; in which state it does not give out its virtue so completely as if it were ground finer: but, in this process, it may be used as fine as it can conveniently be rendered; and, the finer it is, the smaller will be the quantity required, or the richer the extract."

The social breakfast meal dispatched, and the company breaking up, let us first accompany the gentlemen to the

HUNTING PARLOUR,

provided the weather prompts to out of door amusement. The real sportsman, should he even deem a classical library superfluous, will not fail to decorate his hunting parlour, in addition to his fowling-pieces, fishing-rods, and sporting prints, with the best treatises on hunting, shooting, angling, racing, farriery, and the game laws. These treatises are too copious on their respective subjects to permit us to add much novelty to them; but as there are some economic hints which have not yet found their way into such works, we shall so far anticipate the systematic writers as to record them here.

In regard to the purchase of fowling-pieces, we speak not of economy: Nock and Manton may be consulted by those with whom a good piece, and not absolute economy, is the first object—yet in the purchase of a good fowling-piece, even though at first expensive, there may be economy, provided it is afterwards well taken care of. He that sports, because it is fashionable, will leave the care of his gun to his groom or game-keeper; but he that is actuated by a true love of the sport, will take care of it himself. In regard to this, the blacking or browning of the barrel is the first necessary process. Every tyro in philosophy is aware that iron, if exposed to the action of the atmosphere, and of wet, or damp, will rapidly become oxyded—that is, that the oxygen in the air and water having a greater affinity to the iron, will readily unite with it, covering the surface with what is commonly called *rust.* If this is rubbed, or scraped off, and the iron again exposed to the action of oxygen, the same process takes place, until, provided the experiment shall be tried on a gun-barrel, the substance of the metal becomes so thin that it will not stand the force of an explosion, or firing off with a common charge.

To prevent this it has been proposed to silver or to gild the barrels, but the consequent brightness would be an objection not to be got over ; so that blacking or browning are the only methods now practised.

The object of the first of these processes, is in the first instance to prevent oxydation; which is done by a mixture of black lead with hogs-lard, in which a small portion of camphor has previously been dissolved; but this retains so much of the grease as to be unpleasant, so that the second process becomes preferable.

The best browning would certainly be the natural oxydation of the metal; but as the necessary exposure for that purpose would act equally on the inside, which is to be avoided, it is more expedient to hasten the oxydation by an artifical process, which consists in nothing more than washing the outside of the barrel with diluted aqua-fortis, or a solution of blue vitriol, rubbing it well with wax a few days afterwards. This performed, common cleanliness is all that is necessary.

. The care of gunpowder is also an object of economy, especially in the grouse and black cock season, whilst sporting on the moors of Yorkshire, or the mountains of the Highlands, where a fresh supply cannot always be had the moment it may be wanted; so that the best part of the season may be lost from want of a little care and attention.

Whenever, therefore, through accident, or the absolute dampness of the climate, powder may become damaged, it must not be considered as worthless and thrown away, at least as long as the granulation is not destroyed. If circumstances will permit, it must be dried in the sun, or open air; if not, it may be carefully restored to dryness by culinary heat: after which, if it can be got, half a pound of good ought to be put to every pound of damaged powder; adding to every pound and half of this mixture, a quarter of a pound of powdered quicklime, when the powder will be found as good as at first.

Even the best powder may be improved in an extraordinary degree; but it is doubtful whether for sporting purposes. For other uses, however, the process is said to be highly efficacious, the inventor asserting that he has found that saw-dust, particularly of soft wood, mixed with gunpowder, triples its force. The method of applying this discovery to the blowing up of rocks is peculiarly interesting. The mine is charged with a mixture of saw-dust and powder, and the whole covered with dry sand, through which is passed a reed or straw filled with priming powder, so that the danger resulting from the dispersion of the stones is prevented.

In regard to the saving of time and patience, by the much vaunted detonating powders, we have not a great deal to say; but, as several accidents have happened from want of the extreme degree of caution necessary for the management of those dangerous materials, we may here record, that two German chemists profess to have composed a new detonating powder, which is not liable to spontaneous explosion. It consists of fifty-four hundredths of super-oxygenated muriate, twenty-one of ordinary nitre, and seven of powder of lycopodium, or club-moss. A stroke from a very hard body is required to produce detonation, which takes place only on the part that receives the blow; the neighbouring parts being fired by communication, but without violent explosion, so that this powder is absolutely free from danger.

To the veterinary surgeon we must leave the care of the horses; but we would recommend to every one who wishes to save valuable cattle, not to trust them, without his own inspection, to the management of every farrier who chooses to dub himself a Member of the Veterinary College; otherwise, he may meet with the same fate as the Irish gentleman, whose farrier sent him in a bill—" To curing your honour's horse till he died, 2s. 8d½."

The veterinary art, may, however, be carried a little too far; for although we can have no possible objection, on the score of economy, that a horse should be taken to a *watering* place, yet we scarcely know whether risibility or indignation would be

most excited if horses were sent to Bath for their
health. It is true, indeed, that something of that
kind has actually already taken place; and a Mr.
Torchon has obtained a patent for a warm bath for
horses, which is constructed in the following manner:—The bath is sunk in the ground, the top of
it being even with the surface, and above it is a
wooden platform, pierced with a great number of
small holes, and supported by two moveable cross
pieces, serving as the base to a frame, which is
suspended at the end of a lever, by means of a
hook and four iron rods united at the hook. The
horse is placed on the platform, suspended in the
frame by two girths, and then raised by means of
a windlass at the end of the lever: the two cross
pieces which support the platform are withdrawn,
the windlass is turned, and the horse descends into
the bath, where a thermometer is placed, and into
which water, either cold or warm, may be introduced,
by two cocks.

But we may now quit the care of horses, and
point out to the thoughtless sportsman how to take
a little care of himself; for which purpose, whilst
on moorish or northern expeditions, we must particularly recommend to him, when returned from
the day's excursion, to change his clothes instantly,
if wet; but, in all cases, to pull off his shoes or
boots, that they may be wiped clean whilst wet,
and then slowly dried. A strict attention to this
will save leather, blacking and health.

It must be recollected, also, that it is difficult
to keep out wet in a day's shooting, even with
the best new shoes, more or less prepared for the
purpose; and that water-proofing is therefore
absolutely necessary for those who pay any regard to their health, and who wish not in youth

to lay up a store of sickness for middle life and old age.

When the regular process for water-proofing cannot be conveniently gone through, a good suecodaneum may be found in warming and mixing well equal quantities of mutton suet and bees' wax; applying it, whilst hot, to the soles and seams. If it is then permitted slowly to dry, it will take the blacking equally well with the other parts of the shoe or boot.

Or, for a permanent remedy, take a quart of linseed oil, to which add one ounce of rosin, and three ounces of red lead, or of litharge, boiling the mixture until it will stick to the finger when cooled. To this mixture, when cooled, add a pint and a half, or a quart, if necessary, of spirits of turpentine, stirring it up until of the consistence of sweet oil. Let it stand for a day; pour off the clear liquid; add an ounce of lamp black and an ounce of Prussian blue, first intimately rubbed together in linseed oil. Give the boots or shoes repeated coatings until complete.

The new patent water-proof composition consists of the following materials:—Boil six gallons of linseed oil, one pound and a half of rosin, four pounds and a half of red lead, litharge, or any other substance usually called dryers, together, till they acquire such a consistence as to adhere to the finger in strings when cooled; then remove the mixture from the fire, and when sufficiently cooled, thin it to the consistence of sweet oil with spirits of turpentine, of which it commonly takes six gallons. Leave it to settle for a day or two, pour off the liquid from the grounds, and intimately mix with it one pound and a half of ivory or lamp-black, and one pound and a half of Prussian blue, ground in linseed oil. The composition is then ready to be used on any kind of leather or cloth. Stir up the liquid, and apply it with a brush till an even gloss is produced; hang up the material acted upon till the next day, taking care to leave the surface as even as possible, and proceed in the same manner till it has the desired appearance.

But the whole morning need not be allotted to field sports; and before the hour of dressing an hour or two may well be devoted to the

LIBRARY,

than which there is no part of domestic arrangement more useful or more agreeable; not even the larder or wine-cellar, if we are to consider the mental as superior to the bodily faculties; but there is no part more at war with absolute economy, under present arrangements, if we reflect upon the enormous expenditure which a passion for books has, in many instances, produced.

To cherish the love of literature is certainly our wish in this department of the work; but by no means to encourage literary extravagance even though we should not be able to teach much absolute economy. We conceive, however, that as order is the nurse, if not the parent of frugality, so we shall be enabled by pointing out necessary arrangements, and by giving a few useful hints, to save our readers from incurring extravagant and unnecessary expences, and to form a library complete in all its parts at a moderate rate; leaving them to extend or curtail the plan in proportion to their means or their desires.

Some of the most important leading points in rendering a library comfortable, as it is too often

the least used room in a house, consists in producing
an equal temperature; not only in all parts of the
apartment, but, as near as possible, at all seasons
of the year: for which purpose there ought always
to be a free circulation of air, and also for the preservation of the books; besides which it ought to
be well and equally lighted, as far as possible. In
small establishments, where the various members
of the family are accustomed to read in all the
apartments, they must often read in extreme degrees of light, which is peculiarly injurious to weak
eyes. This inconvenience, however, may be obviated in a library by various modes of preserving
the temperament of the light, on the principle that
there is nothing which preserves the sight longer,
than always using, both in reading and in writing,
that moderate degree of light which is best suited
to the eye: since too little strains them, whilst too
great a quantity dazzles and confounds them.

It may also be taken as a general rule, that the
eyes are less hurt by the want of light, than by the
excess of it; unless they are actually strained to
see objects for which the degree of light is inadequate.

It ought to be remembered also that the light
must be graduated according to the size of the
print, and the colour of the paper. For all these
purposes, especially where a gothic library is fitted
up, nothing answers better than windows, not of
gaudy party-coloured, but of light green glass, accompanied also by green shades of various thick-
nesses, which may be temporarily fitted to the windows by an ingenious process.

To point out the best selections of books in
various departments of literature and science, would
require a volume in itself; here we can only hint

that in arranging an old library, or in forming a new one, it is not always the largest quantity of books that makes the best library, much less the cheapest.

On subjects where to possess all the absolute facts is of most importance, the newest works, are, generally speaking, most likely to be the best; but this is very far from being applicable to a library in all its departments. Yet even in works of philosophy or fancy, a careful and economic selection may be made, so as to contain all that is necessary in a small compass, but leaving the extension open to taste and to future circumstances.

Those who can afford it may indeed collect the quaint or queer writers of other days, and never fancy their collections complete; some may pride themselves on embellished manuscripts, or on the excellence of their binding; whilst others may delight in possessing all the varieties of black lettered romance; be it so? In the latter case especially such collections are of some use; for, if they do not absolutely give us the manners of the times of which they profess to treat, they most assuredly do of the times in which they were written, an object of importance in many points.

To expatiate on this will, however, draw us from our plan, we therefore proceed to notice some points on the general management of books, particularly in retired parts of the country, where bookbinders are not to be had at a moment's call.

There is no part of domestic economy in which it is more true, than in regard to the library, that " a stitch in time saves nine." 'Tis a homely proverb, indeed, but not the less useful, and in consonance with it, we must recommend a careful repair whenever necessary, but yet to be done so judiciously that a skilful workman at a future period may be able to undo it without injury to the book.

For the general care of a library, however, we willingly refer to Horne's very useful work on Bibliography—'tis our plan only to offer isolated and unrecorded hints, and we have merely to point out to those who will take care of their own books, that in all repairs, both of books and of prints, whenever paste is necessary, it ought to be made of the freshest flour well kneaded in cold water, and then boiled leisurely ; adding a small quantity of powdered alum, when it will form a white transparent substance, that will not discolour the finest india paper. But when the paste is to be used in bookbinding, or in repairs where the colour is not material, the juice of aloes may be added, forming an infallible preventative against the ravages of the worm. It must also be recollected, that although russia binding is most expensive in the first instance, yet it is in the end the most economical, as books bound in russia leather are not subject to be attacked by moths. When books meet with accidental damage, means ought to be taken instantly to repair it. Ink-spots, in particular, may be removed from books or prints, by the citric or oxalic acids, if carefully applied with a hair pencil; but the muriatic acid must be avoided, as it both discolours the paper and rots it.

When books or copper-plate prints require bleaching or cleansing, whether losing their colour by age or accident, it will always be the safest way to put them into the hands of a professed artist in town ; but the country resident, if he chuses to try one or two experiments upon books of little value, before he ventures upon one of his " lions," may adopt the following process.

Form a bleaching liquid, by dissolving oxymuriate of lime in four times its quantity, (by weight allowing a pint of water to be a pound) of warm water; then take the book from its binding, place the leaves separately between plates of window glass, fixing them vertically in a proper vessel, and then pour on the liquid, in which the paper must remain for twenty-four hours. The liquid must then be poured off, and the paper carefully rinced in soft water, then dried, pressed, and the book rebound.

As this process, though it removes writing ink, does not take out oil or grease, which would endanger the printing, it will be proper to remove those spots before hand; which operation may be thus performed.

First soften the spot carefully by heat, and take up as much of the oil as blotting paper will absorb; after which apply the rectified oil of turpentine with a camel hair pencil to the spot on both sides until the turpentine unites with the oil and forms a soap, which will come off with the brush as it is generated.

Should those spots be taken out of a book which does not otherwise require a general bleaching, the part thus cleansed may be restored to its pristine whiteness, by the application of a brush or pencil dipped in a mixture of spirits of wine, with half its quantity of sulphuric ether.

With a little care and attention this may be done neatly and well.

Prints may also be bleached in the sun upon grass, confined down by netting; but the process will require some days.

Under this head of our work it may be permitted

to us to offer a few economic hints respecting the *Fine Arts*.

It has been said with much energy and great truth, that since the days of the Greeks, no nation or people have possessed so fine a soil for the production of genius in art as Britain, and yet we have twice suffered the thriving plants to be ravished from our land and transplanted to where they have but sickened in the foreign and unhealthy hot-houses of despotism and tyranny. Scarcely had they again sprung up on the spot whence they were rudely torn by the austere reformers in the seventeenth century, and again by the round-heads and self-named puritans of Oliverian Bœotianism, but we would have suffered the false assertions of a Du Bos and a Winckelman, to have destroyed them once more, because French vanity and German pertinacity thought proper to assert that our climate is too hyperborean for their cultivation. We have seen, however, that from the first dawning of classical taste in Britain, the singular height to which that taste has attained by the talents and liberality of those who have graced their country with many of the most genuine and perfect of antique remains, added to our own efforts in painting and sculpture, and all their sister arts, is a most convincing proof of our national superiority.

Much yet remains to be done however to spread not only a taste, but a *respect* for the arts, through the various classes of society. In short the knowledge of the arts we fear must remain circumscribed, until a respect for them is more strongly inoculated, as it were, into the great mass of the people; until a stop is put to those infamously scribbled autographs which disgrace the metropolitan cathedral, and to that avaricious taste of bill-sticking which,

if permitted, would shortly cover even the revered
venerable remains of Henry the VIIth's Chapel.

. This unfortunately operates as a very heavy drawback upon the liberality of art, and leaves us without a word of defence, when it is urged how much
every visitant to France and Italy remembers with
pleasure the liberal admittance which is always found
to their superb repositories of the arts, uninter-
rupted by petty objections, or exorbitant demands
for money, or any change in our feelings from admiration to disgust, by the paltry or mischievous dis-
figurement that attacks almost every object of art
in Britain.

It is true, that many lovers of the fine arts are
endeavouring to imitate foreign liberality in this
respect; but much—much remains to be done.

Perhaps one reason for the sedulous attention
paid to specimens of art almost publicly exposed
in France and Italy is, that in the former country,
the great mass of visitors are led to the Louvre
more by *glory* than by *taste*, and are so busy
shewing themselves, as the best part of the exhi-
bition, that they have not even time to immortalize
their names for a day by scribbling on the Apollo,
the Venus, or Antinous: whilst in Italy, as nobody
goes to look at them, except those possessed of
some taste, that feeling operates as a safeguard.
It is, perhaps, not an unfounded suggestion, also,
that the freedom of spirit which pervades all classes
in this country, prompts, in some measure, to a
disregard of that extreme attention due to the
property of the nation, or of the individual.—
" Don't we pay for it?" says a greasy-fingered
connoisseur, who must feel the object of admiration before he can praise it; "I have paid for
admission, and I shall do as I like."

With the first reflection, our Boeotians must be allowed to indulge themselves, but still they ought not to be made to *pay twice*: as for the second, we trust that it will soon be done away: and this well-founded hope remains, that when the exhibitions of art, in private collections, cease to be a show in consequence of merely being opened during the fashionable season, then the generous possessors may give a more general admittance to foreigners, as well as to Englishmen, of taste, who will readily visit them from a pure love of the art.

But to proceed more particularly to our subject, we certainly recommend to such of our readers as possess good library apartments, to occupy them, in some measure, with specimens of natural history; even to the formation of a cabinet, which may be done at a very cheap rate, and to extend it to objects of art as occasion may permit.

To show how this may be done at the smallest expense, is now our task.

For a general plan, which may be executed in part in any department, and extended at pleasure, we shall insert a description, which we have noticed in a German publication, of a museum of natural and artificial curiosities, which occupies eight rooms. Two are devoted to the animal kingdom, among which are some thousands of conchylia in excellent preservation, a rich collection of butterflies, numerous varieties of the lizard tribe, the eggs of almost every species of European birds, different kinds of dried sea-fish and tortoises, and an extraordinary assemblage of beautiful zoophytes. The next two rooms are filled with productions of the vegetable kingdom, pleasingly arranged; the flowers and seeds of almost all the plants of Germany, many foreign ones, and a striking collection of many hundred species of wood, from the bark to the pith. Two more rooms contain specimens of minerals; and the two others are occupied with artificial curiosities of the Romans, the ancient Germans, the Chinese, and Japanese, which are of great value on account of their rarity. A very numerous collection of coins and medals, and some hundred of sulphur pastes are about to be added. The whole is systematically arranged according to Linnæus, Blumenbach, and Werner, and is estimated at the value of 24,000 dollars, or about £5,500; but this is upon too expensive a scale for any but people of large fortunes, whilst one equally interesting may be formed at a trifling cost, from the productions of our own country. From Cornwall we may have ores of copper and tin, in all their various combinations with sulphur, lime, &c.; from Derbyshire, lead in its various forms, also spars, petrifactions, &c.; from Nottinghamshire and Derbyshire, marbles and gypsum: from the sea coast, shells and aquatic plants of immense variety; from Northumberland, coal, pyrites, &c.; from Lancashire, iron ore, and numerous specimens of stones from the mountainous districts of the Lakes; even from Scotland and Ireland may be collected, cheaply, numerous specimens in all the branches of natural history.

Then how cheap an amusement, yet how interesting, are the *Horti Sicci*, or dry book gardens of leaves, flowers, or garden plants, &c. To prepare these latter may agreeably occupy many idle hours at marine watering-places. The process is extremely simple; nothing more is necessary but that all the smaller plants should be expanded under water, in a plate, upon a piece of writing paper sunk to the bottom. In this state they will assume their natural form and position. The paper, with the plant upon it, must be withdrawn from the water gently; and the plant and paper must afterwards be placed betwixt two or three sheets of blotting paper, and pressed with a book or flat board. When taken out from hence it is to be put betwixt fresh sheets of paper, until all the moisture appears to be gone. It is then to be laid up in a quire of blotting paper, under pressure for a day or two, when, if dry, it may be placed permanently upon writing paper. The larger coriaceous kinds require a good deal of drying, in successive changes of paper, and in a very dry room, or near the fire. When once dried, and put into an herbarium, they never become damp again.

The mode of preserving leaves is as simple :— take two leaves of every sort intended to be preserved; lay them inside of a sheet of blotting paper; place them under a considerable pressure, and let them remain during the night. Open them the next morning, remove them to a dry part of the paper, and press them again for the same space of time. They may then be placed in the book intended for the purpose, and fastened down with a little gum, with the alternate sides turned out, and the name written, with such other observations as the artist may think proper.

The preparation of flowers requires rather more care and application. Prepare a square box, filled nearly with fine sand well sifted, and dried in the sun. On this place the flowers with their stalks nearly cut off, fixing them in the sand at equal distances, and as near the same height as possible. They must then be covered with sand, sifted on them gently, so as just to be covered, but not borne down with the weight. The box must now be exposed to the sun for at least six hours, or more, during two successive days, after which, the flowers must be lifted carefully up, and placed one by one in a sieve, which must be gently shaken until all the sand is off the flowers, when they will be found perfectly dried, firm in their texture, and preserving all the beauty of their forms and colours. They may then be fitted to small cases, in agreeable arrangements, and covered with glass to preserve them from dust and damp.

To make such a cabinet useful as well as pleasing, every species of stone and slate, ought to be introduced for the sake of information, and without regard to beauty; also specimens of various woods, and even small boxes or drawers, with compartments filled with every kind of grain, and dried seeds. If the collector wishes to enrich his cabinet with ornithology, it will be his best and cheapest mode to have his birds preserved by artists who make it a profession, as failure on his part might spoil a fine specimen; but in entomology he may be his own artist, to aid him in which, we add a varnish that will be found extremely useful in preserving insects as well as small animals.

Take one pound of rectified spirit of wine, and two ounces of white succinum; digest the whole in balneo mariæ during forty-eight hours; add thereto an ounce of white sandarac and of white mastic, and an ounce and a half of venice turpentine; digest the whole in balneo mariæ, during twenty-four hours, to an entire dissolution. Take out the intestines of the insects you have a mind to preserve; lay them for some days in rectified spirits of wine, mixed with clarified sugar-candy; afterwards besmear them with your varnish till they are transparent as glass: In this manner you will preserve them for a long time. This varnish succeeds equally with vegetables and fruits, which never rot or decay, when not affected by the exterior air; as has been observed in regard to cherries, which are preserved perfectly well by besmearing them with melted white wax.

The chalcographimania has now reached such an extent that we can scarcely venture to say a word in favour of it upon the score of economy. Yet still even the economical amateur may venture upon a few specimens to complete the arrangements of his library. He may collect a few engravings on wood, by Holbein and Switzer; but if he wishes for copper-plates, he will find nothing before the time of Elstraacke of any value, except for its antiquity. After him follow Deleran, the Passes, &c.; but on this head we must refer our readers to Walpole, Strutt, and other writers on chalcography.

The next department of a good library, is that of medals; they are to it always an ornament, and useful appendage; even considered only as pieces of antiquity, they form a pleasing amusement for the curious; but when properly and in due course applied and made the constituent parts of history, they become most valuable acquisitions. In short they have ever been a popular mode of commemorating great national events, and although deficient in the sublime influence of the higher branches of the arts of design, they certainly possess much of beauty and of interest. Their infrangible and lasting composition enables them to outlive the productions of the pencil or the chisel, and their minuteness and cheapness render them very proper as a medium to disseminate and perpetuate among all classes, the importance and extent of our victories.

Taking them up, on the most economical scale, the young collector must never forget that their absolute value, for himself, and their value at a future sile, consists in the elegance, the history, the size, and the scarcity of the piece, without any particular reference to the metal itself, unless the real value of the medal should be indifferent.

In regard to elegance, he must study the delineation and its entireness, then the beauty of the delineation, and its sculpture.

As to the true œrugo, or classical rust, it is not less valuable whether red or green; for in both cases it equally defends the medal against the injuries of time.

Rarity also causes dearness.

It must be observed that medals are ranked in three classes—the great, the middle, and the small; distinctions determined rather by the size of the head, than by the size or thickness of the medal itself. The sides, or tables of a medal, are the face or obverse, and the reverse; the exergue is a motto sometimes found on the outside of the rim.

Antique medals are seldom seen perfectly round; and their edges in general are cracked. The reason for this is supposed to be that the ancient medallists first melted the metal, pouring it into moulds of the intended size, and when it was hot stamped it with a heavy hammer.

But ancient medals are not absolutely necessary for a cabinet on an economic plan; nor is it best to begin with them, as the larger the collection becomes, the more anxious is the collector for unique specimens, which can only be had for extravagant prices. Nay, where there have been but two medals of a kind known to exist, the desire to render his own an unique, has prompted more than one collector to use undue means to procure or to destroy that of his rival possessor.

To British collections then we would prompt the amateur, since the ancient coins, and medals of this kingdom alone, sedulously sought after, and judiciously studied, will always tend very much to illustrate the ancient history of the British Empire.

With regard to modern medals, we must agree with a judicious essayist, who observes that in France the art of medal engraving has been much more successfully practised than in England.—Simon, who lived in the time of the Commonwealth and of the reign of the second Charles, is almost the only medallist of note which this country has produced, a circumstance at which we are the more surprised, as we conceive excellence in this department much easier of attainment than in those higher arts which in Britain have always maintained an equal rank with her continental rival: our poets, our painters, our sculptors, and our architects, have hitherto sustained the intellectual reputation of the island, and we are certain that native medallists only need patronage and encouragement to enable them to support with equal success the honourable claims of English artists. At present so little is the art practised or understood, that recourse is obliged to be had to French professors to commemorate the defeat of their own countrymen, an employment which is no less disreputable to us than it is ungracious to them.

From this opprobrium we are, however, at length released, as the series of national medals brought forward by the public spirit of one individual must sufficiently testify. We observe also that a medallic museum, for the use of amateurs and the supply of collectors, is recently established.

To form a collection of Roman coins, issued during their occupancy of this island, is a work of little labour and expense—attending a few auctions in London will complete it; or if a small number be afterwards wanted, there is a variety of shops in London where they can be purchased for a trifle. But of British coins, with the exception of those of Carausius, few are to be met with before the time of Alfred.

Gold and silver medals, as we have already noticed, have in general no superior value over the brass, except in the value of the metal, which often becomes a point of very minor consideration. Indeed the brass are almost always finer as medals, being larger, and therefore having more space for legends and devices.

There is nothing in which a tyro may sooner be deceived than in his purchase of medals. To afford him some assistance we offer the following hints: Counterfeit brass medals are generally less worn than the antique, and less corroded. The letters have a modern look. The varnish is black, greasy, shining, and soft upon pricking it; whereas the serugo of the antique is cleanly, bright, and hard as the metal itself.

Counterfeits are always circular; but the real antique are seldom, if ever, so regularly round; especially since the reign of Trajan. Of the era previous to that, from Julius Cæsar to Hadrian, all are suspected, and few now to be met with are genuine.

Nor is the system of counterfeits of very modern date; for even Pliny the elder informs us that false coins were made in his time, and he mentions the fact of a statue being raised in honour of a man who had discovered the means of distinguishing them. It is a curious fact also that some Roman collectors actually laid up the counterfeits as curiosities; and the rage became so general that a false denarius was often purchased at the expense of many that were genuine. So much for Roman economy!

The collecting of *Gems* is too expensive to form a part of our economic lessons, further than to offer a few hints on the *Glyptic* art, and to point out a cheap mode of deriving every real advantage from them, except that of possessing the real ones.— *Gems*, like *medals*, are extremely useful as an adjunct to the library ; because they not only illustrate various parts of classic history, but also oblige us to examine the pages of ancient writers, in order fully to understand them. This is a double advantage, and with this peculiar convenience that these advantages may be enjoyed either by means of sulphur casts, or accurate engravings.

Gems are as old, both cameos and intaglios, as medals or coins, and are to be seen as rings and seals.

It is almost needless to remark that the cameos are raised upon the ground, whilst the intaglios are cut in ; the latter only serving as a seal.

One great advantage of the antique gems is, that they display manners, customs, and facts, besides being models of taste.

They are generally cut upon precious stones, with the exception of the diamond, sapphire, or ruby, the hardness of which the ancient workmen could not overcome ; but rock chrystal is very common from the earliest antiquity, also opal, chalcedony, onyx, and the cornelian which appears to have been most in use.

In Egyptian gems the intaglios predominate ; but in Grecian and Roman the cameo is frequent.

Modern counterfeits are made of glass in peculiar preparations, at which the Italians are very expert. In these the colouring is in general excellent ; though without the real lustre ; but their comparative softness, when touched by an instrument, will always betray them.

In short, on an economical plan, and for real use, we should recommend the plain honest substitutes of engravings or sulphur casts, which will form accurate and well defined cameos, from intaglios, and vice versâ; and indeed will even admit of second casts being taken from themselves, so as to restore the cast to a fac-simile of the original. The process is so simple that any one can practise it; by merely melting sulphur in a crucible until it is liquid, allowing it to remain for some time over the fire; and then pouring it into water, when the impression may be taken with facility. Exposure to the atmosphere restores it to its original hardness, without injuring the finest and sharpest lines.

Steatite or soapstone is sometimes used for copying of gems, with this peculiar advantage that it will receive any colour given to it; but as it requires a tedious process of hardening in the fire, it is not so convenient for common use.

In regard to collecting PAINTINGS, much might be added, were it not that so much has been said by Reynolds and other writers of eminence.

If we were to recommend the forming a collection, to such of our readers as are forced to add economy to a love of the art, it would be on the plan of procuring a series of paintings, one of each painter from the time of Hollbein, as a practical history of our advance in that department of taste. For the real *English School*, however, we must commence with the reign of our late revered Sovereign, so justly distinguished for his general knowledge and love of the arts, and who improved the collection at Buckingham-House, even to excellence.

Incited by his noble example, several of the nobility and gentry began to engage in this branch of virtu with a competition of taste and expense which has, of course, given us many valuable collections. By this the natural taste has certainly been much improved, as well as by the extraordinary influx of genuine works of the Italian school during the revolutionary contest. In short, as it has been well said, painting has been preserved here in the general wreck of nations; nay more, an English school has been formed, which, though less glaring than the Flemish and Venetian masters, possesses all the advantages of bright colour, softened down by all the magic art of the chiaro scuro.

We are, indeed, accused by foreigners of being more partial than any other nation, to portraits. It is true that we are so, because we are a domestic nation, and in addition to our self love, we love our friends and relatives. It may be true also that we display more admirable talents in portrait than in history; but even those who say so allow that in portrait our natural expression of beauty and grace are unequalled. That indeed is a circumstance that ought not to create surprise, when we consider the *models* from which our artists copy in the daily exercise of their art.

Perhaps too, even in colouring, we have an advantage over other nations, in consequence of painting on glass being so much encouraged amongst us.

It is a curious coincidence that glass is certainly the most perfect vehicle both of sound and of colour. Well indeed has an amiable writer judged, when exclaiming, how exquisitely refined are the tones of the harmonica or the musical glasses, when touched with delicacy and skill! and how much have the most exquisite tints of Reynolds and West, gained, by their being transfused over the surface of the storied window!

G

In landscape painting also, we may ask, who can excel us. It is true, as has been said, that the compositions of Claude are all simple and unconstrained; you feel that it is the representation of a scene which you have never had the happiness to behold: but still there is an air of reality which cherishes the belief of its existence. Amid the rigid forms and unnatural hues of inferior painters, you may often discover much to admire, but the illusion is destroyed by defective and obtrusive parts; whilst in the works of Claude you may fancy yourself the distant and unobserved spectator of Arcadian groves. The scenery is the acme of existing beauty —poetical and elevated, but not supernatural. But granting this, need we name a Wilson, a Wright, a Gainsborough, a Morland, a Glover, a Turner, a Calcott, a Collins, a Strutt, and many, many others!

The art of picture-cleaning and repairing, the economist will leave to those who make it a profession; for though he must pay for it, yet he thereby escapes the risk of spoiling a good picture.

In regard to cleaning picture frames, however, we may offer a novel hint, which is in a short and easy method by means of soap on a soft brush, to be used very gently, then to be washed or wiped off, and the frame to be dryed by placing near the fire; after which the gilding must receive its polish by a brush, dry and very soft, dipped in powder of bread charcoal. The point of economy here is to try at first upon frames of little value; as practice and a little tact are necessary.

Sculpture is too expensive for common purposes; but good casts ought not to be excluded from a complete library. In fact every man of taste must congratulate himself that in regard to sculpture, England may now be said to be not only the seat but the refuge of that art, in common with others; and that so many genuine remains of ancient chisels are now preserved in our cabinets. It will also be allowed that no circumstance has tended so much, as Mr. Dallaway observes, to improve the natural style of design and painting, as the introduction of so many antiques into England, together with correct copies.

"The Genius," as Richardson says, "who hovers over these venerable reliques, may be called the father of modern art!"

We have only further to hint upon this subject that extraordinary care ought to be taken of all antiques; for it is proved by the Arundelian marbles, first placed in the garden of Arundel house in the Strand, in the reign of Charles I. and afterwards removed to Oxford, that the short period of exposure to our open atmosphere has done more to injure them, than their twenty centuries of exposure in the genial climate of Greece.

Those who wish to go further into this part of the subject, may consult Dallaway on the fine arts in England.

To enumerate all the philosophical instruments of use in a library, would far exceed our plan; but we may insert two very cheap and useful substitutes for the microscope and barometer, which have been lately offered to the world.

The first, invented by Mr. Sivewright, to form single microscopes of high magnifying powers, is as follows:—Take a piece of platinum foil and make circular holes in it from 1-20th to 1-7th of an inch in diameter, and half an inch apart, put pieces of glass into them large enough to fill the aperture. When the glass is melted by a blow-pipe, it forms a lens which adheres strongly to the metal, and is therefore set for use. An eye or loop, made of a piece of platinum wire, may also be used in place of the foil. The pieces of glass used should have no scratch of a diamond or file on them, as a mark remains after being most intensely heated. Of lenses made in this way, those larger than 1-7th of an inch, were not so good as the smaller, and the best were less than 1-16th: those which contain air-bubbles must be rejected.

Mr. Sivewright has also succeeded in forming a plano-convex lens by fusion. A piece of glass was laid upon a plate of topaz, with a perfectly flat and polished natural surface, which is easily obtained by fracture, and the whole exposed to an intense heat. The glass fused, its upper surface became spherical from the attraction of its particles, and the lower flat and highly polished from contact with the plate of topaz.

The barometer is formed of a common horse-leech, kept in a large phial covered with a piece of linen rag, three parts full of clear spring water, regularly changed twice a week, and placed in a room at a distance from the fire. In fair and frosty weather it lies motionless, and rolled up in a spiral form at the bottom of the glass; but before rain or snow, it creeps up to the top, where, if the rain will be heavy, or of some continuance, it remains a considerable time; if trifling, it quickly descends. Before rain or snow accompanied with wind, it darts about with amazing celerity, and seldom ceases until it begins to blow hard. Previous to a storm of thunder and lightning, it is exceedingly agitated, and expresses its feelings in violent convulsive starts at the top or bottom of the glass. It is remarkable, that however fine and serene the weather may be; when not the least indication is given either by the sky, the barometer, or any other circumstance; if the animal ever quit the water, or move in a desultory way, so certainly will the coincident results occur in 36, 24, or perhaps 12 hours; though its motions chiefly depend on the fall and duration of the wet, and the strength of the wind, of which in many cases it has been known to give a week's warning.

In the country a *Chemical Laboratory* will always be found an agreeable adjunct to a library, even though it should consist of nothing more than a blow-pipe and charcoal.

The first of these is merely a tube with one end large enough to be blown into by the mouth, and the other not larger than a very fine wire; with this the operator forces the flame of a candle upon any object which he wishes to expose to the chemical test of fire upon a small scale. The matter of experiment must be laid upon a piece of charcoal, and that upon a silver spoon.

The charcoal may always be procured; but if intended to be very pure, lay a piece of wood in a crucible, cover it with sand, and set it on a brisk fire until thoroughly burnt to a coal.

We must however hint to our inexperienced readers the propriety of being cautious in their experiments; in illustration of which we shall record a short anecdote of an ingenious continental chemist. By the addition of nitric acid to the solution of pot-ash and phosphorus in alcohol, a nitrate of pot-ash is formed, crystallizes rapidly, and is deposited at the bottom of the liquid. When completely separated from the latter, and strongly heated, it produces the same effects as common nitre; but if the mixture of liquid and salt be heated to desiccation, a violent explosion is the result. " Not being aware of this effect," says M. Sementini, " I evaporated to dryness about 36 grains of the salt mixed with this liquid. The detonation was so violent as to beat me to the ground, completely stunned, and I remained deaf for a whole day. Every thing brittle on the table of the laboratory was broken to shivers. Considering the small quantity of matter capable of producing such an effect, I conceive that, next to detonating silver, this substance is the most violent with which we are acquainted."

Before we close these remarks, we must draw the attention of our readers to two articles which ought to accompany every library, as great savers both in time and books. One is a well classed catalogue, and the other is a set of tickets, or forms of acknowledgement, printed ready for the signatures of those who may wish to borrow books, leaving blanks for the name, date, and volume, in the following manner :—" Received by me this———— day of ————— the ——— volume ——— —— from the library of ————." By this precaution, a gentleman may have the pleasure of accommodating a friend with a book, without fear of finding his shelves gradually thinned, through the carelessness or dishonesty of those whom he may kindly oblige. A wit observed, that all kinds of robbery and theft would be pardoned in the next world, excepting the stealing of a great coat, an umbrella, or a book; articles respecting which many persons who would start at the idea of fraud are, to say the least, grossly negligent, and which yet cannot be forgotten, or wilfully retained without subjecting the delinquent to the charge of ingratitude, or oblivion of benefits received in a moment of emergency.

A common-place book is likewise an article belonging to the library, which ought not to be omitted, as tending to the preservation, and consequently economizing of the information derived from the books themselves; and by adding to the extracts entered into it, the date of the time, or any other circumstance connected with the making of them, an agreeable and often interesting association of ideas will be formed, whenever they may be referred to. A good index should be made of each article, so that it may be readily found when wanted; for in a work professedly on Practical Economy, we cannot too often inculcate the admirable maxim of Franklin, that " lost time is lost subsistence; it is therefore lost treasure."

The bell now calls us to the

DINING ROOM,

a circumstance of such common recurrence, that it will naturally be imagined no hints of novelty can be offered upon a subject respecting the various details of which, so much has been written and printed, so much daily said, and so much daily practised. Nor is it from the *soi disant* sage, who writes of Dinner Parties over his midnight lamp, that the fashionable world will expect much information.

As it is however an old observation, that Providence sends meat, but that *somebody* also sends cooks, we may be permitted to offer one short hint on that subject. Let it always be remembered then that cleanliness is actually an advantage in economy. Hence the cleanest and brightest dishes and plates will always keep meat the hottest.

The philosophy of this hint, for it is the fashion now to philosophize even at dinner—in the epicurean mode at least—is simply thus. If the dish or plate is colder than the meat, it will naturally absorb some of the radiant heat passing off from the smoking sirloin; but the brighter the dish, the more it reflects heat as well as light, and actually returns the radiant heat back again to the joint itself, which attracts it more powerfully than the surrounding atmosphere.

Heaven forbid that *we* should attempt to prescribe bounds to the hospitality of the table; WE, of course, like all the other humble travellers towards the summit of Parnassus—and hard up hill work it is—can never object to the solace of an invitation and refection by the way; nor would we, on any account, recommend the extremes of parsimony to counterbalance profusion: yet even from the miser, may the liberal learn something—and honest, praiseworthy " Lessons of Thrift" may be acquired without any offence to liberal hospitality.

One hint must here suffice. Let him who does not wish to diminish the number of his friends, learn to diminish the number of his dishes and of his servants—the one will facilitate the other: but a little good management will do better than either. At all events, a dumb waiter will soon repay itself; but that which gives the greatest promise is a dinner table which we have seen announced, combining in itself the various offices of sideboard, cupboard, artificial cellar, cellaret, conservatory, and dumb-waiter, besides the use of hot-water plates, and dish-covers, free from their uncouth appearance; adapted to universal family use, from, as is presumed, the most elegant japanning upon tin, down to the humble wicker dining apparatus, for substantial use only below stairs. Its great recommendations are, that it gives to every guest at table the full use and command of all the dishes placed upon it, without being under the slightest necessity of troubling any one in the carving department; next, that it frees both the men of opulence and of business from the liability to the tattle or espionage of their attendants, which exists under the present helpless form of dining; and last, but not least, that it furnishes to the great middle class of society in this country all the elegance and convenience of a living servant in attendance during the daily busy gala hour of human life, without the concomitant inconveniences of want of sufficient employment for them afterwards, as well as enabling them to devote the expense of maintaining one to other purposes.

" Good wine needs no bush," nor does it need animadversion here, though subsequently to be noticed at some length—we may therefore, in due time, proceed to join the ladies in the

DRAWING ROOM,

with all our senses about us.

The economy of the drawing room, according to the fashionable style of crowded routs, may, with a little ingenuity be made more conducive to *saving*, than even the old-fashioned system of *tea and turn out*, so annoying to subalterns in country-quarters— that is, agreeable to the definition given by a frugal cit of his wife's parties—so crowded, or rather crammed, or more truly speaking jammed into two small rooms and a closet, that although there was room to call for refreshments, there was none to hand them in !

We shall take up the subject, however, upon the plan of a more beneficial saving, inasmuch as there is more health actually expended sitting in or coming out of the drawing room, than out of the ball room or crowded theatre ; for, in regard to the latter, habit and early custom have rendered some little care a matter of attention ; but in our own, or our friend's drawing room, we are so much *at home*, that any avoidance of draught, or precaution against exposure is unthought of.

The first objects of consideration in our drawing
rooms then, are their temperature and ventilation,
arising partly from the variableness of our climate,
and partly from the variableness of our customs.

It has indeed been judiciously observed that if
the natural state of our atmosphere be variable,
and if certain parts of the surface of the earth, and
even animal life itself must necessarily tend to vitiate
the composition of the air, our own folly, or the
imperious customs of civilized life, give tenfold
force to these unavoidable enemies of our health.
It is not on the husbandman, the soldier, or the
sailor, who are so much exposed to the conflicting
elements, that their malignant influence principally
falls. It is on the delicate female, the pale me-
chanic, and the sedentary artist, who add artificial
to natural extremes; fly from one to the other;
writhe under the effects of this imprudence—and
then rail against the climate as the cause of all their
miseries!

To examine the matter in a practically philosophical point of view, we may observe that, agreeable
to the existing system, the temperature of our apartments is principally raised by the radiant heat from
the burning materials in the fire-place, whilst in
parts removed from the fire-side it is lowered by
the currents of air which naturally rush in to fill
up the partial vacuum caused by the rarefaction
of the air near the chimney.

To cure this evil, by stopping up all crevices,
and making our doors and windows impervious to
atmospheric air, would only be to encounter a
worse one; inasmuch as the air already in the apartment would speedily be unfit for respiration, the
fire itself would decline for want of draught, and
the heavier external air, by its natural gravity,
descending the chimney would bring all the smoke

along with it, with all the annoyance of partial suffocation. A better system has, however, been proposed, by means of which the combustion of coal may be made complete, the generation of smoke prevented, and even the nuisance of ashes in the grate considerably avoided; whilst instead of part of the company being exposed to the chilling effects of cold currents of air, a stream of warm air, at any desired temperature may be introduced, or its superabundance escape in a similar way, but in a contrary direction. The general principles of the new system are, that the air which is destined to supply the expenditure of the apartment, shall enter at the ceiling over the fire-place; but to be first warmed in cold weather by passing along a culvert or passage under ground, so deep that the temperature shall be higher than that of a winter atmosphere; and, when necessary, by receiving additional heat from a stove. Indeed, from the temperature of the earth, a few feet under ground, being always, or nearly so, equal to the *mean heat* of the climate, the air in winter, if the passage is long enough, will be considerably warmed even without a stove; and in like manner in the summer no artificial heat will be necessary; on the contrary, the air passing then under ground will be cooler than the atmospheric air.

Another great improvement is likely to result to our system of domestic temperature in general, in consequence of the philosophical acuteness of a worthy physician, who directing his attention to the advantage of an equal temperature in rooms occupied by persons suffering under pulmonary complaints, has invented a new apparatus for attaining that object. It consists simply of a glazed metal frame or window, fitted to the chimney-piece, and placed before the fire, so as perfectly to cut off the communication between the room and the fire-place. The fire is fed with air by a tube from without, and ventilation is effected by openings near the ceiling, either into the chimney or stair-case. The inventor asserts that the benefits of this plan are, a nearly uniform temperature throughout the room, the total prevention of currents or drafts of air, the saving of fuel, the general raising of temperature in the house, and the exclusion of smoke or dust. For such blessings he thinks we might bear the eye-sore of looking at our fires through a window, and opening a pane occasionally to admit the poker: and, in fact, it may even be made highly ornamental, independent of its addi-tional security as a safeguard against accidents which have unfortunately in repeated instances de-prived society of some of its most amiable members.

The next point to which we would call the atten-tion of our fair readers, is the danger resulting from unguarded exposure on leaving a crowded or heated drawing room. It is, and has long been the opinion of the most enlightened medical prac-titioners that many lives are annually lost by the ill-judged caution of lingering about the halls and doors of heated apartments, till the body is cool, before venturing into the air. In this state it is highly susceptible of the baleful influence of the night. It would be better to issue forth, even with some perspiration on the surface, than wait till the system is chilled. The greater degree of animal heat in which we are, on going first into the night air, the less injury shall we sustain from it.

It is indeed probable that three-fourths of the disorders to which the human constitution is liable in this climate, originate in, or are, at least, consi-

derably influenced by, aerial transitions; and therefore we cannot be too much on our guard against
this source of danger.

Of course we cannot, in addition to the preceding
hint, enforce too strongly the necessity of guarding
the organs of respiration from the direct influence
of the night air, by such mufflings about the face,
as may not only detain a portion of the air expired
from the lungs each time, but communicate a degree
of warmth to each inhalation of atmospheric air.

We profess not indeed to offer medical advice;
but as useful hints, in a work of this nature, are
more likely to be read by those to whom they are
of most importance, than whilst shut up, as it were, in
treatises which are closed to the female eye, we may
support our cautions by pointing out, agreeable to
the observations of an intelligent physician, that the
defence of the lungs themselves has been hitherto
strangely overlooked; though it requires but a
moment's reflection to be convinced of the vast importance of this consideration. In the space of
one minute the delicate structure of the lungs are
exposed to an atmospherical transition of perhaps
thirty or forty degrees—from the over-heated
theatre to the freezing midnight blast! Is it not
strange, he adds, that we should have been so very
solicitous about heaping fold over fold on the surface of the body, while we never dreamt of the extended surface of the lungs, which we left completely exposed? Is it not still more strange that
this should have been forgotten, when daily observation shewed that the lungs were the organs which,
nine times out of ten, suffered by these exposures?

As the shortest and simplest remedy, we shall
merely add that as the injury is particularly received
through the medium of the skin and the lungs,

so, it is quite evident that the safeguard of the former is warm clothing, constructed of materials that are bad conductors of heat, as woollen, cotton, &c.

Indeed the skin and lungs may both be protected at the same time; as it is already well known that a not unfashionable article of dress, such as is called a *comforter*, folded loosely round the face, will receive a portion of caloric or heat from the breath at each expiration, which portion will be communicated to the current of air rushing into the lungs at each inspiration; and· thus a frigid nocturnal atmosphere is, in a considerable degree, obviated.

We have already alluded to safeguards against accidental ignition of inflammable dresses, and we must again recommend most strongly the projecting wire-work fenders, which prevent the too near approach of muslin dresses. Yet, even with these fenders, sparks may produce accidents, in which cases our fair readers ought so far to have the command over their feelings as not to run after assistance, thereby increasing the danger, but to ring the bell loudly, and then to throw themselves down on the carpet until assistance comes. This precaution has already been enforced in a monthly publication, but cannot be too often inculcated upon the female mind, as well as the recommendation of having a green baize cloth laid upon a table in every drawing room or morning parlour, in which the person whose dress is on fire ought to wrap herself instantly, thereby, if not extinguishing the flame, at least stopping its progress until assistance shall arrive.

SECTION III.

AUXILIARY APARTMENTS.

WARDROBE—*Care of Clothes—Restoration of Colours—Gold and Silver Lace—Boots and Shoes.* BATHS, *temporary or fixed.* CHINA CLOSET.—*Specimens of Porcelain—Hints to Collectors—Dresden, Sevres, and British China—Cleaning and Repairs.*

WARDROBE.

OF late years not only the form, but even the texture of our apparel have been so changeable, that it has become an old fashioned piece of economy *to take care of one's clothes;* yet, in spite of fashion, the change in the times has begun to produce a change in our opinions, and a little economy is not now considered as misplaced. With that in view, we shall venture to offer a few hints to our readers of both sexes, in regard to this branch of domestic arrangement.

As clothes, when laid up for a season, are apt to acquire an unpleasant odour, which generally requires considerable exposure to the atmospheric air,

before it dissipates, it will always be advantageous
to prevent it by a very simple process, which consists in depositing recently made charcoal between
the folds of the garments. Even where the odour
has taken place, the charcoal will absorb all the
unpleasant effluvia.

To drive away, or to prevent the approach of
moths, there are several methods, all efficacious,
which may be adopted ad libitum. Wrap up
yellow or turpentine soap in paper, or place an open
bottle containing spirits of turpentine within the
wardrobe. But as the smell of the latter may be
unpleasant, sprinkle bay leaves, or wormwood, or
lavender, or walnut leaves, or rue, or black pepper
in grains.

A very simple yet efficacious mode of removing
stains from mourning dresses, is by taking a good
handful of fig-leaves, which must be boiled in two
quarts of water until reduced to a pint. Squeeze the
leaves and put the liquor into a bottle for use. The
articles, whether of bombasin, crape, cloth, &c. need
only be rubbed with a sponge, dipped in the liquor,
when the effect will be instantly produced.

But where any reason exists to prevent the substance from being wetted, then apply French chalk
or powdered talc, which will absorb the grease from
the finest texture without injury, if judiciously
managed.

To restore colours, boil the articles in a lye of
equal parts of quick lime and wood ashes, rincing
them out in weak alum water, and pressing them
well when nearly dry; or wash them in water saturated with black soap and salt, rincing them carefully and pressing as before.

As gold lace is now worn in several articles of
dress, it may be useful to know that it is easily
cleaned and restored to its original brightness

by rubbing it with a soft brush dipped in roche alum burnt, and sifted to a very fine powder.

In dying faded articles of dress, it will always be found very advantageous to attend to the quality of the water used in the process. It ought to be the softest and purest; and it will be proper to boil it before mixing the dye stuffs, suffering it to cool under atmospheric exposure.

The various articles, and the manner of using them, will be found in any common receipt book; but we may observe that the expressed juice of the Barberry is useful in family dying. The root boiled in water forms a beautiful green, if applied to glove leather. Very recently too there has been discovered a brilliant yellow matter for dying, in potatoe tops.—The mode of obtaining it is, cutting *the top when in flower*, and bruising and pressing it to extract the juice. Linen or woollen soaked in this liquor, during forty-eight hours, take a fine, solid, and permanent yellow. If the cloth be afterwards plunged in a blue dye, it then acquires a beautiful permanent green colour.

With one word to the gentlemen we shall close. For the cleaning of boot tops, receipts are multiplied far beyond our notice; but with regard to blacking, we may insert that the article sold under the name of *Italian Paste*, is made according to the following receipt: Ivory black, 4 ounces; treacle, 3 ounces; sulphuric acid, 1½ ounce; water 4 ounces; sperm oil, ¼ ounce; calamine stone, prepared, 8 grains; indigo, 8 grains; sal ammoniac, 8 grains; yellow resin, 1½ drachm; wax, ½ drachm. But as the sulphuric acid, unless managed very carefully, is rather an enemy to economy, perhaps a safer receipt will be found in the following:—Ivory black, ground finer than it is usually met with at the shops, 4 ounces; treacle, 4 ounces; vinegar, three quarters of a pint; spermaceti oil, 2 drachms; these will cost about seven pence halfpenny, and will make a pint.

A patent has recently been obtained for a new and improved method of making Blacking, by which a higher polish is given, and the leather better preserved, than by any hitherto known. To make 40 gallons of blacking take 40 gallons of vinegar, (known by the number 18,) 90lbs. of ivory black, 5 gallons (wine measure) of sweet oil, 28lbs. moist sugar, 18lbs. of oil of vitriol, and 26 ounces of gum arabic. Procure a tub with a thin strainer, full of small holes, fixed under its lid, which should likewise have a hole large enough to permit liquid ingredients to be poured through it by means of a funnel or otherwise. Into this tub put the ivory black, sugar, sweet oil, and four gallons of vinegar, and mix them into a thin paste; then pour half the oil of vitriol through the lid and strainer, and after the mixture has stood about ten minutes, add in the same way about two gallons more vinegar. Take off the lid and gradually pour in the remainder of the vinegar, at the same time keeping the whole constantly stirred. This done, pour the remainder of the oil of vitriol through the strainer, put the mixture into a copper, and throw in the gum arabic; as soon as it begins to boil, draw it off, and when cold it is fit to be bottled, but while bottling it should be continually stirred.

From the care of clothing we may naturally proceed to that of the person, in the consideration of which the first great object is the

BATH.

If to preserve health be to save medical expences, without even reckoning upon time and comfort, there is no part of the household arrangemént so important to the domestic economist as cheap convenience for personal ablution.

For this purpose baths upon a large and expensive scale are by no means necessary; but though temporary or tin baths may be extremely useful upon pressing occasions, it will be found to be finally as cheap, and much more readily convenient, to have a permanent bath constructed, which may be done in any dwelling-house of moderate size without interfering with other general purposes.

As the object of this little work is not to present essays, but merely to offer useful economic hints, it is unnecessary to expatiate upon the architectural arrangement of the Bath, or more properly speaking the *Bathing Place*, which may be fitted up for the most retired establishment, differing in size or shape agreeable to the spare room that may be appropriated to it, and serving to exercise both the fancy and the judgment in its preparation. Nor is it particularly necessary, the public having very recently been presented with an excellent popular work on the general subject,* to notice the salubrious effects resulting from the bath, beyond the two points of its being so conducive both to health and cleanliness, in keeping up a free circulation of the blood, without any violent muscular exertion, thereby really affording a saving of strength, and producing its effects without any expense either to the body or to the purse.

Whoever fits up a bath in a house already built must be guided by circumstances; but it will always be proper to place it as near the kitchen fireplace as possible, because from thence it may be

* See Essay on Bathing, by Sir Arthur Clarke.

heated, or at least have its temperature preserved by means of hot air through tubes, or by steam prepared by the culinary fire-place, without interfering with its ordinary uses. Where circumstances do not permit these arrangements, a small boiler may be erected at very small expense in the bath room.

But when a bath is to be built either in a house whilst erecting, or outside of one already erected, it will be found cheapest to form it of bricks, and the ceiling formed into a dome, or segment of a sphere. The entrance also ought not to be in the side wall, like a common apartment, but rather through an aperture in the top, with a descending stair-case in the body of the bath room.

Whenever a bath is wanted at a short warning, to boil the water necessary will always be the shortest mode; but where it is in general daily use, the heating the water by steam will be found the cheapest and most convenient method. As a guide for practice, we may observe it has been proved by experiment, that a bath with five feet water at the freezing point may be raised to the temperature of blood heat, or 96 degrees, by 304 gallons of water turned into steam at an expense of 50lbs. of Newcastle coal; but if the door be kept closed, it will not lose above four degrees of temperature in twenty-four hours, by a daily supply of 3lb. of coal. This is upon a scale of a bath of 5,000 gallons of water.

Another auxiliary apartment, which cannot fail to be interesting to our fair readers, is the

CHINA CLOSET,

whether we refer to it as for mere domestic use, or

for the gratification of a taste elegant and harmless,
if kept within proper bounds.

The passion for collecting China ware, and indeed all things of Japanese manufacture, is by no
means so prevalent as it was some years ago, when
the New Exchange, now Exeter 'Change, was the
grand mart for dragons, bonzes, nodding mandarines, vases, fans, tea and its accompaniment scandal,
and intrigue also, if our comic writers of the last
age are to be credited.

Yet, though no longer the rage, the taste for
collecting handsome or antique specimens of foreign
and also of domestic China ware, is neither inelegant nor useless, if adopted as an amusement,
and not permitted to become expensive.

It must be confessed that the modern porcelain
is much more beautiful than the ancient, but then
it wants the value of the antique, which, of course,
implies a certain degree of scarcity; in consequence
of which, although nearly all the modern colours,
to say nothing of the form and shape, and of the
outline and pencilling, are much superior to any
thing that the China or Japan markets afford, yet
a considerable portion of modern ingenuity has
been turned from the legitimate walks of manufacture, not indeed to *imitation*, which would be
praiseworthy, but to *counterfeiting* the antique
China, a species of robbery as morally reprehensible
as forging a bank note, though not of such important detriment to the common concerns of social
life.

To investigate the principles of *collecting* will
then be to redeem our pledge of pointing out the
means of saving money even in the enjoyment of
elegant superfluities, enabling those who choose
such a pursuit, to indulge it at no greater probable

expense than the interest of their money laid out, the property still retaining its fee simple value, should a change of inclination consign it to the hammer.

The absolute perfections of the old China porcelain consisted in its whiteness, transparency, and fineness of texture; in the elegance of its patterns, neatness of its execution, brilliancy of its colours and gilding, and the magnificence of its form and size. In all these points, however, the Japanese was then, and is still, considered as the most perfect, even in China.

The very oldest Chinese porcelain is a pure white, without any colour whatever, sometimes with figures raised in relief. The earliest colour laid on was the blue, and the oldest and finest was the rich deep blue, so much admired, but now so badly imitated even by the Chinese themselves.

The next in point of antiquity is the black porcelain, of which many specimens, especially when ornamented with gilding, are considered as more beautiful than the more antique manufacture.

The crackled, or marbled China ware, is of more recent date; and so is that called the " Egg and Spinach;" both of which may easily be counterfeited. These latter have no otherwise distinguishing points; but connoisseurs, on taking up the white or blue, always know where to look for the dolphin or dragon marks. There is another species of the real china ware, more curious than beautiful, but valuable from its comparative rarity, as the secret is now lost, nothing further being known than the mode of laying on the colours in various layers on the inside. This species of China is ornamented with various figures, but principally fishes, and its peculiarity is that the figures do not appear until the vessel is filled with water.

Foreign china-ware, or porcelain of modern manufacture, may be divided into the Saxon or Dresden, the French or that of Sevres, and that made at Vienna. These display a most beautiful white, a shining transparency, a fine glazing, exquisite gilding, with elegance and regularity of form ; but, if we leave the point of foreign manufacture out of the question, we have not enumerated a single quality in which they may not be equalled at home; with this remarkable distinction, that the foreign porcelain is all the produce of Royal manufactories, where expense is the last thing thought of, whilst our British manufacture is all the produce of private capital, private industry, and private speculation.

Having thus prepared the amateur to become a connoisseur, we shall suppose the collection to be made, and proceed to the best mode of preserving it entire, and of repairing it, when damaged ; premising that the rules are alike applicable to the china-closet as to the glass-room.

The best material for cleaning either porcelain or glass-ware, is Fuller's earth; but it must be beaten into a fine powder, and carefully cleared from all rough or hard particles, which might endanger the polish of the brilliant surface.

In cleaning porcelain it must also be observed, that some species require more care and attention than others, as every person must have observed that china-ware in common use frequently loses some of its colours. The red, epecially of vermillion, is the first to go, because that colour, together with some others, is laid on by the Chinese after burning. The modern Chinese porcelain is not, indeed, so susceptible of this rubbing or wearing off, as vegetable reds are now used by them instead of the mineral colour. Much of the red now used in China is actually produced by the *anotto* extracted from the cuttings of scarlet cloth, which have long formed an article of exportation to Canton.

It ought to be taken for granted that all china or glass-ware is well tempered; yet a little careful attention may not be misplaced, even on that point: for though ornamental china or glass-ware are not exposed to the action of hot water in common domestic use, yet they may be injudiciously immersed in it for the purpose of cleaning; and, as articles, intended solely for ornament, may not be so highly annealed as others, without any fraudulent negligence on the part of the manufacturer, it will be proper never to apply water to them beyond a tepid temperature. An ingenious and simple mode of annealing glass has lately been adopted by the chemists. It consists in immersing the vessel in cold water, gradually heated to the boiling point, and suffered to remain till cold, when it will be fit for use. Should the glass be exposed to a higher temperature than that of boiling water, it will be necessary to immerse it in oil.

Having thus guarded against fractures, we naturally come to the best modes of repairing them when they casually take place, for which purpose various mixtures have been proposed; and it will here be sufficient to select only those which excel in neatness and facility.

Perhaps the best cement, both for strength and invisibility, is that made from mastic. The process, indeed, may be thought tedious; but a sufficient quantity may be made at once to last a life-time. To an ounce of mastic add as much highly rectified spirits of wine as will dissolve it. Soak an ounce of isinglass in water until quite soft, then dissolve it in pure rum or brandy, until it forms a strong glue, to which add about a quarter of an ounce of gum ammoniac, well rubbed and mixed. Put the two mixtures together in an earthen vessel over a gentle heat; when well united, the mixture may be put into a phial and kept well stopped.

When wanted for use, the bottle must be set in warm water, when the china or glass articles must be also warmed and the cement applied. It will be proper that the broken surfaces, when carefully fitted, shall be kept in close contact for twelve hours at least, until the cement is fully set; after which the fracture will be found as secure as any part of the vessel, and scarcely perceptible.

It may be applied successfully to marbles, and even to metals.

When not provided with this cement, and in a hurry, the white of an egg well beaten with quick-lime, and a small quantity of very old cheese, form an excellent substitute, either for broken china, or old ornamental glass-ware.

It is also a fact well ascertained, that the expressed juice of garlic is an everlasting cement, leaving no mark of fracture, if neatly done.

These are fully sufficient for every useful purpose; but we may still further observe, in respect to the cement of quick-lime, that it may be improved, if, instead of cheese, we substitute the whey produced by boiling milk and vinegar, separating the curd carefully, and beating up with half a pint of it, the whites of six eggs, adding the sifted quick-lime until it forms a thick paste, which resists both fire and water.

SECTION IV.

DOMESTIC OFFICES.

KITCHEN.

IF all books of cookery were treatises on economy, our labours in this department would be short indeed; but even now we shall not trespass far upon the secrets of these Plutonian regions, whose Empress will bear no rival near her throne. The three-headed dog, who guarded the poetic hell, might be entitled, ex officio, to a sop; but the unlucky critical dog, who should dare to enter this modern

Hades in hopes of a sop in the pan, might chance
to have his head broken, had he as many as Cer-
berus himself. The " secrets of this prison-house,"
then we shall not dare unfold, but proceed to notice some improvements which may be judiciously
adopted, even in addition to the convenient arrangements of the Rumford plans which have already,
in a considerable degree, superseded the use of
the immense long ranges, that burned as much
fuel in one day as might suffice for a week. Of the
extraordinary quantity of caloric, or of radiant
heat, emitted from those long ranges, it is almost
impossible to account for the consumption, except
in the belief that a great portion was wasted, beyond what was absorbed by the dressed meat, and
by the cook ; of which wasted portion, some went
up the chimney, whilst the remainder united with
the surrounding air.

To remedy this, much was done by Rumford :
but further philosophic principles have been elicited,
and applied to practice, by means of which a kitchen
may be fitted so as to require less labour and attention; rendering the food more wholesome and agreeable, and preventing that offensive smell, which
makes a kitchen, on the old construction, so great
a domestic nuisance even whilst it is most useful.

Many beneficial effects were produced on the
Rumford plan, by means of hot steam ; but the
new principle is founded upon the application of
hot air, requiring so little alteration as scarcely to
be called a new arrangement, consisting solely of
a stone hearth, a small fire-place on the Rumford
plan, and a roaster for large dishes, serving also for
an oven, together with a steaming apparatus.

The roaster is also supplied with a current of
warm air, sufficient to have a great effect on the
substances to be baked or roasted ; contributing to

the formation of that crusty brown so generally
liked in roast meats, and removing completely that
disagreeable smell which meat is apt to acquire in
a common oven.

In a fire-place of this construction the steaming
apparatus occupies a recess in the wall similar to
that used for the common stew-hearth; and the
vessels which hold the substances to be steamed
are generally of tin, perforated with holes like a
cullender, in order to admit the steam of hot air
freely on every side.

This arrangement may also be made to supply
the scullery at all times with warm water, heated
by the surplus steam from the fire-place.

That fitting up a kitchen, on these principles,
will be expensive in the first instance, cannot be
denied; but the saving, particularly on a large
establishment, will amply repay it in a year or two.
The saving in coals will be considerable; and we
must not forget the saving in cooks, and in all
broils but those intended for alimentary refection.

An important article in kitchen economy is the
use of *good water*—not merely water good in
general—but water which is specially adapted for
culinary purposes. This is a circumstance little
attended to, except in one or two points of cooking;
but it has been shewn by a modern ingenious
chemist, that the effects of different kinds of water
are not only obvious to the eye, but important in
their results. 'Tis not in the solitary case of dry or
ripe peas, one of the first axioms or passing questions in cookery, which cannot readily be boiled
soft in hard water—a fact with which cooks are as
contented, as cooks can be, without examining into
the philosophic principle of hard water being loaded
with earthy salts, and therefore unfitted to dissolve
the farina completely—but in almost every other

ease of culinary preparation; as it is well ascertained that good, pure, or soft water, is best fitted to soften the fibres of animal matter as well as vegetable.

It must be admitted that hard water gives a better colour to green esculent vegetables, than soft water produces; but if the proof of the vegetables, like the pudding, lies in the eating, then soft water will be preferred. The indefatigable chemist, already alluded to, has shewn by an experiment with tea leaves, that soft water will extract a much greater quantity both of the tanning matter and of gallic acid from the leaves, than hard water can produce; but there are other criterions, the simplest of which is to compare two specimens of water by washing our hands in them with soap, when the very touch will be indicative of the quality. To the sight also, the difference in quality will generally be obvious, as good water is beautifully transparent, whilst the hard is tinged with a slight opacity. This however will not always shew itself, if the water is looked at in a glass transversely; but will be evident if the sight is directed perpendicularly into a deep glass vessel.

Good water has neither taste, nor odour; and the best water always containing the greatest quantity of carbonic acid gas, in addition to its proportion of atmospheric air, it will always give out the greatest number of air bubbles when poured alternately into different vessels.

It is true that even the worst water will lose some of its aeriform fluids in boiling, which renders that operation proper for water intended for drinking; but then we must remember that good water also loses its air and carbonic acid, and has a vapid and insipid taste until exposure to the atmosphere restores them. Whenever water therefore is boiled

previous to use, it will be necessary to set it to cool
in large open vessels; and more conveniently to
allow it to filter slowly into a recipient vessel placed
at some distance below, whilst a current of air passes
freely around it. Upon this principle depends the
action of the thunder-pump, so called ludicrously
by the seamen, and in use on board his Majesty's
ships, and also East Indiamen, to prepare the
water for daily use. This instrument resembles a
Dutch oven, but is rather larger. It is made of tin,
with four or five shelves, fitted with ledges, and perforated with a number of small holes; but the
bottom is entire, with the exception of one hole,
about two inches diameter in the centre, admitting
a tin tube or pump which passes through the whole
machine, fitted closely in the shelves, but leaving
a passage for the water, which falls on the bottom
to return into the cask through the lengthened
tube which passes downwards into the bung-hole,
or scuttle. By the action of the pump the water is
brought up to the first shelf, through the holes in
which it passes to the second; then to the third,
and fourth; when it is received on the bottom of
the machine, and returns to the cask. Whilst this
operation is performing, it being continued until it
is supposed that all the water has been pumped
up, the open face of the machine is turned towards
the wind, so that the air comes in contact with
every *drop* of water; its action being formerly supposed to be to deprive the water of something deleterious, acquired by long keeping, but now known
to consist in restoring to the water that which it had
actually lost.

Our fair readers, who amuse themselves with
keeping gold and silver fishes in glass vases, will
learn from this *not* to boil the water with which
they are supplied; as fish will not live in water de-

prived of its atmospheric air : on the same principle, the covers of the vases ought to be open catgut, and not muslin. In the metropolis, the Thames water will be found better for this purpose than that of the New River, as it contains a larger quantity of atmosperic air. In the country, rain water will be best for this purpose; but in London it is too strongly impregnated with foreign substances.

So much has been said on the subject of culinary vessels, that we have little novel to offer. In all cases, but particularly in regard to copper utensils, the utmost cleanliness is necessary. Some cooks may imagine, in their ardour of philosophical research, and of chemical experiment, that where no acids are brought in contact with the copper, no danger of oxyde or verdigrease can arise; but in the kitchen, as well as at college, " a little learning is a dangerous thing;" and they must be taught that even the action of air and moisture will oxyde copper, though not so readily as vinegar or lime-juice. No food of any kind ought therefore to be suffered to remain in the copper kettles or stew-pans, longer than whilst in the process of cooking; whilst even the best tinned ought to be sedulously cleaned and dried after every time of using. It might be a great improvement in the tinning of culinary ware, if that operation were performed upon the copper-plates, previous to their being formed into utensils, as is the case with iron plates for the common tin ware. By this means the copper would be more carefully covered, than according to the present mode, and the danger from careless or inadequate tinning, in some measure guarded against.

As *Leaden* vessels do not come into culinary operation, at least on the fire, we offer no caution to the cook respecting them : indeed it is supposed that even in copper, whilst it is on the fire, and its contents in a boiling state, no verdigrease is produced even by the strongest acids; the danger arising from the oxyde which forms by the action of acids when cold, or of the air afterwards.

This supposition, however, if true, can only apply to liquids in a state of active ebullition, but must not be considered as relevant to liquids simmered in a stew-pan over a charcoal fire. With respect to charcoal itself, let us caution cooks against its use in any quantity, except where there is a free current of air: for charcoal is highly deleterious in a state of ignition, although it may be rendered even actively beneficial when boiled; as a small quantity of it, if boiled with meat on the turn, will effectually cure the unpleasant taint. This is a hint which may be useful, in cooking both hare and venison, where the tenderness of fibre, acquired by long keeping, may be wished for without its *haut goût.*

It may be useful for the economical housewife, who is anxious to dress no more meat than will suffice for the meal, to know that beef loses about one pound in four in boiling; but in roasting, loses in the proportion of one pound, five ounces; and in baking about two ounces less, or one pound three ounces.

Mutton loses, in boiling, about fourteen ounces in four pounds; in roasting, one pound six ounces.

These are grand secrets in culinary free-masonry; but the arch secret, or arcanum, seems to have been discovered by Count Rumford, who says that meat is to be saved by the expenditure of time, instead of the usual mode of saving time by a hasty disposal of the meat, or "bolting," as it is elegantly

phrased by the bacon gorgers of Hampshire.
That indefatigable economist observes, that a scanty
dinner is a matter of no moment, provided we can
prolong the time of consuming and masticating
such short allowance as may be set before us; so
that the glutton or gourmand may rise perfectly
satisfied from table, if we can only contrive to
employ him as long upon two ounces of tasty food,
as he would have been in dispatching a couple of
pounds of venison or turtle in the common way.

For this purpose an Hibernian economist might
recommend the toughest mutton, or a little of that
which sometimes in the metropolis is called *Lamb*,
from its size, though, in age, it may be equal to
that of its oldest brethren on the Welsh mountains,
from whence it emigrated some years ago into Lincolnshire; or the Trans-tweedian housewife might
perhaps set down her " Kebbuck " of cheese,
equal to the best of our *Suffolk* dairy. But Rumford's plan, which he says he saw practised, with
success, by the Hessian soldiery, is first to make
tasty soup, of a few ounces of meat, then to put in
toasted bread, soaked in butter and fried, so that it
remains hard in the mouth, the oily coat and its
artificial solidity having neutralized all chemical
affinity with the soup in which it is floating.

It is true, that some persons with *good* teeth, and
others with *bad* ones, may object to this species of
kitchen discipline; but it is evident that its effect,
if introduced at our fashionable tables, will be to
prolong the social hours of dinner, provided the
guests can be persuaded to stop and perform the
necessary mastication; yet, after all, in regard to
the matter of mere economy, we might perhaps
as well have recourse to the old recipe, which informs us that four and twenty pounds of bone,

boiled in four and twenty gallons of water, for four
and twenty hours, will make four and twenty quarts
of soup for four and twenty Frenchmen !

" *Apropos des bottes,*" however, and whilst we
are talking of bones, it must not be forgotten, that
they may now be eaten as readily as the tenderest
steak or veal cutlet, by the new philosophic mode
of preparing first jelly, and then gelatine.

According to this new principle, for we wish not
to treat it as mere matter for laughter, the old
mode of preparing jelly may be much improved,
and with a considerable saving by the use of bones
only.   It is true, indeed, that bones have long been
employed for that purpose by the London confectioners, but not on so economical a principle as that
which we shall now detail; wherein the bones intended for broth or jelly require little or no selection ; the more veal bones there are among them,
the more readily the broth assumes the form of a
jelly, but it is not on that account better or more
nutritious. The only preparation requisite is to
break them with a hammer into pieces three or four
inches long. The boiler employed is of the common kind, well tinned, or at least kept very clean,
and placed upon a Rumford furnace, which exceedingly facilitates the graduation of the fire, and
produces a great saving in fuel. The boiler must
be provided with a lid, having a vent for the escape
of the steam ; for the heat should not be raised beyond the ordinary temperature of ebullition, and
when that is attained, only a gentle fire should be
kept up, otherwise it is liable to spoil the jelly.
Put into the boiler as much water as it will conveniently hold, with one-sixth of its weight of
broken bones. When it boils, skim, and put on
the lid, which is occasionally removed for the pur-

pose of stirring the bones with a large stick or wooden shovel. When any quantity of fat is seen floating on the surface, take it off with a flat ladle, lest it should be spoiled by long ebullition. This fat, which soon congeals, is one of the alimentary products, and may either be kept by itself, for culinary use, or put again into the jelly, just previous to its being taken off the stove.

It is said to be a great advantage, in this economic system, that the process may be repeated thrice with the same bones, which will each time furnish about the same quantity of broth or jelly as at first; for it appears that water cannot dissolve more than a certain proportion of extractive matter, and that when this liquid is once saturated, it must be renewed, if the extraction shall go on. Thus, one pound of bones will yield at four successive boilings of three or four hours each, four pounds of jelly, containing as much nutritive matter as the broth usually made with six pounds of meat.

After the jelly has thus been extracted, and when a casual observer might suppose that nothing but a caput mortuum was left, the second process begins, of boiling the bones in sal ammoniac, and then laying them up for use; to which they are put by grinding or breaking, and boiled down, until, as it has actually been ascertained by experiment, one hundred pounds of bones, principally beef, yield twenty-five pounds of dry gelatine, the nutritive quality of which, compared with meat, may be thus estimated. Experience proves that one pound of meat will make two of broth. From the analysis published at Munich, it appears that one hundred pounds of beef contain seventy-four of water, six of dry gelatine, and twenty of dry fibre, which serves only to fill the stomach, and not for aliment; so that the 6 per cent. of dry gelatine may be considered as the only parts that are nutritive. The published Instructions add, that eight ounces of beef per day are sufficient for the ordinary nourishment of a man; these eight ounces of meat are scarcely equivalent to half an ounce of dry gelatine. Double the quantity of meat, that is to say, take a pound to make broth for a good ration of soup, and one ounce of dry gelatine will produce the same effect.

The dry gelatine is perfectly insipid, and does not dissolve very easily in water. When it is wanted for use, it is advisable to soak it over-night in water in a warm place. Being then set over a slow fire for four or five hours, it is wholly converted into a nutritious but insipid broth, with which the seasoning and vegetables intended for the soup may be mixed. To give it the flavour of the meat which it has lost, instead of four ounces of gelatine, take but three; add a pound of meat and sixteen pounds of water. Boil it down to one half, and you will have eight pounds of broth, like that made with meat only, and half a pound of *bouilli*.

Where broth is wanted in a hurry, it is found that these cakes broken and thrown into boiling water dissolve very speedily. As this solution is insipid, seasoning and herbs must be added, or a small quantity of meat; the broth is then highly tonic and nutritious. One pound of these cakes will furnish forty pounds of excellent broth; and one ounce of the same, dissolved in twenty ounces of water, furnishes a jelly for table, which may be seasoned to the palate.

With these cakes of gelatine, sugar, and orange-flower water, the apothecaries make a compound for coughs, of a very agreeable taste, and extremely nutritious.

Gelatine in cakes may be used with advantage as a substitute for isinglass (which is much dearer) in all its applications.

The dry gelatine is sold at Geneva at the rate of 4 francs (3s. 4d.) and in cakes at 6 francs 50 centimes (5s. 5d.) per pound of 18 ounces.

To people accustomed to eat their dinners in the ordinary way, it may seem as if a man would never get fat upon the produce of dried bones; but we must remember that the Highland shepherds, who are some of the finest men in the world, live on scarcely any thing more than oatmeal soaked in water, and their dogs often feed out of the same dish.

It is true, indeed, that such food may require something more tasty to give an after-relish; for which the ingenious Count is fully prepared, especially by a mode rendering salt fish perfectly delicious, by keeping it for several hours in water just scalding hot, but not boiling. This, certainly, will be more agreeable to an English palate than the Swedish relish of raw salmon cut into slices, salted, and left for some days in a wooden tray with a little water.

With one word on the boiling of vegetables we shall close this section. We have seen it asserted by a French writer, who seems very anxious to carry all his philosophy into the kitchen, that the hardest and "most unboilable" produce of the garden may be brought speedily into an edible state, by the addition of a small quantity of purified alkali to the boiling water. He tells a whimsical story of a lady who was in that way in which "ladies long to be who love their lords," as the poignant Mrs. Afra Behn expresses herself in the novel of The Noble

Slaves, and who, paying a country visit near to Paris, longed for an immense cabbage, which she saw in the garden standing for seed. Whether she was a tailor's wife, or not, he does not inform us; but she was in a hurry, and under the usual plea in such cases, not only insisted on having the cabbage, but on having it in half an hour. In vain did the unfortunate cook declare that it was impossible—she asserted, that to a *good* cook nothing was impossible. His honour was touched—his glory was at stake—and Monsieur, pulling up the cabbage and pulling off his ruffles, began "*faire l'impossible.*" Fortunately for the honour of his art, as the poor cook knew nothing of philosophy, our Author stepped in to dine, and was informed of the circumstance; when, slipping into the kitchen, he unseen deposited a small quantity of purified alkali in the cabbage-kettle, and to the surprize of all, but the conjuror himself, the cabbage was served up within the half hour, and the so much feared mark avoided! It had been well if the family cooks of many of the present great men in Paris could have boiled their mushrooms as speedily!!!

The same writer tells another anecdote of the astonishment which he excited amongst the ladies, directresses of a soup establishment, in boiling their haricots in two hours, instead of seven, by the same chemical application, after he had prophecied the result, thus fulfilled—" the time revolved—they found their haricots *en purée!*" or boiled into pease pudding; as an Hibernian might translate it, without adding a bull to the soup, in defiance of economy. And now whilst we mention economy, we must beg leave to remark, that as a nation we are very deficient in the practice of this virtue, as far as our culinary operations are concerned. A French family would live well, on what is wasted in an English kitchen, the bones, drippings, pot liquor, remains of fish, vegetables, &c. which are too often consigned to the grease pot, or the dust heap, might, by a very trifling degree of management on the part of a cook, or mistress of a family, be converted into sources of daily support and comfort, at least to some poor pensioner or other, at an expense that even the miser could scarcely grudge.

It would be of little avail to offer directions for culinary practice, if strict attention were not to be paid to the

LARDER,

a department in which the eye of a careful housewife will always find employment.

It is needless to say that the greatest cleanliness is necessary; but it is proper to remark that a thorough current of air ought always to be kept up; and if the situation of the larder will not admit of opposite windows, then a current of air must be admitted by means of a flue from the outside. Shelter from the sun is expedient, and as equal a temperature ought to be obtained as possible. Though joints of meat ought, in general, to be exposed to this current of air, and game also, yet fowls may be rendered peculiarly tender by a shorter process than mere atmospheric exposure; which is to lay them, as soon as killed, in a heap of wheat; when they will become tender and palatable in a couple of days.

With respect to game, observe that when the weather is very warm, it will always have a good effect to put a stopper of charcoal in the vent, tying at the same time a string tightly round the neck.

The beneficial effects of charcoal in stopping putrefaction, are now well ascertained; nay even fish or meat may be restored by boiling charcoal with them.

It is not irrelevant here to notice that meat, tainted to an extreme degree, has been speedily restored by washing in cold water, and afterwards in strong camomile tea, after which it may be sprinkled with salt, and used the day following; or if steeped and well washed in beer, it will make pure and sweet soup, even after being fly-blown.

Many other hints might be offered, but they are rather subjects for works professedly on cookery; we proceed therefore to record all the recent useful applications of philosophical principles to facts connected with the preservation of articles of food, both in summer and in winter.

An ingenious German professor has made many successful experiments with pyroligneous acid, as a means of preventing the corruption of animal substances. He has entirely recovered several anatomical preparations from incipient corruption, by pouring this acid over them. With the oil which is produced from wood by distillation in the dry manner, he has moistened pieces of flesh already advanced in decay; and, notwithstanding the heat of the weather, soon made them as dry and firm as flesh can be rendered by being smoked in the smoking-room. All traces of corruption vanish at once, when the vinegar of wood or the oil of wood is applied to the meat with a brush.

This explains why meat, merely dried in a stove, does not keep, while that which is smoked becomes unalterable. We have here also an explanation of the theory of hams; of the beef of Hamburg; of smoked tongues, sausages, red herrings, and of wood smoked to preserve it from worms, &c."

It is sufficient to plunge meat for a few moments into this acid, even slightly empyreumatic, to preserve this meat as long as you may desire. Cutlets, kidneys, liver, rabbits, may be prepared and kept as fresh as if they had been just procured from the market.

Another foreign chemist has recently made some curious experiments on the preservation of flesh in the gases. Into a receiver of the capacity of three cubic inches, filled with very pure sulphurous acid gas, he introduced, through mercury, a piece of fresh beef; in a few minutes it had absorbed almost all the gas, and the mercury filled the capacity of the receiver, except some air bubbles, probably owing to the atmospheric air. The flesh soon lost its natural red colour, and assumed that of boiled meat: it underwent no other apparent alteration, and the air in the bell-glass preserved its volume. At the end of seventy-six days, during which time the temperature had varied from 0 to 10° Reaumur, the beef had acquired scarcely any smell of sulphurous acid, and was harder and drier than roasted meat. After being left four days in the open air, it became more compact without being putrified, and did not change colour: it merely lost the weak smell of acid, without acquiring any other. A piece of ox beef was treated in the same way in the fluoric acid gas, and the results were in every respect similar: the phenomena were only less visible, because the acid attacked the glass, and a thin coating of mercury was deposited on the flesh. Beef deposited in a receiver filled with ammoniacal gas exhibited very different alterations: a total absorption of the elastic fluid had taken place; the meat assumed a fine red colour, nearly resembling the effect of nitrous gas, and retained this fresh appearance seventy-six days; it was much softer than in the foregoing experiment, without smell, and having the colour and consistence of fresh meat. When exposed four days to the open air, it did not putrify, but lost its red colour, became brown, dry, and covered with a kind of varnish.

These experiments are, indeed, fitter for the laboratory, than for the larder; but the pyroligneous acid may be successfully applied by those who have no knowledge of practical chemistry, beyond the boiling of salt brine. It is also easy not only to check, but to cure putrefaction in tainted, salt, or dried meats, by simple washing with a brush dipped in the acid.

An ingenious Spaniard, has discovered that meat may be preserved fresh for many months, by keeping it immersed in molasses.

A plan has recently been patented for methods or processes of preserving such animal and vegetable substances separately or mixed together as are fit for the food of man, and for such a length of time as to render them fit for ship or garrison stores.

As the principles of the plan are easily applicable, in many points, to domestic economy, even upon a small scale, we shall enter upon it at some length; first premising that the object of the invention is effected by cutting off all communication between the atmosphere and the articles to be preserved, by one or other of the following means; by pouring into the vessel in which the pieces of food to be preserved are packed, melted and hot fat, or pouring in a strong hot animal fluid jelly in such a manner that not only all the interstices between the pieces, but the whole interior of the vessel shall be so completely filled as to displace entirely all the atmospheric air; or secondly, by coating the different pieces with melted suet, before they are packed in the vessel in which they are to be preserved; then packing them when cold, and afterwards displacing all the air between the pieces and from the whole interior of the vessel; by pouring in, cold, a saturated aqueous solution of common sea salt or mineral culinary salt, that is to say, a solution of muriate of soda; or thirdly, when the article is such as to permit it (as for example butter) by filling the vessel so completely with the article itself, as to expel the air, using due precautions to prevent the access of air afterwards, by percolation, or otherwise, through the substance of the vessel. The vessels employed are adapted to the nature of the article, the manner of preservation, and the quantity to be contained in them. For quantities not exceeding fifteen pounds the patentee employs vessels of tinned iron, either square, cylindrical, or of any other convenient form, also of earthen-ware, glass, or even wood. These vessels he prepares in one or more of the following ways: 1. By applying in a hot state all over their outside, and that of their covers, some good varnish or resinous substance.—2. By saturating them, as much as the nature of the material will admit, and as completely as possible from their inside, with a saturated aqueous solution of common salt.—3. By lining them with a coating of any substance or mixture not deleterious or injurious (as suet or wax, or a mixture of them) that can prevent the articles put in from coming in contact with the vessels or their covers.—4. By inclosing the vessels within other vessels or boxes, leaving a little space between them to be filled up with tallow or wax, or any other substance capable of excluding the contact of the atmosphere from their sides and bottoms. Their covers are to be coated in like manner. If the vessels are of metal or earthen-ware, use the first and third, or the third and fourth means; if of glass the fourth; if of wood the first and second, or the second and fourth, or the third and fourth, having previously charred the inside of the vessel.

The articles to be preserved are cooked in any of the usual ways, put hot into the vessel, which is then filled with melted fat or fluid jelly so strong as to be solid when cold. The cover is then put on and soldered air-tight, after which it is to be filled completely through a hole left in the cover for that purpose. The last operation is to stop this hole with a cork, over which rosin or tallow is melted, and a tinned iron cover fitted over that. When meat is to be preserved coated, separate pieces of 3 to 6lbs. weight are placed in a mould while hot, and surrounded with melted suet. When cold the entire mass is taken out of the mould, and any number of these pieces may then be placed in one sound case or vessel made of wood, to contain from 18 to 50 or 100lbs. or more.

It is evident that all the varieties in this specification depend, in a great measure, upon the same principle as that which directs the covering of potted meats with mutton suet boiled down to fluidity; but, nevertheless, the variations in practice may be found strictly applicable to the use of the larder.

We shall now conclude with one point of very important consideration, both in regard to public and private economy, dependent upon a process for curing herrings, pilchards, mackarel, sprats, &c. which may become of extensive utility, by preserving large quantities of these various kinds of fish for food, which might otherwise be wasted in very abundant seasons. This is sufficiently evident from the fact, that in January, 1814, sprats pickled by this method were selling to the poor of Spitalfields at the rate of one penny per pound. In the same year upwards of 25,000 mackarel, 300 barrels of herrings, and 50 of sprats, were cured at Ramsgate by this process, which is as follows :—Reservoirs of any size, vats, or casks, perfectly watertight, should be about half filled with brine, made by dissolving about 28 parts of solid salt in 72 of fresh water. The fish, as fresh as possible, gutted or not, must be plunged into this fully saturated brine in such quantity as nearly to fill the reservoir, and after remaining quite immersed for five or six days, they will be fit to be packed as usual with large grained solid salt, and exported to the hottest climates. As brine is always weakest at the upper part, in order to keep it of a uniform saturation a wooden lattice-work frame, of such size as to be easily let into the inside of the reservoir, is sunk an inch or two under the surface of the brine, for the purpose of suspending upon it lumps of one or two pounds, or larger, of solid salt, which effectually saturate whatever moisture may exude from the fish, and thus the brine will be continued of the utmost strength so long as any part of the lumps remain undissolved. The solidity of the lumps admit of their being applied several times, or whenever the reservoirs are replenished with fish; and the brine although repeatedly used, does not putrify; nor do the fish, if kept under the surface, ever become rancid.

One other point, of some importance, connected with this process is, that all provisions are best preserved by this method, especially bacon, which, when thus cured, is not so liable to become rusty, as when done by the usual method of rubbing with salt, and is nevertheless effectually cured.

As there is no part of rural economy more compatible with elegance, and even with modern refinement, than the

DAIRY,

so may it be found perfectly consistent, even with

affluence, to render the ornamental dairy subservient to utility and economy.

It must be pleasing to shew to one's friends, not only the elegance of the dairy itself, but also its agreeable produce; not in the common routine of mere milk and cream, but in their more artificial combinations.

We wish also most particularly to point out to families inclined to economize, fairly, carefully, and judiciously at home, by means of a little exertion, that attention to the management and produce of the dairy farm is a most important component part of their system.

If indeed they prefer sour wine to good milk, and to sit idle instead of adopting a little household exertion, let them continue to grumble against the times, or set off for a domiciling visit to France, where they will soon learn to grumble still more: but if a real love of their country impels them to remain at home, let them put their own shoulders to the wheel; and, instead of complaining of high prices, endeavour to secure all the necessaries and many of the comforts of life at half-price, by a small proportion of labour, which will soon become an amusement. It is not enough to grumble at what is bad, or to wish for what is good—we must exert ourselves to overcome the one and to procure the other, or we shall be contented no where.

But we shall give a truce to moralizing, and proceed at once to offer a few economic hints for the management of the dairy itself, which ought to be erected in a situation remote from dirt or dust, with an aspect open to the north if possible, in which direction it ought to have one window, with another to the south. By this means its atmospheric temperature may, in some measure, be regulated in the different seasons; but it will be proper that the

windows when open, and indeed the lattices generally, should only be pervious to air and light.
Glass may certainly be used, but gauze, or oiled
paper within the lattice will be found the best.

A temperature of about fifty-five degrees will be
found most favourable to the separation of the
cream from the milk.

Where expense in the erection is not absolutely
an object, then the apartment ought to be vaulted;
at all events, however, it may be ceiled; the walls
ought to be well white-washed, the floor well flagged
or paved with proper tiles, and every thing so arranged as not to interfere with the utmost tidiness
of preparation. If its size will permit, it is better
to have shelves, of table height, arranged all round
it, but if not sufficiently large, then another and
higher shelf may be added. Where the floor can
be laid on a bias, with a gradual descent, either to
the middle, where a small grating may lead to a
drain, or else to one of the sides, it will be found a
most convenient arrangement. No extra damp
ought to be permitted to lie until it evaporates; and
it ought to be an invariable rule that the cheese
presses shall be placed in another apartment.

If the inequality of the ground permits the
dairy to be so placed that a pipe may be laid from
a natural spring, with a small reservoir and stop-
cock, great advantages from freshness and cleanliness must ensue: otherwise there ought to be a
good sized reservoir, with ready means of replenish-
ing it, so that the idea of trouble shall not tempt
the dairy maids to avoid the necessary expenditure
of water.

In regard to the vessels used for the reception of
milk, those of wood are unquestionably the sweetest;
though they require more care with respect to
scalding and rubbing than other materials. Those

of lead have been in much request of late years, under the idea that they keep the milk cooler, but they may from accidental causes become prejudicial to the health, and they likewise require great attention. They should be scoured with salt, or Calais sand. Vessels of pottery are often badly glazed, and that too with materials prejudicial to health. Before any of these are applied to use, it will be proper to test them, by means of a short and simple process,

Fill the vessel with vinegar, into which put some fat of beef, salted. Set this upon a stew-pan to boil for half an hour; then set all by for twenty-four hours, and if the glazing is badly executed, small particles of the lead will be discovered of a black colour, proving the vessel to be unfit for use.

It has been recently stated, that the kind of oily coat which is formed by repeated coction on the internal surface of earthen vessels, and which is substituted for the glazing generally used in potteries, removes all the uneasiness respecting the possibility of poison, which has been felt since Ebell's examination of the danger of glazing with lead. This new invention is owing to Mr. Kirchoff, at St. Petersburg: the vessels covered with this kind of coat, serve not only for cooking, but also for preserving all kinds of acid, salt, and fat substances.

This application, however, even if efficacious, might sometimes lead to a false security, wherefore we consider constant manual cleanliness as a much better preservative.

The dairy being arranged, the choice of cattle, for its supply, becomes the next object of consequence. To be well managed, indeed, a dairy at first sight, appears expensive; but a moderate number of cows will always pay for the extra attendance of keeping them as clean and comfortable as horses.

Perhaps no mode of managing cows can be found preferable to that adopted by Mr. Harley, of Glasgow, whose cow-house is an object of curiosity to all who visit that thriving and interesting city. When we saw Mr. Harley's *cow establishment*, it contained ninety-six inhabitants, each of whom was confined to a post by a chain across her neck, of sufficient length to allow her, by means of a sliding-ring, to lie down when she pleased. The cows stood in pairs, one before another, on each side of the cow-house, leaving a space sufficiently wide for the attendants to pass backwards and forwards between them. Each pair has a grating before them, and the hay for the whole party is cut by means of a small steam-engine. The temperature is regulated with great exactness, the whole premises kept in the most delicate state of cleanliness, and the cows themselves are regularly curried and rubbed down, which supplies to them the place of exercise; as they never go out, except at a given period after the birth of their first calf, when they are always sold; not being retained by Mr. Harley long enough to have a second. It will therefore be easily imagined that the quality of the milk must be as desirable to the purchaser, as the quantity of it must be profitable to the proprietor.

The milk is all sold in Glasgow; and to prevent its being adulterated by the people who take it out, the barrels which contain it are covered by lids which have padlocks on them, and there is to each a lock-cock by which the milk is drawn out. A large stock of pigs are likewise kept on the milk of this establishment, and twenty roasters are selected from them every Wednesday, and sold at half a guinea each.

By adopting the cleanliness and judiciousness of

such of these regulations as may be practicable
on a small scale, a private family may keep a cow
with less trouble and expense than are attendant on
keeping a horse.   The `scarcity and consequent
dearness of milk is an evil daily increasing; not only
in the capital, but even in country towns; on account
of the enclosures which have taken place within late
years, and of the pride and self importance of
modern farmer's wives, who look upon the concerns
of the dairy as objects of such minor importance, as
to be beneath their notice: yet when we consider
the privations that the children of the lower classes
sustain, in consequence of the utter impossibility on
the parts of their parents to procure them this their
natural aliment, and the prejudicial effects both on
their health and future habits, which result from
their being reared with beer and spirits, and other
destructive potions, in its place ; we cannot but recommend it most earnestly to the consideration of
the benevolent, as well as the economical, that by
keeping cows in all families where it may be practicable, they will not only be enabled to supply themselves with a variety of nutritious, delightful and
elegant dishes, at a very small expense, but also to
minister, without any perceptible deduction from
their own stores, to the wants of their poorer neighbours ; and especially to those of the patient little
tribe who, continually pinched with cold and hunger,
endure for hours together, whilst sitting on the
threshold of the rich and luxurious, such privations
as would try the philosophy of most of our pro-
foundest theorists.

Let it be kept in remembrance, that cows are
profitable in all respects, not only in their present
produce, but in their rearing calves for agricultural
and dairy purposes, and in their fetching nearly
their first cost, when age requires that they should
be fatted for the market.

In a moderate establishment, where several cows are kept, it will always be found that after serving the family, the overplus cheese and butter will pay the expence of keep, and go towards paying the first cost, so as to make the fattening of the cattle, when no longer fit for the dairy, an object of actual profit. This need not be doubted, when it is known that milch kine, well housed, will each give nine gallons of milk per day for some months; and, with care and judicious feeding, will not fall much below it, for some time longer. They become, therefore, very fair objects of consideration to those who wish to adopt a rational practical system of economy, and to obtain at the same time an increase to their enjoyments, instead of any diminution of them. Even the calves form an object in the scale of saving. If thought necessary, or expedient, to take them from the cow at the earliest age, they may easily be taught to drink a mixture of hot water and oatmeal, in the proportion of a pound of oatmeal to four quarts of water, adding to it about three pints of the skimmed milk; or they may be fed with hay tea, containing one quart of flax-seed to every two gallons of water. This, however, must only be practised, where, on a careful calculation, the milk thus saved will cover the expence of the artificial food. Where cows are, indeed, very prolific, the extra calves must either be killed or fed in this manner. Where they come singly, it is not so much an object; but in many instances there are twins, and even more. Of this fact it is needless to enumerate instances; but a more extraordinary instance of the fecundity of a cow than the following, we believe, is not on record,—she produced in July, 1815, five calves; in May, 1816, three ditto; in March, 1817, three ditto; in May, 1818, two ditto; and in April,

1819, three ditto; making together 16 in the space of four years.

In choosing cows, from the various breeds, some consideration is always necessary.

Where amusement, more than absolute profit, is the object, the Alderney breed may be selected; not, indeed, that these are to be considered as unprofitable, for their milk is so very rich that the average of their annual butter may be reckoned as upwards of two hundred weight; and, though small, they always fetch a good price in the market when unfit for the dairy—but because their very high price, as milch cattle, places them rather beyond the limit of actual economy in the curtailment of outgoings.

If a distinction can conveniently be made, we would recommend the Alderney cattle for *butter*; but for *cheese*, the long-horned Lancashire breed, the produce of whose milk in the latter article is equal to that of the Alderney breed in the former. The very worst of the Lancashire will yield four gallons of milk per day; some of them half as much more; and they will finally pay for themselves in the market.

But if milk in its natural state be the principal object in the dairy, the best breed is the Holderness, sometimes called *Dutch*, perhaps from their coming up from that district of Lincolnshire, which bears the appellation of *Holland*.

Though considered the most valuable for agricultural purposes, we may, perhaps, place last on the list the Devonshire breed; but, without any disparagement of their peculiar good qualities.

The food of dairy cattle is an important object in this branch of economy; but it will not be uninteresting, previous to that investigation, to record some recent and highly curious experiments in the properties of milk, and their philosophical application to domestic purposes, which have been tried in Switzerland. It appears from the literary records of the day, that Dr. Schübler, Professor of Chemistry applied to agriculture in the celebrated institution of M. de Fellenberg at Hofwyl, has been led by his investigations into the nature of milk, and its immediate principles, to results equally curious and interesting to the farmer of every country.

"Morning's milk," he says, "commonly yields some hundredths more cream than the evening's at the same temperature. That milked at noon furnishes the least; it would, therefore, be of advantage, in making butter and cheese, to employ the morning's milk, and to keep the evening's for domestic use.

"In milking cows, this singular phenomenon is observed, that the milk obtained from one and the same milking differs considerably in quality; that, contrary to what might be expected, the milk first extracted is not the best; but that which is obtained last contains invariably the largest proportion of cream. To satisfy myself thoroughly on this point, I caused a meal's milk of one cow to be milked into five vessels of the same size, and then separately examined the milk in each, in the order in which it was taken. The results were as follow :

	Areo-meter.	Specific Gravity.	Cream.
No. 1	56	1034,0	5 p. cent.
2	55	1033,4	8
3	54	1032,7	11,5
4	52	1035,5	13,5
5	48	1029,0	17,5
Average	53	1032,1	11,05

"To ascertain whether the quantity of caseum differed in like manner, I had a young and healthy cow milked clean into ten different vessels. The first milked was, as usual, the heaviest, and the last contained the most cream.—After the milk was nicely skimmed, I found its weight in an inverse ratio; now the first milked was the lightest, and the last the heaviest, and richest in caseous matter; so that the milk obtained last is better also in regard to the quantity of caseum.

"In an experiment of this kind, I caused the milk to be drawn first from the left side of a cow's udder, and afterwards from the right; the latter was the best. The following day I reversed the experiment; and still the milk last extracted was the richest.

"The subjoined table exhibits the gradation in the quality of the milk found by the above experiments :—

	Num. of vessel.	Sp. Grav. of the fresh milk.	Mean Sp. Gr.	Proportion of Cream.	Sp. Grav. of the skimm'd milk.	1000 pts. of skimmed con. cas. pts.
Right Side.	1	1033,1				
	2	1033				
	3	1032,7	1032,7	8,3 p.ct.	1035,6	49
	4	1032				
	5	1031,6				
	6	1030,7				
	7	1031,7	1031,7	12, 7	1036	50,1
Left Side.	8	1030,6				
	9	1028,6	1026,3	26,6	1036,6	52,3
	10	1024				

"Thus the milk of the 7th vessel, with which the left side was begun, proved of inferior quality; and in some succeeding experiments, it became as poor as that of the first. The increase of cream was found beyond all proportion in the vessels last milked, especially when compared with the augmentation in the early ones. The diminution of weight in the first portions was from 0,1 to 0,3 and 0,7; and in the last it was in the proportion of 1,1 to 2 and 2,6. In one of my experiments, after having caused both sides to be well milked, I attempted to begin the operation for the second time on the left side, and afterwards on the right: I obtained again a small quantity of milk from both sides, which was much richer in cream than that previously extracted; and the whole of this last essay was still better,—it yielded 42 per cent. of cream.

" I have repeated these experiments with several cows; the difference between the milk of the right and left, according as I caused them to be milked first on the one side or the other, was frequently less considerable than in the case above cited; sometimes, indeed, but trifling; yet the milk obtained last from each side, and also from each particular teat, was constantly richer both in butter and cheese."

The preservation of milk, beyond the mere use of the day, cannot be of any peculiar importance in England; but, unwilling to omit any thing which may eventually be useful to our readers, we trust to be excused in here stating, that the foreign journals inform us, that Kirchoff, the chemist who discovered the process of forming sugar from starch, gives the following simple mode of preserving that agreeable fluid. Fresh milk is to be slowly evaporated by a very gentle heat, till it is reduced to a dry powder. This substance should be kept in a dry and well stopped bottle. Diluted with a sufficient quantity of water, it possesses considerable analogy, both in its taste and other properties, with new milk. This would be a very convenient form of taking milk to sea, where a cow cannot be accommodated.

Passing on, however, to more practical purposes, we may observe, that in addition to the expenditure of the skimmed milk in feeding calves, &c. it is now become an object of some importance in home commerce, as a means not only of fining down wine, but spirits also.

The economic *dairyist* will find advantage in noting, that of all green foods, sainfoin is indubitably the best to increase milk and cream, both in quantity and quality; but when the cattle cannot procure green succulent food, it will be judicious to give them their preserved fodder, either boiled or steeped in warm water, allowing it to stand until cold; a process, in fact, which is said to produce a saving equal to three fourths of the food. The cattle must be permitted not only to eat the hay, but also to drink the water; but when water is given solely for drink, then it will always be much improved by boiling in it half a dozen handfuls of hay to every twenty gallons of liquid.

It has often been objected, when cattle are artificially fed, that the butter becomes affected by a peculiarly unpleasant taste—a circumstance which may always be guarded against by the simple operation of putting a piece of saltpetre, about the size of a nutmeg, into each vessel which may be large enough to hold as much cream as will make six pounds of butter.

Parsnips are said to have the least effect in giving an unpleasant or peculiar flavour to milk; so much so, indeed, that it is by some agriculturists considered as judicious to sow even the best land with that root. Carrots rank next with respect to flavour, producing also an additional quantity of milk, when given in the very latest period of the winter season, or before the green food begins to shew itself.

Turnips, of course, rank last; but where no other food can be procured, the disagreeable odour given to the milk may be counteracted, in a great degree, by a weak solution of nitre in spring water, applied in the proportion of one small table-spoonful to every two gallons, as soon as the milk comes into the dairy. The objection against cows' milk, fed on turnips, may also be removed by the following simple process in the preparation of the milk for dairy purposes.

Let the bowls, whether of lead or wood, or earthenware, be kept constantly clean, and well scalded with boiling water before using. When the milk is brought into the dairy, to every eight quarts add one quart of boiling water; and then put the milk into the bowls to stand for cream. By keeping strictly to this practice, sweet and well-tasted butter has been made all the winter from cows house-fed, upon turnips solely.

A little hay may, however, be given at intervals; and a mash of bran with warm water, every evening.

One other species of winter food must yet be noticed. The attention of agriculturists was some time since directed in a particular manner to the Mangel Wurzel, which was stated, on the authority of Lord CREWE, Mr. COKE, Mr. TOLLET, to be pernicious to cattle. It seems now to be decided that the disorder complained of proceeds rather from the manner in which this root is given, than from the root itself; and that cattle feeding greedily upon mangel wurzel, thrown to them on a bare pasture, without any other food to qualify the excessive proportion of water contained in it, cannot be expected to escape injury. Whatever the food, it will always be found that in salting butter for winter use, a great improvement will be found to arise from mixing one ounce of crude sal ammoniac, and two ounces of salt-petre finely powdered, with one peck of salt. This requires a smaller quantity to be used, and gives a more agreeable flavour than the usual mode of applying common salt alone.

There is a very ingenious mode recommended to ensure good butter in winter, which is by preparing half the supposed quantity required in winter, during the course of the summer. The process is to salt, and dye it a deep colour with marygold or anotto. Then, in winter, put as much of this into the churn as it is expected the milk will produce. They will thus be intimately mixed together, and equally salted; and the whole mass will have a flavour equal to that of summer butter.

A new method has lately been proposed, which may appear, at first sight, as tedious in the process; but which certainly requires less labour than the usual mode. It is thus:—Put the cream intended for butter into a strong linen cloth; tie it up tight with a string, dig a hole in the earth fifteen inches deep, and let the bottom of it be sufficiently capacious to allow the cream to lie about four inches deep all over it. Put another cloth around that which contains the cream, to keep the dirt from it. When deposited in the hole, cover it up with the earth, (but do not tread it down) and let it remain 24 or 26 hours; then take it out and pour the cream, which will now be very thick, into a bowl or other vessel, and stir it well, from five to ten minutes, with a wooden spoon or ladle; when the butter will be completely formed, and may be taken out and washed as usual. The advantages of this mode of making butter, are as follow :—1st, the cream yields a larger quantity of butter, or an addition of about one pound in ten; 2nd, in hot weather, butter is obtained without a tedious process, and is free from the rancid taste that long and hot churned butter generally possesses; and 3rd, a very small stock of cream may be operated upon equally, as well as a larger quantity.

A species of churn has been for some time in use in the neighbourhood of Rootan Hall, in Wales, which saves both time and labour. It is called the Cradle Churn, being made upon the principle of a common rocking-horse; and can with ease be worked by a child of five or six years old. Sir R. Vaughan is so well convinced, from experience, of the superiority of this churn over every other, that he has had many made and distributed among his tenants. The shape is of no consequence, provided it be made considerably wider at the top than at the bottom, that it may churn either a large or small quantity of milk equally well; but the usual form is that of a canoe.

We may conclude our economical hints on butter with one observation respecting the best mode of preserving it; which is, that when vessels of pottery are employed, it is preferable when, instead of being glazed within, they are impregnated with melted wax or tallow, or saturated with a solution of muriate of soda. If wooden vessels are employed, they should be saturated in the same manner, having first been well varnished on the outside. If any empty space should be left, the air must be expelled, by pouring in, as before directed, a saturated solution of soda. Butter may also be preserved, deposited in the middle of its containing vessel, and surrounded completely with the same solution. In this case, the vessel is provided with a false bottom and cover.

In regard to *Cheese*, we profess not to write a treatise, but still we may offer some economic hints as to the imitations of various kinds; which, with a little care and attention, may be made fully equal to those which they are intended to resemble. At the same time we enter a caveat against all professed adulterations, or colouring with deleterious substances. Let us refrain from imitating Gloster cheese, if we can only do so by the use of red lead; a practice already too common, but which may always be detected by a little chemical skill; scraping the cheese into water in which sulphurated hydrogen is combined, with a small portion of muriatic acid, when the adulterated cheese changes its red colour for a deep black or brown.

Fresh cheese may be made at all times of the year, with a little care, equal to that which comes from Lincolnshire in the radish season; by merely adding new milk to that of the preceding milking, letting them stand, and pressing them gently two or three times, after which they may be turned daily for a few days, and used at pleasure; and a fair economist may produce her own *Stilton* by the following simple process :—To the new milk of the cheese-making morning, add the cream from that of the preceding evening, together with the rennet, watching the full separation of the curd, which must be removed from the whey without breaking, and placed in a sieve until of such a consistence as to bear being lifted up and placed in a hoop that will receive it without much pressure. The cheese, as it dries, will shrink up, and must therefore be placed from time to time in a tighter hoop, and turned daily until it acquires the proper degree of consistence for use or keeping.

If it is intended to imitate Parmesan, let the day's milk be heated to the degree of 120 of Fahrenheit, then removed from the fire until all motion ceases. Put in the rennet, allow an hour for the coagulation, after which set the curd on a slow fire until heated to 150, during which the curd separates in small lumps. A few pinches of saffron are then thrown in, together with cold water sufficient to reduce it instantly to a bearable heat, when the curd is collected by passing a cloth beneath it, and gathering it up at the corners. Place the curd in a circle of wood without a bottom; lay it on a table covered by a round piece of wood, pressed down by a heavy stone. The cheese will acquire sufficient consistence in the course of a night to bear turning, when the upper side is to be rubbed with salt, to be continued alternately for forty days.

In Italy they next cut off the outer crust, and varnish the new surface with linseed oil; but that may well be omitted, as well as colouring one side of it red.

It may be also noted that the day's milk is formed from the evening milk skimmed at morning and at noon; and from the morning's milk skimmed at noon.

Perhaps one of the greatest comforts connected with a dairy, is the certainty of having milk and cream free from adulteration. A point of similar importance, in regard to the next object of discussion, is the

BAKERY.

There is no article of more home importance in

domestic economy than the bread, which forms so material a part of our daily nourishment, together with the flour which enters into so many culinary preparations; and there can be no doubt that when every part of the process can be home-made, there must always ensue. a considerable *saving* both in health and comfort—a saving, at the end of the year, of much greater importance than the sum total of petty, but ill-judged, economy can ever amount to.

The superior nutritious qualities of bread, have been doubted; but the question has recently been set at rest in France, by some chemical researches into the proportional nutriment of various edible substances.

M. M. Percy and Vauquelin were appointed to make the experiments on which the solution of these questions rested, and they have published the results in an interesting report on domestic economy. They have ascertained that bread contains 80 nutritive parts in 100; meal 34 in 100; French beans, 92 *idem*; common beans, 89 *idem*; peas, 93 *idem*; lentils, 94 *idem*; cabbages and turnips, the most aqueous of all the vegetables compared, produce only eight pounds of solid matter in 100 pounds; carrots and spinach produce 14 in the same quantity; whilst 100 pound of potatoes contain 25 pounds of dry substance. It must be recollected, that the solid parts, when separated from the aqueous or humid parts, may contain a small quantity of extractive or ligneous matter probably unfit for food; and next, that the same substances do not act uniformly on all stomachs, and are relatively more or less nutritious. But as a general result, the learned reporters estimate that one pound of good bread is equal to two pounds and a half, or three pounds of potatoes; that 75 pounds of bread and 30 of meat, may be substituted for 300 pounds of potatoes. The other substances bear the following proportions: four parts of cabbage to one of potatoes; three parts of turnips to one *idem ;* two parts of carrots and spinach to one *idem ;* and about three parts and a half of potatoes to one of rice, lentils, beans, French beans, and dry peas.

Where a family grow their own corn, they may be certain of its purity. Its goodness, as a mere article of trade, is measured by the comparative smallness of the quantity of bran which it produces. This, indeed, in family economy, is not of high importance ; but if it is wished to make a distinction, then select such wheat as is round and plump, rejecting that which is shrivelled as yielding most bran. Where plump and shrivelled grains are found together in the same binn, they may be separated by simple immersion in water. If the grain be all sound and of equal quality, the smallest grains will still be proportionably the lightest, and will swim whilst the others fall to the bottom; and should a very strict separation be wished for, that may be produced by a judicious application of weak brine, which being gradually poured in, so as to increase the specific gravity of the water, the lighter grains will proportionally rise : this however must be stopped in time, otherwise the water will be so impregnated with salt that the whole of the grain will rise to the surface.

If the grain is dried immediately afterwards, it will not receive any damage from the experiment.

Should the whole of the harvesting appear at first sight to be damaged, it is not on that account to be absolutely rejected. A gentleman of considerable science and experience has communicated to the Royal Society a process for sweetening musty corn, by simply immersing it in boiling water and

letting it remain till cold. The quantity of water
should be double that of the corn to be purified.
He has found that the musty quality rarely pene-
trates through the husk of the wheat, and that in
the very worst cases it does not extend beyond the
amylaceous matter immediately under the skin. In
the hot water all the decayed or rotten grain swims
on the surface, so that the remaining wheat is effectually cleaned from all impurities, and without any
material loss. The wheat must afterwards be dried
and occasionally stirred on the kiln, when it will be
found improved to a degree scarcely credible without actual experience.

The first adulteration may be suspected to take
place at the mill; but even this, with a little care,
may be guarded against by an expense, at first, of
about six guineas for a portable mill, which will
grind any kind of grain with little comparative
trouble.

This mill was originally constructed for the purpose of supplying the French armies with flour,
during their march to Moscow; in the course of
which service its merits were fully proved. It was
brought from Paris by Sir John Sinclair, and presented by him to the Society of Arts, by whom it
is considered one of the most useful machines ever
submitted to the notice of that scientific body.
With the power of one man it will grind about a
bushel of wheat in two hours, and as the labour is
not severe, he may grind from four to five bushels
per day. It will last for many years, is not liable to
go wrong—the only precautions required in the use
of it are, not to drive it above twenty revolutions a
minute, as in that case it would heat—(sixteen or
seventeen revolutions are as many as is necessary,)
not to allow the handle to be turned when the mill
is empty; and to prevent pieces of iron or hard

stone from getting into it. The corn should be dry, or otherwise it would clog the plates, which would make it necessary to take the mill to pieces to clear them. It can easily be attached to any power, either of horse, steam, or water.

People in the flour trade generally knead a small quantity by way of experiment; if good it immediately forms an adhesive, elastic paste, which will readily assume any form that may be given to it, without danger of breaking : pure and unadulterated flour may likewise be easily distinguished by other methods. Seize a handful briskly, and squeeze it half a minute; it preserves the form of the cavity of the hand in one piece, although it may be rudely placed on the table. Not so that which contains foreign substances, it breaks in pieces more or less; that mixed with whiting being the most adhesive, but still dividing and falling down in a little time. Flour mixed with ground stones, bones, or plaster of Paris, loses its form at once, and the more bran there may be in it, the sooner it will be flat on the board. It may also be observed, that genuine flour will longer keep the impression even of the grains of the skin, than that which is adulterated, the latter very soon throwing up the fine marks. Let a person of a moist skin rub flour briskly between the palms of both hands ; if there be whiting among it, he will find resistance; but white pure flour none. If there is time carefully to try the unsoundness of flour, put a tablespoonfull into a basin and mix with cold water until it is of the consistence of pudding-batter ; then set a small pan upon the fire with half a gill of water ; when this water is hot, but before it boils, pour in the batter, and let it boil three minutes. If sound, the flour will unite as a good sound pudding; if unsound, it breaks, curdles, and appears somewhat

watery. Some attention, while it is warm, will lead
to a judgment on the different degrees of unsoundness.—Again; drop the juice of a lemon, or good
vinegar upon flour; if the flour be pure, it remains
at rest; if adulterated, an immediate commotion
takes places. This is the readiest method of detect-
ing the presence of stone-dust and plaster of Paris.
—Or, after having dipped the fore-finger and thumb
partially in sweet-oil, take up a small quantity of
flour; if it be pure, you may freely rub the fingers
together for any length of time; it will not become
sticky, and the substance will turn nearly black;
but if whiting be mixed with the flour, a few times
rubbing turns it into putty, but its colour is thereby
very little changed. Among the means of adul-
terating flour, great use has lately been made of
bones, the price of which has accordingly advanced
within these few years from ten-pence a bushel to
eighteen-pence, to the first purchasers. The collecting of bones is in fact pursued as a regular trade
in the metropolis.

The admixture of fine pulverised clay in the
prime necessary of life, is likewise a practice in
many parts of the kingdom; and that in one or
two instances, to a very great extent: the industrious
adulterators thinking perhaps that the white, or
Cornwall clay, might be equal in its nutritious
qualities to the German clay, which was thus described some years ago in a German Ephemeris:

" In the lordship of Moscaw, in the Upper
Lusatia, a sort of white earth is found, of which
the poor, urged thereto, no doubt, by the calamities
of the war in those parts, actually made bread. It
is taken out of a hill where they formerly worked
saltpetre; when the sun has somewhat warmed this
earth, it cracks, and small white globules proceed
from it as meal; it does not ferment alone, but only

when mixed up with meal. M. Sarlitz, a Saxon gentleman, was pleased to inform us, that he has seen persons, who in a great measure lived upon it for some time; he assures us, that he procured bread to be made of this earth alone, and of different mixtures of earth and meal, and that he even kept some of this bread by him upwards of six years: he further says, a Spaniard told him, that this earth is also found near Gironne in Catalonia."

We trust, however, that no rapacious millers or flour factors will again be enabled to force their countrymen to swallow clay instead of bread. Though man may originally be made of clay, it is not necessary that he should return to it before the good time ordained by Providence.

As the economical housewife will assiduously avoid the use of alum in her bread, so must she shun all other chemical adulterations, except in cases where the flour to be used is unavoidably musty, or where it is new flour after a wet season, when the bread often comes out of the oven with an unpleasant heaviness about it, which may induce families to give up their own wholesome home-baked, for the produce of some *scientific* baker. The evil spoken of has been obviated by the carbonate of magnesia, but the best remedy is the carbonate of ammonia. If the flour be not very unsound, for 14lbs. of it, use one ounce of carbonate of ammonia, taking particular care to purchase where you can rely upon having it *pure*, as much depends on this. This ounce of carbonate of ammonia should be dissolved in a little warm water, and then put into such further quantity of water as may be requisite for kneading the dough quite stiff. As this carbonate is volatile, and all flies off, there is no impropriety in increasing the quantity. It is generally used by bakers and confectioners. In case the flour be very bad, it might be well to make the experiment with 7lbs. of it, as a much larger quantity of the ammonia would be needful; but the very worst of flour may be rendered useable if sufficient of the carbonate of ammonia be introduced. When purchased, the ammonia should be tightly corked up in a phial, in order to prevent evaporation, to which it is greatly liable. An ounce of carbonate of ammonia costs three-pence, which is only half the price of carbonated soda.

A considerable increase in home-made bread, even equal to one-fifth, may be produced by using bran water, for kneading the dough. The proportion is three pounds of bran for every twenty-eight pounds of flour, to be boiled for an hour, and then strained through a hair sieve. The bran need not then be lost, but mixed up with dry food for the poultry yard.

In baking bread at home there are many experiments that may be tried for amusement as well as utility. One mode was formerly actually practised generally in the County of Essex, even so late as the sixteenth century, and was as follows. Take peeled turnips; boil them until they are soft; press out the juice and mix them, beaten very fine and small, in their own weight of wheat or flour; add salt dissolved in warm water; knead the whole like other dough, and bake it.

Excellent paste for meat or fruit pies may be made with two-thirds of wheat flour, one-third of the flour of boiled potatoes, and some butter or dripping; the whole being brought to a proper consistence with warm water; and a small quantity of yeast added, where lightness is particularly wished for.

This will also make very pleasant cakes for breakfast; and may be made with or without spices, fruit, &c.

Mr. Whately, of Cork, received a gold medal in the year 1813, from the Society for the Encouragement of Arts and Sciences, for a machine for the expeditious rasping of potatoes, and for his experiments in making bread with the farina of them. The bad harvest in 1816 again turned his attention to his favourite theory, and he thus expresses himself on the subject:—" Having by me a considerable quantity of the former which I had prepared in the year 1813, I began to use it in bread, and find that it has not only very much improved from age, by losing the strong flavour of the raw potatoe, which it retains when recently made, but that it serves to render the flour made from the wheat of last season more palatable. The proportion that I make use of is one-fourth; which has the effect of making the bread lighter, drier, and, beyond comparison, better than the bread made from the wheaten flour alone of the last crop; and I can safely and strongly recommend its adoption to all those who find bread from new flour heavy, glutinous, and difficult in the preparation. It should be remarked, that the farina I am using was made at a late period of the spring and early in the summer of 1813, after a considerable vegetation had commenced in the potatoes; consequently, it is neither so good, nor so profitable, as if it had been made before the vegetative process began. The best time for making it is during the first three or four months after the potatoes have been dug from the ground; and although they yield farina to a very late period of the year, it is neither so nutritive in quality, nor so great in quantity, as when it is made at an earlier period. The experiment proves how extremely advantageous it would be for the public, in years when the crop of potatoes is very abundant, to convert a portion of it into farina; which experience proves, when properly dried, will keep good for almost an indefinite length of time. In such seasons, the farina, which is about one-seventh part of the potatoe, would be produced at about two-pence halfpenny or three-pence per pound.

"It might remain stored up in casks, until the seasons called for its use; and become a very great and profitable resource in times of scarcity. Indeed, from the peculiar quality that it possesses, of continuing for years to afford its nutritive properties, not merely uninjured, but really improved by age, I know of no article of food which can with such advantage be furnished, from the bounties of Providence, in one season, to administer to the wants of another. It offers such strong inducement in this respect to speculative men, that I shall hope hereafter, in an unproductive year, to see very great relief afforded from it.

" The manufacturer has only to prepare it after the manner of starch at those times when the price indicates a very plentiful supply of potatoes, and to reserve it in his warehouse until a sufficiently tempting price calls it forth, greatly to his own advantage, and to that of the public. Perhaps it is not unreasonable to calculate, that every seventh year would give him the opportunity of doubling or trebling capital thus employed, and I consider it would be well worth the attention of any speculative individual, residing in a country where potatoes are cheap and distant from market, to put this experiment in practice upon a large scale." An account of this process, which is very simple, and a drawing of the machine, may be seen in the

volume of the Transactions of the Society of Arts
for 1813.

Whilst the connection between potatoes and
flour is thus before us, it may not be amiss to observe, that there are few articles in families more
subject to waste, both in paring, boiling, and being
actually thrown away, than this valuable and most
useful root—there are few cooks but what boil
twice as many potatoes every day as are wanted,
and fewer still that do not throw the residue away,
as totally unfit in any shape for the next day's
meal. Yet if they would take the trouble to beat
up the despised cold potatoes with an equal quantity of flour, they would find them produce a
much lighter dumpling, or pudding, than they can
make with flour alone; and by the aid of a few
spoonfuls of good gravy, easily manufactured from
the browner parts of the dripping-pan, whilst a
joint of meat is at the fire, they will provide a
cheap and agreeable appendage to the dinner-table,
which the younger branches of the family will
relish far more than that part of their meal that is
furnished by the butcher.

To preserve yeast through the winter, it may be
beat up with a whisk until it appears thin and
even; then spread it in thin coats upon plates,
coating each over again as they dry, until about
half an inch in thickness, when they may be taken
off the plates, broken into small pieces, and kept
for use in bottles closely stopped.

If there be a cheese press, or screw press at hand,
the yeast may be preserved by a simpler method.
Fill a canvass bag with the yeast, and submit it to
the action of the press, which will squeeze out all
the moisture, when the residue may be well packed
in paper, so as to keep it from the air and from
moisture. The following mode of making yeast is

both easy and expeditious. Boil one pound of good flour, a quarter of a pound of brown sugar, and a little salt, in two gallons of water for an hour. When milk warm, bottle it and cork it close. It will be fit for use in 24 hours. One pint of this will make 18 pounds of bread.

There are other offices of culinary activity which require notice, but as they are principally connected with the social circles of superior affluence, we shall first proceed to examine the

LAUNDRY,

as an office of more general use, and one which requires specific investigation.

This most important department of domestic economy naturally includes the *Wash-house*, into which philosophy has found its way for the application of many useful principles, and much useful practice; especially on the new plan, by means of which linen is washed, not by hand, but by a machine constantly turning round, in which the linen is inclosed. All that is required is to rub the linen with soap, the night previous, and then the cylinder into which it is put ought to move so rapidly as not to whirl it completely round, but that it shall be heard to fall at every half revolution; and, if moved at a proper velocity, each change of linen will be washed in less than half an hour, without rubbing, but with the addition of alkali or pot-ash, which may be now used of a greater strength than when washing by the hand. The linen is then rinsed, and a little hand-washing applied where necessary.

Boiling is next requisite; after which the linen is drained on a tray full of holes over a reservoir, which receives the soapy water for further use.

The process of wringing is also shortened, and improved, by placing the linen in a square box of strong sacking,. kept open by iron rings, and shut up in a cast iron box, with a sliding plate forced against the end of the bag by a rack and pinion, and turned by a winch. By this process the clothes are squeezed much drier than by the common method, and the pressure upon all parts being uniform, less injury is done to the texture of the linen.

But, whether washing is carried on by the new mechanical process, or by the usual manual mode, a choice of the best materials will always be of high importance. The quality of the water, in particular, requires due observance: for it must be remembered that water, impregnated with earthy salts, can never be used to advantage ; and, if tinged with the minutest solution of iron, it will always give a yellowish hue to the linen or muslin, which will be extremely difficult to get rid of.

When water is hard, and will not readily unite with soap, it will always be proper to boil it before use ; which will be found sufficiently efficacious, if the hardness depends solely upon the impregnation of lime, in the form of what modern chemistry designates as a subcarbonate. The philosophical reason for this is, that the lime, by some secret process of nature, is united to a portion of carbonic acid, which causes it to be suspended in the water; but, in the process of boiling, the carbonic acid unites with the acquired caloric, and is carried off with it into the atmosphere.

Even exposure to the atmosphere will produce this effect in a great degree upon spring water so impregnated, leaving it much fitter for lavatory purposes. In both cases, the water ought to be carefully poured off from the sediment, as the neutralized lime, when freed from its extra quantity of carbonic acid, falls to the bottom by its own gravity.

Boiling, however, has no effect, when the hardness of the water proceeds from lime united with the sulphuric acid, or sulphate of lime of the modern chemistry : and it must be neutralized, or brought to its proper state, by the application of common wood ashes from the kitchen grate, or of barilla, now called soda, or the Dantzic ashes, or pearl-ash; or by the more scientific process of dropping in a solution of subcarbonate of pot-ash. Each of these unite with the sulphuric acid, and separate it from the lime, which gravitates, as in the former case, to the bottom.

Having thus philosophically explained the arcana of the washing-tub, we may offer a saving hint in order to economise the use of soap, which is to put any quantity of pearl-ash into a large jar, covered from the dust; in a few days the alkali will become liquid, which must be diluted in double its quantity of soft water with its equal quantity of new slacked lime. Boil it half an hour, frequently stirring it; adding as much more hot water, and drawing off the liquor, when the residuum may be boiled afresh, and drained, until it ceases to feel acrid to the tongue.

Much soap and much manual labour also may be saved by dissolving alum and chalk in bran water, in which the linen ought to be boiled, then well rinsed out, and exposed to the usual process of bleaching.

Soap may also be totally disused, or nearly so, in the getting up of muslins and chintzes, which should always be treated agreeable to the oriental manner; that is to wash them in plain water, and then boil them in *congee,* or rice water: after which they ought not to be submitted to the operation of the smoothing iron, but rubbed smooth with a polished stone.

The economy which must result from these processes renders their consideration important to every private family; in addition to which we must state that the improvements in philosophy extend to the laundry as well as to the wash-house.

One of the first of these principles is, that by proposed improvements it is intended that, even in the confined laundries of a town residence, a much greater quantity of air may be made to pass through the linen, so as to give it all the results of a more open exposure.

Amongst other advantages intended to arise from the plan of heating dwelling-houses and offices by warm air running through tubes, properly directed for that purpose, is the very important one that a much greater degree of heat can be introduced, both in the wash-house and laundry, than could otherwise be borne by the female assistants. Upon this principle it is proposed to introduce hot closets, through which a current of heated air is made to pass from a stove, which also heats the smoothing irons; and it is proved that if the clothes are properly washed and got up, they will, when solely dried by this hot air, preserve their whiteness as perfectly as if dried by exposure to the open atmosphere.

Thus far we may be considered as having attended solely to the common lavatory process; but it often happens from unavoidable circumstances, that linen suffers from accidental causes, beyond the mere wear and tear of a family. It is true, that there are numerous books which profess to contain infallible recipes for every possible occasion, and we deny not their efficacy; but having sedulously selected from all the discoveries of the passing day, whatever appeared easily applicable to this branch of domestic economy, we offer them in addition to the existing stores of our fair readers.

When linen is soiled and discoloured by town washing, or by age, or lying by, out of use, the best bleaching materials are the natural verdure of the ground, with the dews and winds of Heaven. A more speedy mode may however be wished for, in which case a little chemical skill is useful. The linen must undergo a process of two ablutions, the first in a mixture or lye, formed in the proportion of one pound of common soda to a gallon of soft water in a boiling state, where it must lie for twelve hours, and then be boiled for half an hour in the same liquid; after which it must pass through the second ablution, in a mixture of the common bleaching powder (hyperoxymuriate of lime) with eight times its quantity of water, or a pound to a gallon, which must be well shaken in a stone jar for three days, then allowed to settle, and being decanted off clear, the linen must be steeped in it for six and thirty hours, and then washed by the usual process; this will take out all but ink stains.

Grass bleaching is always best for discoloured linen, or muslin; but in town, or when in a hurry, mix a pound of oxymuriate of lime with six quarts of soft water, and put a portion of this into the tub where the articles are steeping.

To remove iron moulds, take some chrystallized citric acid; pound a small quantity to a fine powder, and apply it to the spot; drop some hot water on, and rub it in, upon a pewter plate over a stove, until the oxyde of the iron unites with the acid, when a little warm water washes all out.

, Where spots from iron or ink are of too long standing to be readily removed; a more chemical process is required. Take sulphurate of potash, or muriate of tin; apply it to the spot, and let it remain about five minutes, when it must be washed out. Then apply to it some citric acid. The older the spots, the oftener must the process be repeated.

Ink spots in linen may be taken out by melting part of a mould candle, and dipping the spot in it, before the linen is put into the washing-tub.

The most difficult spots to remove, are those upon coloured stuffs, so as to preserve the similarity of colour. Stains of acid vegetables, such as orange juice, &c. are destroyed by the application of alkaline salts; the best of which are a mixture of alcohol and liquid ammonia.

Stains from an alkaline substance, on the contrary, must be neutralized by the acid of vinegar, diluted.

Muslin, when stained by wine, will be best restored by rubbing with soft soap and common whitening, before washing; after which it must be kept wet, and exposed to the sun and air.

To remove spots of grease, moisten them with a few drops of concentrated solution of subcarbonate of pot-ash; rub the spot between the fingers, so that the alkali may unite chemically with the grease, forming a species of soap, which a little warm water will wash out.

To remove spots of wax, moisten them repeatedly with alcohol, or strong spirits of wine, when the wax will become dry and brittle, yielding easily to the action of a brush.

If, however, the spots are of long standing, it will be a readier mode to apply a few drops of rectified turpentine, rub it well in, and wash out with soap and water.

To remove oil paint, apply oil of turpentine, and wash it out.

These are all applicable to linens, cottons and woollens; but silk requires another process to remove spots of grease. Take some fullers' earth, powder it, and mix into a paste with water. Apply it to the spot; let it dry and then brush out; after which remove the marks with a little sulphuric ether, which must again be washed out with spirits of wine.

For *Marking Ink*, several processes are recommended. The simplest is to mix the juice of the sloe with green vitriol; but as the sloe juice cannot always be had, there is another process equally permanent.

Take a drachm of nitrate of quicksilver, commonly called lunar caustic, dissolve it in a glass mortar in double its weight of pure water; this is the ink. Dissolve a drachm of salt of tartar in an ounce of water, in another vessel; this is the liquid with which the linen must be first wetted, then allowed to dry, and finally to be written on.

A cheap and easy marking liquid may be made, much better than what is commonly sold in the shops, and advertised as infallible.

Take vermillion, as much as will lay on a half-crown piece; of the best salt of steel, about the size of a small nutmeg; grind or levigate well together with linseed oil. You may make it thick or thin at discretion.

The price of starch, it should be remembered, is regulated by the price of flour; and as it will keep for some years, if covered up, in a warm dry place, the economical laundress will lay in her stock of this article at the time when bread is cheap.

It has been recommended, for the sake of economizing flour, that the starch used for stiffening muslins, and other fine stuffs in the laundry, should be made of the flour of Canary seed, which is also considered as superior for that purpose ; and also for the purpose of manufacture when in the loom ; but perhaps a much better substitute may be found in the starch of rice flour, which forms the dressing paste, or *conjee*, in the Indian looms, as well as the starch in getting up muslins in India.

It must be recollected, too, that much of the softness of the Indian cotton depends upon the palm-oil, which, even when not specifically applied, constantly oozes out of the fingers of the spinner and the weaver.

So much superior is the mode of getting up muslins in India, that formerly our home nabobesses used to send out their soiled dresses to India, once a year, for the purpose of oriental clear-starching.

When the linen is well dried, and deposited in the wardrobe, nothing more is necessary than to secure it from damp and insects; and the latter operation may be most agreeably performed by a judicious mixture of aromatic shrubs and flowers, cut up and sewed in silken bags, to be interspersed amongst the drawers and shelves.

These ingredients may consist of lavender, rosemary, thyme, roses, cedar shavings, powdered sassafras, and cassia lignea, &c. &c. in which a few drops of otto of roses, or other strong perfume may be thrown.

We shall close this section by noticing, that as linen may sometimes be scorched or browned, in the getting up, without being actually burned through, even the effect of this may be removed. The process is simple. Add to a quart of vinegar, the juice of half a dozen large onions, about an ounce of soap rasped down, a quarter of a pound of fullers' earth, one ounce of lime, and one ounce of pearl-ash, or any other strong alkali. Boil the whole until it is pretty thick, and lay some of it on the scorched part, suffering it to dry. It will be found that, on repeating this process for one or two washings, the mark will be completely removed, and the linen without any additional damage, provided its texture has not been absolutely injured, as well as discoloured.

The offices of general use thus disposed of, we shall proceed to one, which may be made as conducive to elegance as to economy, although not usually considered as forming a part of minor establishments, where the kitchen is considered as including also the

CONFECTIONARY.

Where these departments can be separated with convenience, it will be for the advantage of both, and also for the sake of propriety; as the females of the family who may choose to superintend this department, are more removed from the view or interference of the domestics.

Those who seek for common recipes in this branch of domestic management, must refer at once to the usual works on the subject; yet in this reference we neither enforce the economy of time, of money, or of health, all of which may be wasted by a strict adherence to the variety of directions which

the culinary taste of their writers and their readers,
appear to have rendered necessary.

It happens unfortunately, in utter despite of all
economy, that the confectionary of the present day
is more for shew than use, and is a mere waste of
the materials which a bountiful Providence has
given to us in almost endless variety, for the purpose not only of gratifying the taste, but also of
increasing the quantity of food, whilst prompting to
the use of edibles not so superabundantly nutritious
as animal food, whether fish, flesh, or fowl.

In fact, in the old English household arrangement, confectionary, in all its branches, acted as a
certain and speedy aid to the larder in days of hospitality, when either visits or visitations were un-
expectedly made at the castle, the abbey, the hall,
or the grange; and was almost invariably joined in
the cookery of all dishes, except the plain solid sirloins or rounds, under which even their heavy
boards groaned, before sympathetic or sliding
tables came into fashion.

It is then, to the useful adoption of confectionary
that we would call the attention of our readers, not
only as aiding a small income to make a good appearance, but as tending to the preservation of
health, and affording a pleasing variety of occupation to such young ladies as may wish to be
valued for something more useful than the mere
amusement of the hour.

It is indeed a powerful objection to the practice
of kitchen superintendance for young ladies of the
present day, that the society to which they would
thus be exposed would be unpleasant, if not dangerous. This arises from two causes, especially in
London, and in almost all houses of modern construction: the first is the want of room, which

throws all the servants, male and female, into one apartment; the other, the fear of increasing the impertinence of male servants, if the younger part of the family were permitted to mingle so much with them as a personal superintendence of the kitchen would expose them to, especially where men cooks are employed. But the first objection will not hold good in a country mansion, and the second may be got rid of by a very beneficial change in domestic economy—in the dismissal of men cooks, a silly custom copied from France, and the diminution of male servants in general, thereby saving many miserable females from a life of infamy and desolation, into which they may be forced, from the impossibility of meeting with proper employment.

Having copied one silly custom of France, it were well if we could remedy the evil by the adoption of another which is evidently beneficial—we allude to a school established at *Ecouen*, near Paris, where every species of domestic economy and management is engrafted on the new system of tuition, without interfering with the useful, or even the ornamental parts of fashionable female education. But if we hope to avail ourselves of the introduction of such a system into English education, we must instantly commence a reform in the lower regions, that is of our own dwellings, and the kitchen must no longer be a *sanctum sanctorum*, into which even the mistress cannot enter without being considered as an impertinent intruder, and liable to the sauciness of those whose grand secret it is to become the domestic tyrants, in whatever comes within the scope of their management.

But even under existing circumstances, if the kitchen is not a proper place for the young ladies of the mansion to enter, the same objection will not lie against the confectionary if it be in a convenient apartment, distinct from the absolute domestic offices, and only liable to the entrance of female servants. On that principle then, we shall offer a few general hints for its management, which will ultimately be found conducive to economy in this part of the domestic duties.

In the first place, we recommend particular attention to the vessels intended either for the preparation or the preservation of the various preserves, pickles, &c. These ought invariably to be either of glass, or the coarse brown, or speckled stone ware. The very best earthen-ware, especially the cream coloured, is always glazed with a preparation which contains much of the oxyde of lead. This glazing will withstand the effects of any culinary heat that may be applied; but acids, even of preserved fruits, act upon it speedily, and decompose a slow but subtle poison. The same objection applies to its use in pickling; or indeed in any way where acids are made use of, or likely to arise from fermentation.

For boiling then, let tin, iron, or glass be used; for preservation let the vessels be of glass or unglazed stone ware.

Copper vessels are not quite so dangerous as leaden ones; but the constant labour and scouring requisite to keep them in a clean wholesome state, wear them out more than culinary use. Where copper vessels indeed are indispensible, due attention, daily, to their cleanliness will suffice to prevent any very dangerous accidents; and to that we would more willingly trust than to a mode recommended by a French economist, who declares that his method succeeded perfectly in preventing the accretion or even the formation of verdigrease during a period of eight months. He describes his copper boiler as being twelve feet long and three wide, fitted on an economic stove. Its use was intended for the evaporation of vegetable syrups, marmalades, &c.; but its size made it difficult to be taken down, and it was placed in a damp under-ground story. All these circumstances operated against its good preservation; and rendered some permanent precaution necessary. This was performed in the following manner. After being once used, and still warm, it was well cleaned out with a sponge and hot water, and as soon as it was nearly lukewarm, the whole interior surface was spread over with a coat of paste, made from potatoes diluted with water. This coat was suffered to dry before further use, and completely succeeded during eight months in preserving the copper from verdigrease without any further trouble.

The only real objection to this mode is on the score of absolute cleanliness, which it must be difficult to preserve without processes that would rub off the coat of paste; but some may object that the colour of their preserves or pickles must be injured by want of the coppery tinge. This, however, is an error that must be carefully guarded against. All the artificial modes of colour are pernicious, and we must learn not to please our eyes at the expense of our health. We shall not go the length of an ingenious modern chemist upon this subject; not indeed because we think he has gone too far, but because we trust his book is now in so many families as to be permanently useful; at the same time we must not omit, whilst guarding our fair readers against artificial colours, to warn them also against the factitious flavours which it has long been too fashionable to give to our confectionary.

If almonds cannot be had conveniently, 'tis bet-

.ter that our custards and puddings, should want the peculiar flavour imparted by them, than to have the poisonous cherry laurel substituted in their place. Indeed a much more agreeable flavour than either almonds or the laurel can impart, may be produced by grated cocoa nuts, which are now imported in such quantities as to be sufficiently cheap for any culinary purpose. In Virginia and the Southern States, a very favourite pudding is made, the principal part of which consists of the grated cocoa nuts, with bread or flour, milk and eggs, and the other common ingredients of a pudding.

The chesnut, either of home or foreign growth, may also be applied to this purpose, with great propriety; not indeed to the extent of being a substitute for flour entirely, but in a proportion of one-half, or two-thirds, in which case it might be used with safety even by the most phtisicky persons, without the inconvenience which it often produces when eaten raw—nay our common hazle nuts, or filberds, if carefully cleared of their outer coating, might be judiciously used for the same purpose.

Where the flavour of saffron is specially wished for, it ought to be used with great prudence, as it possesses strong medicinal powers. Its stimulative tendency to raise the spirits, formerly rendered it an approved remedy in hysterical cases, with considerable success, and it may certainly be used for culinary purposes in moderation; but perhaps the safest mode will be not to extend its use beyond the slight tinge of colour which a small quantity affords, and which will be fully sufficient to impart a flavour pleasing to the palate, without acting particularly as a stimulant. In purchasing it, the English saffron ought to have the preference.

Sugar is to the confectioner what gravy is to the cook, the very basis of all his excellence and fame. There is scarcely indeed any article in the consumption of a family in more daily use, and therefore the following hints relative to the purchase of them may not be unacceptable to our readers. The coarsest in quality, and consequently the cheapest in price, is far from being the cheapest in the end, as it is heavy, dirty, and of a very inferior degree of sweetness. That which is most refined is always the sweetest. White sugars should be chosen as shining, and as close in texture as possible. The best sort of brown has also a bright and gravelly look, and is often to be bought in its pure imported state. East India sugars appear finer, in proportion to the price, but they do not contain so much saccharine matter, consequently they are less fit for wines and sweetmeats, though when they are good of their sort they do as well for common household purposes as any other.

The indiscriminate use of sugar, however, in confectionary, both in regard to health and economy, deserves some notice. That sugar possesses strong nutritious powers cannot be denied, especially before granulation; a fact proved by the fatness of the negroes in the West Indies during the cane season, from eating the juice in the form of syrup; and even by the improved condition of the mill cattle, which are fed on the crushed canes; but we must not forget that in its prepared state, perhaps principally owing to its impregnation with lime, sugar is pernicious both to the teeth and bowels. Reasoning from these facts then, we should recommend the use of those fruits, in confectionary, which contain most sugar in their own composition, in preference to those which require sugar to make them palatable. It is unnecessary to spetify all the varieties; but we may notice the apple as that English fruit which, of all others, contains the greatest proportion of sugar; whence the addition of prepared sugar is almost totally unnecessary in the different preparations of the fruit, whether boiled, baked, or even in marmalade.

To have the sugar of the apple in perfection, however, it is necessary that the fruit should undergo culinary operation, or else a slight fermentation. A modern writer considers cyder as nothing more than sugared water, because the fermentation either neutralizes the malic acid, or, more properly speaking, combines it with the mucilage of the fruit, and thus forms the sugary compound. This may be exemplified by an easy experiment—Squeeze or press some apples which may have lain by for the winter: throw part of this juice into some milk, and it will produce curds in an instant; but if the remainder is boiled for about a quarter of an hour, it will unite with milk or cream without the slightest tendency to separate their constituent parts.

A few words on the shortest and cheapest method of preserving fruits must close this article. The grand secret is to deprive the fruit of its water of vegetation in the shortest time possible; for which purpose the fruit ought to be gathered just at the point of proper maturity.

An ingenious French writer considers fruit of all kinds as having four distinct periods of maturity—the maturity of vegetation, of *honeyfication,* of expectation, and of coction. The first of these, he considers as the period when, having gone through the various vegetable processes up to the ripening, it appears ready to drop spontaneously. This however is a period which arrives sooner in the warm climate of France than in the colder orchards of England; but its absolute presence may be ascertained by the general filling out of the rind, by the bloom, by the smell, and by the facility with which it may be plucked from the branch. But even in France, as generally practised in England, this period may be hastened, eitheroby cutting circularly through the outer rind at the foot of the branch, so as to prevent the return of the sap, or by bending the branch to a horizontal position on an espalier, which nearly answers the same purpose.

. The second period, or that of *honeyfication*, consists in the ripeness and flavour which fruits of all kinds acquire if plucked a few days before arriving at their first maturity, and preserved under a proper degree of temperature. Apples may acquire, or arrive at this second degree of maturity upon the tree; but it too often happens that the flavour of the fruit is thus lost, for fruit over ripe is always found to have parted with a portion of its flavour.

The third stage, or of expectation, as the theorist quaintly terms it, is that which is acquired by pulpy fruits, which, though sufficiently ripe to drop off the tree, are yet, even then, hard and sour. This is the case with several kinds both of apples and pears, not to mention other fruits, which always improve after keeping in the confectionary—but with respect to the medlar and the quince this maturity of expectation is absolutely necessary.

: The fourth degree of maturity, or of coction, is, completely artificial, and is nothing more nor less than the change produced upon fruit by the aid of culinary heat.

. We have already pointed out the first object necessary in the preservation of fruit, its maturity of vegetation; and we may apply the same principle to flowers or leaves which may be gathered for use. The flowers ought to be gathered a day or two before the petals are ready to drop off spontaneously on the setting of the fruit; and the leaves must be plucked before the season has began to rob them of their vegetable juices.

The degree of heat necessary for the purpose of drying must next be considered, as it differs considerably with respect to different substances.— Flowers or aromatic plants require the smallest increase of heat beyond the temperature of the season, provided that season be genial; something more for rinds or roots; and a greater heat for fruits; but this heat must not be carried to excess. Philosophic confectioners may avail themselves of the thermometer; but practice forms the best guide in this case, and therefore we shall say, without speaking of degrees of Fahrenheit or Reaumur, that if the necessary heat for flowers is one, that for rinds or roots must be one and a quarter, that for fruits one and three quarters, or nearly double of what *one* may be above the freezing point.

The best method of ensuring the process is by a current of warm dry air, for damp is destructive. To warm the air, artificial heat may be applied, but the action of the sun-beams will always be sufficient for flowers; and it is injudicious to dry them in the shade, as thereby they lose their colour and are apt to crack and shiver. With regard to fruits which require long drying, it must be remembered that the night air is always hurtful to them, even in the dryest weather; they must therefore be sedulously protected from it; as in one damp night they will often acquire more humidity than they possessed at first.

The necessity of drying several kinds of fruit, previous to their application to useful purposes,

depends upon that process actually giving them a
degree of artificial ripeness which they would not
otherwise acquire.   This fact is proved by a simple
yet very curious and satisfactory experiment.
Take a pound of fresh almonds; squeeze or press
them, and scarcely a drop of oil will exude; but
take another pound from the same tree; dry them
judiciously, and they will yield nearly half their
own weight !

Cold as well as heat, may be applied to the preservation of fruit, and that too in a green state,
through the winter.   Let cherries, strawberries,
raspberries, plumbs, peaches, or any other succulent fruit whatever, be put into a vessel somewhat like that used by common confectioners for
freezing ice-creams, around which put salt and
ice, exactly as they do.   The fruit will soon be
frozen, when it should be carried to the ice-house,
and placed in a hole dug out in the centre of the
ice, and over the top of the hole a quantity of
powdered charcoal should be placed, secured by a
common watch-coat blanket.   When the winter
season arrives, the containing vessel may be opened,
and the fruit taken out in its frozen state; then
place it in cold water to thaw, and it will be found as
delicious as when first gathered.   When salt and
ice, in the manner employed by the confectioners
in general, shall be found inadequate to freeze
some fruits hard enough, the mixture for producing
an intense cold, as spoken of by Chaptal, the celebrated French chemist, of salt, saltpetre, and glau-
ber salts, will effectually freeze it very hard.

Chemistry also offers artificial means for the
same purpose.   We find in a recent scientific work
that M. Dumont, in a letter to Count Chaptal, has
announced the important practical discovery, that
fruits may be preserved by means of carbonic gas,

Cherries, grapes, pears, apples, and chesnuts, were placed in glass veesels, filled with carbonic gas, obtained from carbonate of lime by sulphuric acid. Neither the colour nor the taste of the cherries were altered at the end of fifteen days; and at the end of six weeks, they were in the same state as if they had been preserved in brandy.

Intimately connected with this department of elegant housewifery is the

STILL ROOM,

but we are well aware that it is only in very large domestic establishments, or in the antique mansion of some rural Lady Bountiful, that an apartment is now dedicated to purposes of distillation. On this consideration then we shall not enter far into the subject, but content ourselves with a few hints that may be of general use in regard to various liquids connected with it.

To those who may choose to make their own rose water or cordial compounds, it may be matter of convenience to know that where there is sufficient space, a flat condenser, supplied judiciously with water, is much more powerful than the spiral worm, and more rapid in its condensation.

But there is even a more simple mode of distillation, which any one may try, and which depends upon the principle that the bladder of an ox, though actually pervious to water, has yet the property of retaining alcohol. The process founded upon this is merely to put the liquid intended for distillation into a bladder, until half full. Close the orifice, and expose the bladder to the action of the sun, of the air, or the heat of a stove, when the watery particles will evaporate, and leave the spirituous part behind.

We must beg leave here to offer one important caution to all domestic chemists, in regard to the factitious flavours recommended in most books that treat of this branch, and which are often directed to be produced by substances which are highly deleterious.

The foreign papers have recently announced the death of a celebrated chemist of Vienna, named Schavinger; in consequence of having spilled upon his naked arm a quantity of prussic acid, which he was preparing, and which proved fatal in a few hours. It is well known to chemists that the principle of this acid, one of the most subtle poisons with which we are acquainted, exists in the leaves of the peach tree, the wild laurel, the almond, and most of those which bear fruits with kernels. The late Duke Charles of Lorraine, had well nigh lost his life by swallowing a few drops of *eau de noyau* too highly impregnated. It is also generally known how dangerous it is to chew the leaves of the wild laurel. The odorous principle of the prussic acid is of the same nature, and a small quantity of it inhaled when the acid is in the state of gas, is sufficient to produce death, without convulsions, in a few seconds. A tea-spoonful of water or spirits, impregnated with a small quantity of this acid, will kill the largest dog. It is believed that the sudden death of Scheele, the celebrated Swedish chemist, while engaged in some experiments upon prussic acid, was caused by the deleterious nature of the gas.

Those who have any regard for their own health, or that of their friends, will scrupulously avoid in their distillations and confectionary the so often recommended leaves of the cherry laurel.

Those who chuse to prepare their own alcohol, may do so by a very easy and cheap mode; as they will find, that ripe potatoe apples, when they are plucked, mashed, and fermented with one-twentieth of a ferment, yield from distillation as much spirit as is obtained from the best grapes. Numerous experiments made in France with them upon a large scale, leave no doubt respecting this valuable application of the plant.

The alcohol thus prepared may be tinted any colour, or impregnated with any particular flavour that the domestic chemist may please from whole-some materials.

This simple spirit will form a pleasing liqueur with cherries and sugar; but where cherry brandy is preferred we can recommend the following recipe with great confidence to our readers:—Stone six pounds of black cherries (guines;) pour on them four quarts of the best brandy; bruise the stones in a mortar, and put the kernels in with the cherries; cover them close, and let the whole stand for a fortnight; then squeeze them clean from sediment, through muslin. Boil two pounds of very white sugar to clear syrup; mix it with the strained brandy, and bottle it into clear dry bottles. It may be used in two months, and should be kept in a cool cellar.

We are not very anxious to recommend the distillation of liqueurs as a private amusement, as it may lead to disagreeable habits; but those who chuse to practice it will find the heat of a sand bath quite sufficient for their purpose, when they use spirits that have been already distilled, first steeping in them the substances whose flavour they may wish to impart.

These substances may be cinnamon, mace, cloves, rose leaves, lavender, orange flowers, mignionette, &c.; to be sweetened afterwards agreeable to the palate.

Marasquin may be made of the vinous spirit produced from a tartish kind of cherry, distilled with bay leaves: this is wholesome.

Ratafia may be made different ways; one mode is to boil equal quantities of gooseberries and sugar into a thick jelly, over which a sufficient quantity of white wine must be poured, and suffered to remain for some days. Press out and filter the mixture, add half the quantity of brandy, with any spices that may be agreeable.

Even a simple mixture of one pint of brandy, one gallon of water, and a pound of sugar will make a pleasant ratafia that may be flavoured at will, with any essential oil distilled in spirit. This ratafia makes also a good basis for noyau with apricot stones, which must be broken, the shells dried in the air, then powdered in a mortar and steeped in brandy, exposed to the heat of the sun, or of a stove in a bottle well closed; taking care that the artificial heat is not too great, otherwise the bottle will burst.

The simplest and best, however, of all these recipes, is to put as much of the full blossom of the white thorn, picked dry and clean from the leaves and stalks, as a great bottle will hold lightly, without pressing down: fill it up with French brandy, let it stand two or three months, then decant it off clear, and add as much sugar as may make it of a proper sweetness.

As *Noyau* is of all liqueurs that which seems the most generally adopted in England, we shall subjoin a recipe for the making of it, which will furnish sixteen clear quarts of a liqueur no way inferior to the *Veritable Martinique*, at an expence of not more than five pounds, which is not half the cost of the foreign article.

Blanch and pound one pound of bitter almonds, half a pound of sweet almonds, and two ounces of cassia buds, *separately*. Put them with two gallons of British gin into a barrel, and shake it every day for a fortnight. Then make a syrup of twelve pounds of sugar and three quarts of water, and put it into the barrel milk-warm. Add three quarts of spirits of wine, a pint of ratafia, four ounces of orange flower water, the juice of two lemons, and a piece of calcined alum, about the size of a walnut. Shake the barrel occasionally for three or four days. Then add half an ounce of isinglass, dissolved in half a pint of gin, reserved from the two gallons, for that purpose. Shake the barrel only once afterwards, let the whole remain three or four days, and then filter it through an earthen-ware cullender, with filtering paper laid on it, changing the paper every time it is empty. In two days and nights full sixteen clear quarts will be produced; when bottled, dip the corks in melted rosin.

Under the head of *liqueurs*, though not strictly speaking of distillations, we may notice a beverage much talked of, the Regent's punch, of which the composition is champaign, mixed with various liqueurs, with a small portion of an infusion of green tea, which is the only water used in the mixture.

As for the common distilled waters, we have nothing of novelty to report; consequently we pass them over, but must record a very wholesome beverage long used upon the Continent, yet never introduced here, and made from the leaves of the branc ursine; the process is easy.

A discretional quantity of the dried leaves of branc-ursine are boiled in a sufficient quantity of common water, and, when the decoction assumes a yellowish colour, it is taken off; and, a little leaven, made with rye-meal, being put into it, the vessel is well stopped, and laid on a stove, in order that the liquor may ferment. When the fermentation is over, the liquor has an agreeable smell, and a tartish taste; nothing more is wanting than to strain it through a woollen bag, and to keep it in a cool place for use.. This beverage is exceedingly wholesome, and attended with excellent effects in cases of obstructions, intermitting fevers, &c.; some years ago, when it was kept a secret, the price was so exorbitant, that few but persons of wealth or quality purchased it.

Here let us also notice, that ginger beer of a very superior quality, may be prepared as follows: —Powder of ginger, one ounce; cream of tartar, half an ounce; a large lemon sliced; two pounds of lump sugar, and one gallon of water, added together, and simmered over the fire for half an hour; then fermented, in the usual way, with a table spoonful of yeast, and bottle it close for use. It should be put into such bottles as are used for soda water, and closely corked.

As vinegar forms such an important part of ornamental cookery, it must be always important to asertain that it is unadulterated. The chemical process is simple. In a test glass of vinegar, put three or four drops of acetate of barytes, which will produce a white precipitate. Filtrate through paper, and heat the powder in a tobacco-pipe until red hot. Then put it into spirit of salt, or diluted aquafortis.. If the precipitate dissolves, the vinegar is genuine. If it does not, then the vinegar is adulterated with oil of vitriol. If metallic adulteration is suspected, especially in distilled vinegar, take the following tests: add liquid ammonia to vinegar until its odour predominates; then if the mixture assumes a bluish tint, you may depend upon the presence of copper.

Again, add water, impregnated with sulphuretted hydrogen, to the suspected vinegar. If it becomes black, or yields a black precipitate, the presence of lead is obvious.

We shall dismiss this Section of Domestic Economy, with some brief notice of the

ICE-HOUSE.

It will readily be admitted, that this branch of domestic arrangement has little to do with domestic economy, strictly speaking; yet, even where an ice-house is thought too expensive a part of the establishment, it may be agreeable to know the various modes of producing ice for culinary purposes, at a trifling expense, and with very little trouble.

One very simple and easy method, is merely to fill a gallon stone bottle with hot spring water, leaving about a pint vacant, and putting in two ounces of refined nitre; when the bottle must be stopped very close, and let down into a deep well. After three or four hours it will be found to be completely frozen; but the bottle must be broken to procure the ice. If the bottle is moved up and down, so as to be sometimes in and sometimes out of the water, the consequent evaporation will hasten the process. The heating of the water assists the subsequent congelation; and it has been proved, by experience, that hot water, in winter, will freeze more rapidly than cold water, just drawn from a spring.

When the ice is thus procured, it may be increased in quantity by various processes. A very active and ingenious chemist, in a recent philosophical work, suggests that a very convenient and effective mixture for producing a diminution of sensible heat, which has hitherto escaped the attention

of chemists, is that of snow and alcohol. The
greatest effect takes place when equal weights of
each are used, and the solution accomplished in the
least possible time. The temperature both of the
snow and alcohol being 30° the solution in several
experiments fell to —17°, or 19° of Fahrenheit;
but as the alcohol was not of a very low specific
gravity, it is imagined that it would not be difficult
to produce an additional degree. This circumstance explains the greater degree of cold generated
by mixing snow with strong wines, than by plung-
ing the containing vessel into ice and water : and the
same effect may be produced by pounded ice as by
snow.

An easy chemical process, when necessary to be
had recourse to, will produce a degree of cold sufficient even to congeal mercury, or reduce the gaseous nitrous acid to a liquid form.

This process is simply to mix together sulphuric
ether and muriatic ether, when an instantaneous
evaporation takes place.

Some experiments have been tried in making ice
by absorption, in which several substances have
been used, particularly rotten trap, or toad-stone.
Very recently, however, the ingenious Professor
Leslie, of Edinburgh, has communicated an improvement in his method of producing ice. He
has discovered that parched oatmeal has a stronger
and more extensive power of absorbing humidity
than even decayed trap rock. With about three
quarters of a pound of meal, occupying a surface
of seven inches in diameter, he froze nearly a quarter
of a pound of water, and kept it almost 20 hours
in the form of ice, till one-half of the congealed mass
was again melted.

An easily practicable plan for a portable ice-house,

has also been proposed by a scientific Frenchman, M. Belenger, which may be rendered cheaply convenient for domestic purposes.

Take an iron bound butt or puncheon, and knock out the head, cutting a very small hole in the bottom, about the size of a wine cork. Place inside of it a wooden tub, shaped like a churn, resting it upon two pieces of wood, which are to raise it from touching the bottom. Fill the space round the inner tub with pounded charcoal; and fit to the tub a cover, with a convenient handle, having inside one or two small hooks, on which are to be hung the bottles, during the operation. Place on the lid a bag of charcoal, about two feet square; if the charcoal, in this bag, is pounded, it will answer better; and over all place another cover, which must cover the head of the outer cask.

When the apparatus is thus prepared, let it be placed in a cold cellar, and buried in the earth above four-fifths of its height; but, though cold, the cellar must be dry; wet ground will not answer, and a sandy soil is the best. Fill the inner tub, or nearly so, with pounded ice; or, if prepared in winter, with snow, well pressed down, and the apparatus will be complete.

Whenever it is wished to make ices, take off the upper cover, then the sack or bag of pounded charcoal, and suspend the vessel containing the liquid to be frozen to the hooks inside of the inner cover; then close up the whole, as before, for half an hour, when the operation will be complete, provided proper care is taken to exclude external air.

SECTION V.

STORE OFFICES.

COAL CELLAR—*Management of Coals—Qualities of Coals—Economic Management of Heat.* BEER CELLAR—*Home Brewing—Materials and Substitutes—Management of Ale and Beer.* WINE CELLAR—*Choice of Wines—Tests—Tricks—General Management—Made Wines.* SPIRIT CELLAR.

COAL CELLAR.

THERE is no part of domestic economy which every body professes to understand better than the management of a fire, and yet there is no branch in the household arrangement where there is a greater proportional and unnecessary waste, than arises from ignorance and mismanagement in this article. It is an old adage, that we must stir no man's fire until we have known him seven years; but we might find it equally prudent if we were careful as to the stirring of our own. Any body, indeed, can take up a poker and toss the coals about; but that is not *stirring a fire!*

In short, the use of a poker applies solely to two particular points—the opening of a dying fire, so as to admit the free passage of the air *into* it, and sometimes, but not always, *through* it—or else approximating the remains of a half-burned fire, so as to concentrate the heat, whilst the parts still ignited are opened to the atmosphere.

The same observation may apply to the use of a pair of bellows, the mere blowing of which, at random, nine times out of ten will fail; the force of the current of air sometimes blowing out the fire, as it is called, that is, carrying off the caloric too rapidly, and at others, directing the warmed current from the unignited fuel, instead of into it. To prove this, let any person sit down with a pair of bellows, to a fire only partially ignited, or partially extinguished; let him blow, at first, not into the burning part, but into the dead coals close to it, so that the air may partly extend to the burning coal. After a few blasts let the bellows blow into the burning fuel, but directing the stream partly towards the dead coal; when it will be found that the ignition will extend much more rapidly than under the common method of blowing furiously into the flame at random.

The reason of this, both in regard to the poker and the bellows, is, that fire cannot exist without the presence of atmospheric air, seventeen parts in one hundred of which are pure oxygen, which forms the *pabulum* or food of fire, in addition to its own combustible qualities. It is on the same principle that water is thrown on the forge fire, in order that the existing heat shall produce decomposition; when its component particles, oxygen and hydrogen, both become combustible, and increase the ignition; just as a little water sprinkled on a parlour fire appears to increase the smoke, whilst it unites the small coals, and prevents the atmospheric air, from the draught of the apartment, from passing through, before its oxygen has been decomposed by the fire, adding its own oxygen and hydrogen to the amount, as well as its own caloric, which is by no means inconsiderable.

With these principles in view, we may now proceed to a more practical illustration of the subject, the first point being the qualities of the material, of which there is a great choice in the London market; amounting to upwards of sixty species, from the mere bituminous slate, up to the brilliant Cannel coal. For common use, in London, however, we recommend the best of the sea coal, which is generally supposed to be from the Walls-end Colliery, which comes by the Newcastle ships, and contains a sufficient quantity of bitumen, mixed with purer materials than any other species, thus affording heat and possessing durability. According to the present system, indeed, the consumer is quite at the mercy of the coal merchant, but a little management may remedy even that. If the consumer, instead of ordering a large supply at once, will, at first, content himself with a sample, he may with very little trouble ascertain who will deal fairly with him; and, if he wisely pays ready money, he will be independent of his coal merchant; a situation, which few families, even in genteel life, can boast of. Indeed we cannot too often repeat the truth, that to deal for ready money only, in all the departments of domestic arrangement, is the truest economy. Ready money will always command the best and cheapest of every article of consumption, if expended with judgment; and the dealer, who means to act fairly, will always prefer it. Trust not him who seems more anxious to give credit, than to receive cash.

The former hopes to secure custom by having a hold upon you in his books; and continues always to make up for his advance, either by an advanced price, or an inferior article; whilst the latter knows that your custom can only be secured by fair dealing. On this point, however, every ones experience may convince him; we therefore proceed to the more practical management of the subject in question.

There is, likewise, another consideration, as far as economy is concerned, which is not only to buy with ready money, but to buy at proper seasons; for there is with every article a cheap season, and a dear one; and with none more than coals: insomuch, that the master of a family, who fills his coal cellar in the middle of the summer, rather than the beginning of the winter, will find it filled at half the expense it would otherwise cost him; and will be enabled to see December's snows falling, without feeling his enjoyment of his fire-side lessened, by the consideration that the cheerful blaze is supplied at twice the rate that it need have done, if he had exercised a little more foresight.

We must now call to the recollection of our readers, that chimnies often smoke, and that coals are often wasted by throwing too much fuel at once upon a fire. To prove this observation, it is only necessary to remove the superfluous coal from the top of the grate, when the smoking instantly ceases; as to the waste, that evidently proceeds from the frequent intemperate and injudicious use of the poker, which not only throws a great portion of the small coals among the cinders, but often extinguishes the fire it was intended to foster.

The philosophy of the matter is simply this. When the heat begins to operate, the gas is extricated, and carrying some of the grosser particles along with it, a heavy smoke is thrown up, which will not rise in the chimney, and by its own gravity is forced back into the room, on which the warm air of the apartment, being lighter than what comes in, instantly ascends towards the ceiling, and the lower part becomes cool. But if a portion of the fuel is taken off, then the small quantity of active caloric acts with greater force on the unconsumed coal, brings out its latent heat more rapidly, and thereby producing a quicker decomposition of the gases by the increasing combustion, the smoke becomes thinner and lighter, and though it carries up certainly more caloric with it, proportionably than before, yet the quantity of radiant heat is greater, and the general temperature of the apartment is more equalized.

Taking off the superabundant fuel has also the advantage, of permitting a freer draught through the fire, and of course presents a greater quantity of atmospheric oxygen as food for combustion, rendering a poker almost useless. In short a few minutes patience will do more for a fire, than stirring and knocking the coals about for half an hour. The true secret is that stirring a fire is only necessary to keep the bottom clear, except when the top absolutely requires breaking, or rather perforation only.

Attention to these hints will save nearly one-third of the coal expenditure; certainly an important object not only in London house-keeping, but in all parts of the Empire.

We may add that although a well acting chimney carries up a greater portion of caloric than a smoky one in the same period of time, yet it does not diminish the active heat of the fire, but rather increases it; for as a smaller quantity of coals is in the grate, so a greater proportion of that quantity is in active combustion, throwing out more radiant heat, and burning until nothing is left but a mere *caput mortuum*. 'Tis true that there will be fewer cinders, and that these will be less serviceable than under other circumstances; but then the quantity of coals consumed will be much less in proportion. According to this method too, the warm air of the apartment is prevented from rushing up the chimney before it has passed through the fire; an arrangement which we attempt to produce artificially by the application of a tin blower, or register.

These hints apply both to parlour and kitchen fires; but with respect to the latter, if it were facile to make cooks practical philosophers, it ought to be explained to them that when water is once made to boil, all that is further necessary, is just to keep the water at that temperature, which Count Rumford has proved by repeated experiments to require a very minute, though frequent addition of fuel. Meat will thus be as well boiled, and in the same time; with this advantage that a smaller quantity of the water will be evaporated: and less additional water to fill up, being thus required, consequently the fire will not so often demand copious additions of fuel—to say nothing of the injury done to the meat by the frequent dashing in of cold water.

It has been ascertained that 100lbs. of beef may be kept boiling hot for three hours, by means of 2½lbs. of pit coal in a confined place, so prepared as to prevent the radiating of the heat, except in the direction required, and at an expense of about three farthings, when coals are £4 per chaldron.

When fuel was comparatively cheap, this saving might not be considered as of high importance; nor is it easily practicable in England to make great savings in fuel, whilst rounds and sirloins are boiled and roasted. But in small families there

is less economy in cooking a large joint in one day
to last for seven, than there would be in smaller
dishes, cooked as in the warmer climates, in both
the East and West Indies, and even in Spain and
Italy; where, according to the national mode of
cooking, less fire is consumed in dressing a large
dinner than an English cook-maid will require to
boil a tea-kettle. Even in both the Indies, the
native cooks contrive to dress English dinners with
a smaller consumption of fuel, than beef steaks for
half a dozen can be cooked at home.

The steam cooking is also another important
saving in domestic economy; though, at first the
preparatory expense is considerable. With many
indeed there exist strong prejudices against meat
thus dressed; but that may be obviated in large
establishments, when by a very simple process the
steam may be applied, not to the meat itself, but
to the warming of the water in which the meat is
boiled. The practice of heating water in this
manner by steam is now becoming general in breweries and in large manufactories, such as dyeing
houses, &c., and even on a small scale might be
made convenient for private families at a moderate
expense; requiring, indeed, rather more patience
and attention than English cooks are disposed to
bestow upon economical practices.

But even without this, much may be done to
prevent an extravagant and unnecessary waste of
heat, by attention to the preparation of the general
cooking apparatus.

On turning over the various philosophical repositories of the present day, we find that many
attempts have been made of late to preserve a
uniform temperature in breweries and distilleries,
by confining the warmth to substances which are
bad conductors of heat. The cement invented for

this purpose by Mr. Kurten, the architect at Wiesbaden, has been highly commended. It is stated to have the property of concentrating in stoves, and especially the economic stoves, almost all the heat, so that it is expended only upon the things to be heated, and never in vain. The Polytechnic Society at Munich, which has lately analysed this cement, finds that it is indeed useful, but however, not so advantageous as the inventor supposed. According to the analysis of this Society, Mr. Kurten's cement consists of earthy marle, sand, and ochre, and though not perfectly adequate to the purpose, may yet be applied judiciously, until better means are found to produce the desired effect.

We may here conclude, by hinting that much saving would take place from paying more attention to the sifting of cinders and mixing them, for use, with small coal. A patent has lately been obtained for an improved apparatus for this purpose. It consists of a bin, or box, containing a sieve suspended upon swinging pivots: this is moved in a manner similar to the sieves of winnowing machines, by the intervention of a crank connected with the handle, and its motion may be regulated by a flywheel. There is a contrivance, by means of a sliding lever and handle, to discharge the contents of the sieve after it has been sifted, into a scuttle placed beneath; and by this means the operator is protected from all the dust which naturally arises. We would also recommend to the attention of the public the mode practised by the people in Wales, in preparing their coal for the hearth, by which the quantity is doubly increased, besides the durability of the fire, which lasts thrice as long as it would if made of coal alone. It is as follows:—
To every bushel of small coal (the smaller the

better,) add one bushel of clay or river mud, mix
them intimately together with some water to soften
the clay, then form this mass into small balls,
about twice the size of a hen's egg.   According to
the state of the weather, the balls are fit for use in
from six to twelve hours.   A fire made with these
balls throws out a regular, ardent, intense heat,
and if made with clay will burn eighteen hours,
but if with mud about twelve hours; so that by
this mode of preparation, a bushel of coal will last
as long as four, consumed in the usual way.   There
is another advantage, as small coal, the very refuse
of the coal-hole, answers best: this, it is presumed,
may be purchased at a lower price than coal in
general.

The economy of the

BEER AND ALE CELLAR,

is an object of necessary attention even in small
establishments, the expenditure of malt liquors
costing more in proportion than almost any other
article of common demand in house-keeping. But
the true economy consists not so much in the re-
duction of quantity, as in the regulation of that
quantity upon a liberal principle, aided by modern
chemistry in the preparation of fair and wholesome
ingredients.

The saving in excise duties will always repay the
time and trouble of home brewing; independent of
the comfort and salubrity of wholesome potations
instead of the sophisticated mixtures so generally
imposed upon the public—but we propose not to
write an essay on brewing; that subject has been
treated of sufficiently in numerous publications;
it will be more important to point out, from modern,

discoveries and recent practice, the best mode of applying the various articles of water, malt, and hops, so as to produce the greatest quantity of the best article at the smallest expence; to describe some lighter substitutes for table beverage; and to shew how far chemistry may prevent the waste resulting from liquors spoiled by accident or inattention.

‘ In choice of water, always select that' which is softest. This offers a three-fold saving; in time, in coals, and in malt; as it operates sooner, and with less heat, besides extracting a much greater proportion of the essence of the malt. 'Tis true that it leaves less extractive matter for a second brewing; but as it permits a diminution of malt in the first mash, the operator can afford to add fresh malt to the second brewing, which will always improve it in flavour as well as in quality.

Though March and October have long been the two great brewing eras in old English house-keeping; yet a considerable saving will be found to accrue from brewing small quantities at a time, and brewing often; nay if the great brewing in each of these months shall be divided into several, the advantages resulting will be found to counterbalance the additional trouble.

It has recently been proved by actual comparative experiments, that as small brewings allow the malt to be boiled in the infusion, with the hops and wort prepared in the usual way, so is the beer always stronger and better. The process is to make the usual infusion for the wort, during a steeping of three hours: then 'putting in the hops, to boil the whole together for three quarters of an hour, straining it afterwards, and proceeding in the ordinary way for working. One important improve-

ment has recently been patented, which offers a
complete safe-guard against an accident that often
spoils a whole mash.

The mode is this : the patentee had observed that
in the common way of boiling the wort, the extract
is often, if not always, more or less, burned ; to
prevent which, he never suffers fire or flame to come
in contact with the vessel in which the wort is
boiled, but performs that process by means of steam,
applied on the outside of that vessel.   For this purpose, he incloses the brewing vessel in another
vessel called the case or jacket, made either of
metal or wood, with a sufficient space left between
them for the admission of steam from a boiler, by
means of tubes, or other convenient communication.
In arranging this simple apparatus, attention
should be paid to the following particulars :—the
brewing vessel must be so well secured in its case,
that there may be no way for the steam to escape
but through a valve or cock.   The brewing vessel
should rise somewhat higher than the case, as it is
not advisable to apply the steam to that vessel
higher than the worts within it rise to, as some
portions of the hop are apt to adhere to the sides of
the vessel, and these, if exposed to a greater heat
than the worts, might injure the flavour of the
beer.   The boiler which supplies the steam should
be furnished with a steam-valve, and placed somewhat lower than the brewing vessel ; so that the
water produced by the condensation of the steam
in the case may be returned to the boiler by a
tube.   The tube which connects the boiler and the
case, should be furnished with cocks, that the steam
may be excluded or admitted at pleasure.   By
employing a close brewing vessel with a safety-
valve, the temperature of the wort may be raised
above the common boiling temperature of 212°,

and a larger portion of extract may thus be obtained from the hop. The flavour of the beer thus brewed is represented as superior to that boiled in the common way, and as being, when properly fermented, more vinous, spirituous and palatable.

It ought also to be remembered that the brown malt yields less extractive matter, or gives weaker wort than the pale malt ; in consequence of certain principles being destroyed by the more powerful action of the fire upon the grain. It will be found beneficial always to steep the hops, before using, in soft hot water ; after which boil the hops, and the infusion must be poured into the mash previous to the general boiling.

Where the smallest savings form a necessary part of domestic economy, substitutes for hops may often be judiciously applied.

Gentian root may be used with complete success as a substitute for hops in brewing, in the proportion of one ounce, or one ounce and a half to four ounces of hops for each bushel of malt. The root may be bought at about three halfpence per ounce, which produces an effect equal to a pound of hops. It is cut into thin slices, and put into boiling wort, as hops are ; but if previously boiled in water, the bitter principle, which is more grateful than that of the hop, will be extracted with greater certainty. A small quantity of hops thrown into the cask when bunged down, will impart the full flavour of the latter.

It is also known that one pound of buckbean will bitter one strike of malt for fresh drink, and give it a very agreeable flavour. The roots only, in the season, are as good as the leaves in the month of June.

Various substitutes have been offered for malt liquors, but these, however, may be found in any

book of receipts; but as a ready light summer
drink we may recommend the mixing a bottle of
ale or porter in ten quarts of water, adding a pound
of coarse brown sugar, and two ounces of ground
ginger. This is not exactly ginger beer; but if well
mixed, then bottled and corked loosely, it will be
found fit for drinking, and forming an agreeable
beverage in a day or two afterwards, particularly
in hot weather.

To those who have vines in their gardens or conservatories, it may be agreeable to know that their
vine prunings, either fresh or dry, when mashed in
hot water, yield a very fine beer; and if the infusion
is permitted to ferment, it will be found to make
very good wholesome vinegar.

Considerable ingenuity and fancy have been dis-
played in producing beer with the flavour of various
flowers, plants, and shrubs, but with much unnecessary expense of time, fire, and trouble. It
will be found much better, and equally agreeable,
to bottle off strong ale in its pure state, leaving the
space of about three table spoonfuls, into which
may be poured the extract of any fruit or flower, &c.
made strong or weak as wanted. These extracts may
even be added after the ale has ripened, by being
dropped in after the cork is drawn for immediate use.

The following recipe will be found to produce a
very pleasant and wholesome beverage. To a
quarter of a peck of sweet wheat bran, add three
handfuls of hops, and ten gallons of water. Boil
the whole together in a copper, until the bran and
hops sink to the bottom: then strain it through a
hair sieve into a cooler, and when luke-warm add
two quarts of molasses, or three pints of treacle if
thick. This will be sufficient for a nine gallon
cask. Before you pour in the liquor, which must
be done as soon as the molasses or treacle is melted,

put two table spoonfuls of good yeast into the barrel. When the fermentation has subsided, bung the cask close up, and in four days it will be fit to use. If you should choose to bottle any part of the beer, it will be much improved by so doing, and will be ready to drink in six or seven days.

To make any attempt to ripen beer before the proper time of its own chemical confection, is a dangerous experiment, as it often spoils a good cask; but where it is particularly wished for, it will be found that the proportion of twenty drops of spirit of salt to a gallon of beer or ale, will take off the newness, or extra sweetness, correcting it also when it is either too stale or eager.

Where it is intended to keep beer for any time on draught, it will be prudent to take ground malt in the proportion of one pint to every twenty gallons of the cask's contents; enclose it in a small linen bag, hang it in the cask as soon as broached, but keep the bung well closed, never opening it but for the purpose of lowering the bag, as the beer sinks from expenditure.

When beer turns ropy, without being sour, it may readily be restored by mixing one spoonful of mustard to every fourteen gallons, in a little of the beer, which is to be poured into the bung-hole; and in the course of the ensuing day, the beer will be fit for use.

But when it is actually sour, it may be restored by hanging a linen bag in the cask, containing equal quantities of pounded chalk and calcined oyster-shells. This will operate successfully in the course of a day and night; or for immediate use apply salt of wormwood, or a small quantity of carbonate of soda.

These articles form the base of all the advertised specifics for this purpose.

When beer is first tunned, it may be improved by putting a handful of coarse oatmeal into each barrel.

This may be applied with propriety to beer *purchased* in casks, if not intended for immediate use. But where beer is intended to be kept, it is the safest way to have it home-brewed, as its absolute strength is then known and can be depended upon. Where circumstances, however, prevent this, a simple test of its powers may be found in mixing a little pure alcohol in a small quantity of the beer. If the beer be not well fermented, and possess more mucilage than spirit, it will immediately become turbid; which clearly manifests that it will turn sour long before the period proposed for bottling, or for draught.

We now come to a more expensive, though perhaps not more important department of domestic store in the

WINE CELLAR,

and we shall divide this interesting portion of our work into the separate heads of choice of wine; testing of wine; tricks of wine-coopers; management of wine in cellar, in wood, and in bottles; and close with some novel and cheap modes of preparing home-made wines; confining ourselves, however, to short hints upon each division, leaving more detailed essays to systematic writers upon the subject.

As the goodness of wine, especially in a medical point of view, depends upon the quantity of astringent matter, or *tannin*, contained in it; this may readily be ascertained by dropping a solution of isinglass into it, when a gelatinous precipitate takes place in proportion to the tannin, whether it be port, claret, or burgundy.

Let every purchaser of port wine, however, recollect that even when he gets wine that is really unadulterated, still it is extremely probable that half his pipe consists of a rough Spanish wine; wholesome indeed, but by no means equal to the real port, either in strength, in body, or in flavour.

Wine that is really genuine will at once speak for itself, and show that no chemical test is necessary; but where there is cause to suspect adulteration, then it is proper to examine it more accurately.

The presence of sugar of lead may be detected by filling a wine glass, and adding a few drops of Harrowgate water, when the wine will become blackish, if lead has been infused to correct acidity: or use the common chemical test of water impregnated with sulphurated hydrogen gas, and a small portion of muriatic acid, filling a glass about one-third, and the rest with the wine to be tested. If a black precipitate falls it is lead: which may be easily proved by the common experiment of the blow-pipe.

The most frequent adulteration of port wine is with alum, in order to give it astringency when mixed with lighter bodied wines. The process to detect this is simple. Take some fresh prepared lime water, mix the suspected wine with it, in any fair proportion; allow the mixture to stand about a day; then if the wine is genuine, a number of chrystals will be found deposited at the bottom of the vessel; if alum is in the wine there will be no chrystals, but a slimy and muddy precipitate.

The lime water need not be very strong. The proportions of lime water and wine may be equal.

There is another way of ascertaining the presence of alum, but more scientific. Drop some solution of sub-carbonate of potash into the wine, when, if alum be present, there will be a violet-coloured precipitate, or at least cloudiness; which will vanish again if a few drops of caustic potash, or of muriatic acid are added to the mixture.

Where colouring matter has been, added to the wine, put a quarter of a pint into a small phial with an ounce of fresh charcoal finely pulverized. Shake the mixture well for a few minutes, when the natural colouring matter will be chemically destroyed, and the wine when filtered will yield a clear limpid fluid: but if the wine is artificially coloured, that colouring matter cannot be acted on by the charcoal, and the mixture will appear unchanged.

Wine-coopers know too well that a little Brazil wood saw-dust mixed with some natron or impure carbonate of soda, and put into a tumbler of water, immediately communicates to it the colour and appearance of red wine: but if this coloured fluid is poured into another glass containing a few drops of lemon juice, it instantly loses its colour and becomes like white wine.

It is also important to notice that none of the substances used in giving the red colour to wine, form with the acetate of lead, that greenish grey precipitate which is the result of its union with genuine red wines. When coloured by bilberry, campeachy wood, or elder, the precipitate is deep blue ; and when with fernambouc, red saunders, or red beet, the precipitate is red.

It is needless here to enumerate the various tricks of giving a factitious crusting to wine bottles, by means of Brazil wood and potash ; or the colouring of wine corks to represent long residence in the neck of a bottle, though perhaps only driven in yesterday ; nor the crusting even of the wine casks, with chrystals of the super tartrite of potash. Those who wish to know those secrets will find them fully explained in Accum's work, with many other " Secrets worth Knowing;" but we may observe that the older port wine is, the less of the tartar, or supertartrite of pot-ash is contained in it, and the greater the deposition on the sides of the cask or bottle. But new wine may be put into old casks or old bottles. Therefore, to ascertain the quantity of the salt, take a pint of wine, and boil it down to one-half, into which drop a solution of muriate of platina; when a precipitate takes place, greater or less, in proportion to the quantity of the salt contained.

In choosing, or in forming a wine cellar, remember that the deepest are the best; yet they cannot have too much air, provided it comes through air holes with a northern aspect. They ought also to be as far as possible from *all drains*, as much good wine has often been spoiled by inattention to this circumstance. Both casks and bottles ought to be so arranged as to admit of a free circulation of air. This prevents the rotting of hoops, and very often saves a cask of old wine.

Where wine is intended to be kept in casks for years, considerable advantage will be derived from painting them with a coat of oil and any common ochre; sprinkling over it, whilst wet, some very fine sand, adding a second coat of oil and sand, which forms a complete stony encrustation against damp or dry rot.

It is positively averred, that to pour oil on wine when in the cask will prevent it from turning musty; but if wine in the wood turns musty or sour, put a quantity of clean wheat in a linen bag, and hang it in the cask. In a short time the wine is fined, and may be drawn off the lees, into a clean cask.

Nothing can be more injurious to young wines than to hasten them in colour or in flavour, whether by things in themselves harmless, or by the deleterious ingredients too often used by wine-coopers.

But then, let it be remembered, that the natural ripening of wine will be always impeded in proportion to the irregularity of temperature in the cellar.

An ingenious person, a few years ago, endeavoured to procure a patent for ripening Madeira and other wines. The effect was to be produced by the casks being kept in a regular temperature and state of motion, similar to that which they would experience during a voyage. The scheme had much of plausibility in it; but, like many other schemes devised for the benefit of society, it fell to the ground for want of pecuniary means to carry it into execution.

For the clearing of turbid wine, chips of hazel are a harmless, and generally an efficacious remedy: but where a more rapid clarification is necessary, then powdered gypsum or alabaster may safely be tried : stirring it up in the wine, which, after settling, must be drawn off into a fresh cask.

Here we may hint at a mode of ripening claret, even in bottle, which is very much practised in France, and may be practised here, without injury to the health; though we certainly are far from recommending the practice to the venders of wine, however it may be adopted in a private cellar.

The process is to operate upon wine perhaps only a year in bottle. Draw the corks, and pour about a glassful out of each, re-corking them tightly; then place the wine, thus drawn, in an oven, suffering it, at the end of an hour or two, to cool gradually. Draw the corks again, and fill up the bottles, which must be carefully replaced in the cellar; and in a day or two the wine will have every appearance of being ten years old.

Before wine is drawn off into a fresh cask, it will always be proper to dip a rag into melted brimstone, and to insert it as far as the centre of the cask, by means of a wire; stopping up the bung-hole after it is set on fire. The reason for this may be shewn by a curious experiment.

If two or three drops of the oil of tartar are poured into half a glass of very fine red wine, the wine will lose its red colour, and become opaque and yellowish, like turned and pricked wine; but if two or three drops of the spirit of sulphur, which is a very strong acid, are afterwards poured into the glass, the same wine will entirely resume its beautiful red colour; whence the reason is easily perceived, why sulphur is burnt in hogsheads in order to preserve wine, since it is not the inflammable part of sulphur that causes this effect, but its acid spirit, that enters and permeates the wood of the vessel.

Naturalists seem not yet agreed on the reasons why vehement thunder disturbs wine, and other liquors in cellars, and makes them become vapid or acid. Some think, that the tremulous motion of the air occasions this alteration; and others, that there is a certain occult fermentation in the air, that disturbs and corrupts the usual motion of insensible parts. The latter opinion is held to be the more probable by Mr. Boyle, who, by hermetically sealing a glass vessel, filled with beer, found that this liquor, after great thunder, lost nothing of its strength and taste; whereas the same in hogsheads, becoming sour, the exhalation diffused through the air must have penetrated the hogsheads but not the glass. Whence he advises, in time of thunder, to light coal fires in vaults and cellars, which, he says, will preserve liquors from corruption; either because the fire discusses the sulphureous and corrupt-

ing vapours, or that it breaks their force, whilst it
changes the figures of the vapours, or their magnitude, or texture.

Some may consider this as a vulgar error; but
we are not of that opinion; though we do not
agree with Mrs. Tabitha Bramble that double
locking the cellar door ought to be a specific preventative!

With respect to wine in bottles, it is now ascertained, that the dry rot, however injurious to
others, is of great advantage to wine merchants,
as it soon covers the bottles with its mouldy appearance, and consumes the external parts of the
corks; so that with a trifling operation on the
bottles after they are filled, and then deposited in
cellars pretty strongly affected with the dry-rot,
they can send out wine as having been bottled for
seven or eight years, before it has, in fact, been there
so many months.

· This, however, can be of no advantage in a private cellar; and therefore we record a better plan
than even corking wine to preserve it, nay to improve it materially in quality, though with a diminution of quantity whilst in bottle.

It is well known, that water passes with facility
through animal substances, such as bladders, &c.
whilst alcohol is almost perfectly retained by them;
as already noticed under another head. To apply
this principle, close wine bottles, with pieces of
bladder instead of cork, and after some time the
wine will be found diminished in quantity, but its
strength will be much improved.

To guard against " corked wine," dip the corks
in a size made of white wax melted with half its quantity of beef suet; let them dry rapidly, and repeat
the dipping until their outsides are saturated.

· The properties of cork have been lately investigated deeply by an ingenious French chemist, who, for this purpose, has contrived a machine which consists of a Papin's digester, closed by a valve supported by a spring; the force of the spring, which may be changed at pleasure, determines the degree of heat that the liquid ought to receive in order to its escape. The produce of each degree is successively collected by means of a tube, which conducts to a receiver. The solid matter to be analysed is held in the digester by a moveable piece, by which it may also be compressed, and the remaining liquid squeezed out of it. M. Chevreul has operated upon cork by this method; he subjected it twenty times to the action of water, and fifty to that of alcohol; and after having thus detached from it very various matters, there remained a cellular tissue, which he calls *suberine*, and which when treated with nitric acid is transformed into suberic acid. Among these matters extracted from cork, there is one which he believes to be new, and which he calls *cerine*, because it possesses several of the properties of wax.

It must be acknowledged, however, that no particular advantage to the wine cellar has yet resulted from this discovery.

Various methods are in vogue for cooling wine: it is enough here to record that it has been found that equal weights of alcohol and mace, rapidly mixed, produce a diminution of temperature from 32 to 17. - This explains the reason why a small quantity of mace mixed with a strong wine produces more cold than if the wine be merely plunged in mace water.

Some writers are actually of opinion, that home made wines, or wines made from fruit, are more wholesome than those made from the grape, because the latter is said to contain saline principles

M

injurious to health; whilst the former has for its basis, the salubrious juice of fruit, whose slight acid may be changed, by repeated boiling, into saccharine matter. But there is another cause of difference—that grape wine contains the tartaric acid, whilst the acid of fruit wines is the malic, and which is imparted to excess by the pressure and boiling of the seeds and husks.

As the great quantity of sugar, required to correct this overplus, affects the flavour of the home-made wines, it has been proposed to remedy that defect by the addition of the super-tartrate of potash.

Of this acid, there is a portion in the gooseberry; and gooseberry wine, of a most excellent flavour, may be made by a very simple process, so as even to pass with the best judges for a fine foreign wine.

For this purpose, to every two gallons of full ripe gooseberries mashed, add an equal quantity of soft water, milk-warm, holding in solution one pound of single refined sugar. Stir up the whole quantity in a tub, and cover with a blanket, to preserve the heat of fermentation. Stir frequently for three days, then strain, first, through a sieve, and, secondly, through a coarse cloth; the liquor must then be put into a cask, kept full, and allowed to ferment from ten days to three weeks; when two or three bottles of brandy, or more, according to the size of the cask, in proportion of one to eight, may be poured in with the same quantity of sherry, together with a small quantity of isinglass perfectly dissolved in water.

Close the cask tightly. If at the end of a fortnight it is not sweet enough, add more sugar. Close finally for six months, and then bottle; or sooner, if it is wished to imitate sparkling champaign.

To make a wine nearly equal to the Rhenish,

you must to every gallon of the juice of the apple, immediately after it comes from the press, add two pounds of common loaf sugar; boil it as long as any scum rises; strain it through a sieve, and let it cool; add some good yeast, and stir it well; let it work in the tub for two or three weeks, or till the head begins to flatten, then skim off the head, draw it clear off, and tun it. When made a year, rack it off, and fine it with isinglass; then add half a pint of the best rectified spirits of wine, or a pint of brandy to every three gallons. This wine will be found very superior.

For a fine currant wine, take black currants, red ditto, white ditto, ripe cherries, raspberries, and strawberries, of each an equal quantity. To every four pounds, well bruised, add one gallon of clear soft water. Steep three days and nights in open vessels, and stir the mass frequently. Then strain through a sieve, and press the pulp to dryness. Add together both liquids. To each gallon put three pounds of good rich moist sugar. Let the whole stand three days, skim off the top, and stir frequently. Tun it into casks, to purge at the bung, for about a fortnight; then to every nine gallons add a quart of good brandy, and close the casks. Isinglass finings may be applied, if necessary.

But of all home-made wines, that which may be procured from the mulberry, is most congenial to the palates and constitutions of Englishmen; and it is much to be regretted that the mulberry tree is not more cultivated in this country; as the soil and climate are so favorable to it, that in the course of a very few years, half the consumption of the united kingdom might be supplied, by this means, at the cheapest possible rate, with a pure, delicious, and salutary wine, free alike from foreign matters, and from foreign duties,

Dr. Mac Culloch, in his Remarks on the Art of making Wine, reprobates the practice of adding alcohol or brandy to wines, either home-made or foreign, under the idea of making them keep longer. He contends, that to this practice, as applied to port wine, the frequency of liver complaints in this country must be attributed; and insists, from various experiments, that the notion of the preservative power of spirits, when added to wine, is founded on error. It is certainly a subject in which all habitual wine-drinkers are deeply interested, and consequently deserves their serious attention.

We can state, from our own knowledge, that some of the finest flavoured, and strongest bodied made-wines, we ever met with, were made without any addition whatever of brandy; and the excellence they had attained from age, was a sufficient proof that it was not necessary merely to enable them to keep. Time is a very good economist on some occasions, however destructive he may be on others; and if left to himself, will often perform for nothing, what, by endeavouring to hasten his operations, must be gained at considerable expense.

Before closing this part of the subject, we may add a few words in regard to the

SPIRIT CELLAR.

In which department, however, there is but little room for novelty, except to inform our readers, that *new rum* is much improved in flavour by steeping in it a small quantity of ground rice and charcoal for about a fortnight; frequently stirring it, then allowing it to settle for decanting, and, where the quantity is not very great, filtering it through paper: and that new brandy may be made equal to old, by pouring four or five drops of volatile

alkali to every quart, shaking it well and then allowing it to settle.

Cyder and perry afford little that is not generally
known respecting them, except to recommend their
use in preference to the sophisticated stuff so often a
disgrace to the very name of wine, the dearness of
which, at present, acts as a severe check upon those
who would administer it charitably in their various
neighbourhoods. Indeed, unless it is genuine, we
must agree with the physician who recommended
poison in preference, as acting more rapidly, and
therefore more humanely. In fact, the universal
complaint of bad wines at inns and public houses,
(from whence the poor have usually drawn their
little stock) will, perhaps, too much justify the
above observation. We have lately, in this country, been taught to seek for substitutes for the
necessaries of life. Prohibited the use of port
wine, we would, therefore, recommend cyder to the
poor, when attacked by the low contagious fever;
but not luscious, sweet cyder, such as is usually
sold at our inns, or is to be found in the cellars
of the merchants; for this has generally been adulterated, and mixed with we know not what, to
render it agreeable to the palate. The best cyder
for cases of fever and sore throat, is the natural produce of apples, such as the farmers of
Herefordshire keep for the entertainment of their
friends; which they call rough and stout, in oppo-
sition to the soft and luscious sorts, that are made
to adapt themselves to the taste. Such home-made
cyder, we are sure, is genuine; has no mixture in
it of acid spirit, as most of our wines have; and
is quite as strong an antiseptic. If perry be used
instead of cyder, the same attention should be had
to its quality. The best sorts of perry for such

uses, are those called by the several names, Cara-
dine, Houghcap, and Barland.

We shall now conclude generally, that it is most
important for health, to be able to ascertain the
purity of cyder, or perry, before stocking a cellar
with them. The principal adulteration of these
liquors is lead; either accidentally from the leaden
bed of the press, or intentionally, for the purpose
of neutralizing the super-abundant acid.

To ascertain this, nothing more is necessary than
to test the suspected liquor, with a solution of mo-
lybdate of potash; when a white precipitate will
take place, even though the lead should exist in
the smallest possible quantity.

The purity of spirits may easily be ascertained
by setting fire to a little of it in a spoon, when, if
it be unadulterated, it will all burn away, without
leaving any moisture behind.

SECTION VI.

EXTERNAL CONVENIENCIES.

KITCHEN GARDEN.— ORCHARD.—FLOWER GARDEN. APIARY.— POULTRY YARD.—PIGGERY.—FARM YARD. ORNAMENTAL GROUNDS. — CONSERVATORY.—HOT-HOUSE.—AVIARY.—IMPROVEMENTS.

KITCHEN GARDEN.

THIS is one of the most important parts of general domestic economy, whenever the situation of a house will permit a family to avail themselves of its assistance, in aid of butchers' bills. It is, indeed, much to be regretted, that small plots of ground, in the immediate vicinity of the metropolis more especially, are too often frittered away into shrubberies and baby-gardens, when they might more usefully be employed in raising vegetables for the family, during the week-day residence in town, than wasting their sweetness on the smoky air, in all the pride of lilac, hollyhock, and batchelors' buttons, to be merely smelled to, by the whole emigrating household on the day of rest.

With a little care and attention, a kitchen garden, though small, might be rendered not only useful, but, in fact, as ornamental as a modern grass carpet; and the same expense incurred to make the ground a labyrinth of sweets, might suffice to render it agreeable to the palate, as well as to the olfactory nerves, and that even without offending the most delicate optics from Snowhill or St. Mary Axe.

For the general management of such a wished for change, we must of course refer to the numerous didactic books on the subject. It is only in accordance with our plan, to give the hint, and to record such novel points as may facilitate the proposed arrangement.

It is one objection to the adoption of a kitchen garden in front of the dwelling, or in sight of the family apartments, that its very nature makes it rather an eye-sore, than otherwise, at all seasons. This, however, is an objection that may be readily got over, by a little attention to neatness and good order : whilst the plants themselves, if judiciously attended to, and the borders sown or planted with ranunculus, polyanthus, mignionette, &c. in succession, will really be ornamental : but then, in cutting the plants for use, the business must be done neatly, all useless leaves cleared from the ground, the roots no longer wanted taken up, and the ravages of insects to be guarded against by sedulous extirpation.

It will also be found a great improvement, where space will admit of it, to surround the beds with neat espaliers, with fruit trees, or even gooseberry and currant bushes trained along them, instead of these being suffered to grow in a state of ragged wildness.

One great difficulty, however, is to preserve the

plants from the ravages of insects and vermin; as their depredations too often render the utmost care and neatness totally useless. We shall, therefore, offer several hints which, we have reason to believe, are not yet engrafted in the various treatises on this subject.

It has lately been satisfactorily proved that the ammoniacal liquor, produced in the manufacture of gas from coal, will effectually extirpate the grub and other worms, which so often destroy the rising hopes of the gardener, particularly in early crops: nor is any harm to be feared from the liquid injuring the tenderest plants, as they appear rather to be invigorated by its application. The water in which potatoes are boiled, will likewise, as we have elsewhere observed, if sprinkled over grain or plants, completely destroy all insects in every stage of existence, from the egg to the fly.

Many specifics have been offered, as infallible in getting rid of moles; but absolute extirpation is the only certain remedy. To do this, however, does not require the aid of a professed mole catcher; as the secret by means of which they succeed in driving these vermin from their holes, so as to be killed easily by proper weapons or by dogs, is now known. It has often been observed, that moles will not attack garlic, onions, or leeks, whilst growing; and their antipathy to them is so great, that if any of these, particularly in a green state approaching to ripeness, are put into their holes, they will immediately leave them, and expose themselves to be taken.

Though ponds in gardens are seldom objects of beauty, in consequence of the quantity of aquatic weeds with which they are generally overrun, yet they may be kept in good order, when large enough, by means of swans, two of which will be sufficient for an extensive piece of water when once thoroughly cleared.

It remains for us now to offer some new discoveries in regard to the economic culture of several hortulane productions, which we shall notice in alphabetic order, for more ready reference; but without pretending to give any thing like general directions for a kitchen garden, which must be sought for in appropriate treatises.

The first of these which we shall select, is a cheap and easy way to raise *Asparagus.*—Make the bed quite flat, five feet wide of good soil, without any dung, long or short; sow it with onions—then sow two asparagus seeds (lest one should fail) about one inch deep near each other; twelve inches each way sow two more; and if the spring is cold and dry, let the weeds grow until rain comes. In October, cover the bed with manure or rotten hot-bed. The next spring remove the weakest of the two plants, and keep the bed from weeds. Samples have been sent to the Horticultural Society, cut the third year, and very large. To raise seed, select the largest stems; after blossoming sufficiently, take off the tops to make the seed strong. This is also the best way to raise double ten week and Brompton stoke—six pods are sufficient for any strong plant; setting them to flower near double ones is of no use. The excess in petal arises from cultivation, and transplanting into rich soil. Wild flowers are seldom double. Keep all small seeds in the pod until they are sown.

Beet-root, though considered injurious to the stomach, when eaten to any extent, is yet a very useful and economic plant, independent of its choice for salads; as it has been proved capable of making very good beer, in lieu of malt. This, of course, depends in a great degree upon its saccharine qualities; and the process is to submit it previously to sufficient pressure so as to get rid of nearly all the juice, when it may immediately be applied to the purpose of malt, or dried and kept to a proper season. It is unfortunate, however, that a considerable portion of its sugar is expressed along with the juice, which, under strong pressure, will amount to nearly half the weight of the root itself, yielding nearly one-tenth of its own weight of sugar after evaporation. But to evaporate the juice for a saccharine supply, would be futile in the extreme; yet it may be expedient to boil it down considerably, and then to mix the residue with the beet malt, by which means nothing will be lost.

The culture of the *Cucumber* scarcely comes within our province, except to offer a hint respecting a point, on which common foresight might readily be negligent; nor should we venture to record it, were it not that the fact has been already clearly ascertained.

As this plant cannot be well raised here, except in hot-beds, or under glass, attempts have been made to concentrate the Sun's rays upon them, by means of copper sheet reflectors. This, however, has been ascertained to render the plants reared by them, completely deleterious, even to the loss of life. It is not impossible that the rain water and dew dripping from these reflectors may have aided much in the unhappy consequences; but, in whatever way the morbific action may have taken place, it would be the height of imprudence to adopt, or to prolong a practice, the results of which have been fatal in more than one instance.

There is a wild plant which might, with great propriety and advantage, be introduced more frequently into our smaller kitchen gardens. We allude to the *Sea kale* which in taste much resembles asparagus, and is dressed and served up in the same manner. It makes its appearance very early in the year; viz. in February and March, and does not begin to fail till the month of May, so that asparagus is at it were a continuation of it. It is, in botanical works, designated as the *Crambe Maritima*, and is found wild upon the sea shore in divers parts of England, particularly in Sussex and Dorsetshire. It is found also upon the southern coast of Devonshire, where it shoots itself up among the sands.

The best mode for general cultivation, is that it should be propagated either by seeds or roots; if the former, it should not be cut till the third or fourth year; if the latter, i. e. by transplanting, it will be fit for use the second year.—The seed must be sown very thick, and remain in the seed-bed one year, the roots are then to be taken up, and transplanted at the distance of a foot from each other, which space they will soon fill up; indeed this plant propagates itself so fast, that we may almost say it is with difficulty eradicated. It should, however, be covered during the winter with long dung, to preserve it from the frost. When exposed to the air, it turns green, and then is not fit for the table: for the space, therefore, of ten or twelve days previous to its being cut for use, it must undergo the process of blanching—which is done by burying it, during that time, in coal ashes or sand.

But there is another species of Kale, the *Cæsarian Kale*, which must not pass unnoticed; and it is to be expected that this valuable and most excellent vegetable will soon rank high, both in cultivation and esteem, there being no species of vegetable in this country resembling this prolific plant.

It must be sown in spring or the beginning of

summer, broad cast, and transplanted at the distance of about two feet.—When sown with turnips, it answers an admirable purpose, as few crops are more subject to fail than that of the turnip, whereas the Cæsarian kale seed may be depended on. It is so prolific and hardy, that it will vegetate well in almost any soil or climate, and prosper even in the shade of fruit or other trees. The farmer, grazier, dairy-man, kitchen gardener, &c. would find it greatly to their advantage to grow this beneficial plant, as well as families living in towns, and who find it difficult to procure sufficient pasture and meadow for a cow: as it has been ascertained that during the winter, particularly in severe frosts and deep snows, when other green fodder for cattle cannot be had, this plant, from its elevation, (growing to four or five feet) and its natural hardiness, yields abundant and successive supplies, which is an important desideratum. The mode of using it for cattle, is by cutting off the large leaves, as wanted, when a regular succession takes place continually through the winter. Very early in the spring (previous to most other vegetables), it produces vast numbers of large delicious sprouts for the table, equal in sweetness to asparagus—so that it may be said to produce two crops—Cows fed on this plant give a greater quantity of milk, and the butter is of a richer flavour than when fed on any other vegetable. A matter also of great utility, is that of its comforting and cheering qualities in the feeding of ewes in the winter, while suckling house lambs.

With respect to *Kidney Beans*, considerable economic improvement may now be expected, as an ingenious botanist has discovered that both the common and dwarf kidney-bean (*phaseolus vulgaris* and *p. nanus*), as well as the common garden bean (*faba vicia*) and all its varieties, hitherto considered by botanists as annual plants, are, in reality, perennials. If they are cut down in the autumn before the appearance of sharp frosts, and the roots covered with stable litter, they will shoot up again in spring; and though the pods do not come to maturity so early in the second and succeeding years, yet the crop is not so liable to be injured by the vicissitudes of the weather as that of fresh sown plants.

Onions have recently been much improved by a simple and facile process; as by an experiment carefully tried, it was found that if some were transplanted early in March, whilst the remainder were left in the original bed, the transplanted bulbs, in a ripe state, exceeded the others more than threefold, both in size and weight. Half a dozen onions treated in this manner were found to weigh eight pounds and a quarter. Their shape was flattish; and in flavour they were as mild as the best Portuguese or Spanish. A new method has also been introduced of producing an earlier crop than usual. If onions are sown about Midsummer, a crop of bulbs will be obtained of the size of a small horse bean. These, on being transplanted early in the next spring, will not run to seed, but produce an earlier and more certain crop of fine large bulbs in the following season. The Americans practise this mode of sowing onions with much success. Dibble the small bulbs singly in rows about three inches apart or a little more.

But above all things we wish to see the greatest possible encouragement given to the culture of the *Potatoe*. One acre for one year will support twenty persons, including women and children; and leave sufficient for the feeding of one or two pigs. That its produce must be great, is evident from the fact, that the farmers in Essex, with their high rented, well manured, and dearly worked lands, including cartage and various incidental expences, have been able, in good years, to sell them at three shillings or four shillings the cwt. in the London markets: that is to say, five or six pounds of good food for two-pence. In fact the produce per acre has been thirteen tons on a moderate average.

It may also not be inappropriate to mention that two crops of potatoes may be raised instead of one. Potatoes were set on the twenty-eighth of March, and taken up on the twenty-fourth of June; then cut and set again on the twenty-sixth, in the same spot of ground with only the addition of a little lime. On the twenty-eighth of October they were again taken up and yielded a more plentiful crop than the summer produce. It may likewise be observed in this place, that in some lands, but not however in light or stony lands, (for the rule does not apply invariably) by taking off the blossoms just when they are beginning to unfold, the produce of the roots will be increased in almost double the quantity.

Scarcity of manure has, indeed, sometimes been urged as a reason for the neglect of this useful root. But that may easily be got over; for whenever manure is difficult to be procured, it will be found fully sufficient, even in light soils, to plant them a good distance asunder, and give three ploughings between. By such culture the potatoe crop will pay for the land; but the produce of an acre may be much increased by a judicious intermixture of other plants, especially if we introduce a new sort of potatoe, called the bread-fruit-potatoe, which, from its uncommon productiveness, is getting rapidly into estimation. A farmer, near Bridge-water, planted in the common way, in a heavy soil,

without manure, or any extra attention, two potatoes of that variety, weighing four ounces; the
produce was 264 ounces, being an increase per
acre (allowing six sacks to be the proper quantity
to seed an acre) of 396 sacks. Heligoland beans
may be cultivated with the bread-fruit-potatoe,
with success, by dropping about half a bushel per
acre in the channels with the potatoes when planted;
as they grow and ripen at the same time, without
deteriorating the crop of potatoes.

Nor are its esculent uses the only advantage to
be drawn from the cultivation of the potatoe. An
ingenious French chemist has, within these few
months, obtained a new and very lucrative product
from potatoes, by burning the stalks and leaves of
the plant and extracting the potash which they
contain in abundance. Just when the flower begins to go off, at which time the stalk is in full
vigour, the plants are cut with a sharp instrument
about five inches from the ground. The stumps
soon throw out fresh shoots which suffice to bring
the roots to maturity. The plants after being cut
are left eight days in the field to dry. They are
then burned in the same manner as soda manufac-
turers burn kali, in a hole five feet in diameter and
two feet deep. The ashes are washed and the ley
evaporated. By this process 2,500 pounds weight
of the salt is obtained per acre; the author of it
calculates that the potatoes grown upon an acre
will produce 225 francs, over and above the expense
of cultivation; and that the salt from the same area,
deducting the cost of making, will be worth 816
francs, making a total of 1041 francs, upwards of
£43 sterling.

Many experiments have recently been tried to
obtain new potatoes throughout the winter. Three
of these modes have been so successful, that we

shall record them; giving, however, the precedence to the invention of a very ingenious lady * of Chester, for which she has most deservedly obtained the gold medal from the Society of Arts. Her mode she describes to be, to prepare a proper quantity of red sand, rather of a loamy nature, and to mix it up with a portion of lime in powder, viz. about one-third or one-half, about 14 days before use. This soil is to be spread about three inches thick at the bottom of any old wooden box, or on a very dry brick cellar floor. The cellar ought not to be exposed to the frost, nor yet too much confined from the air. Then procure a measure or two of large potatoes of a prior year's growth; the best sorts are the red apple potatoe, the pink eyes, or Mr. Curwen's purple potatoes. Set these on the soil whole, about three inches apart, with the crown or the principal eye to the soil in preference, but put no soil over them.

It is a matter of some importance, that the original potatoes for planting whole, for sets in September, should be such as were of perfect growth in the October of the preceding year, and well preserved during the winter; the sprouts which shoot from them should be removed by the end of April, and these sprouts, which will be from six to twenty inches long, may be planted, with all their fibres, in a garden for a first crop. About June 15th the potatoe sets must be sprit again, and the sprouts planted for a second crop; and in September the potatoe sets must be sprit a third time, and the sprouts of this last produce thrown away as useless. At the end of September the original or seed potatoe is to be gently placed on the soils as before-mentioned, for a Christmas crop. At the end of three months at farthest the old potatoes should

* Miss Anne Clague.

be carefully twisted from the new ones, and the sprouts taken off the old potatoe; and the old potatoe is then to be placed on its bottom or side, on a fresh bed of soil prepared as before, and left to produce another crop from fresh eyes placed next the soil; as we are to observe that the old potatoe should not be set or placed twice on the same side, and we must take care at that time to remove the sprouts, to prevent the moisture rotting the old potatoe. By the above method, this lady had four crops of new potatoes from one potatoe, exclusive of those produced from the sprouts planted in the garden in April and June, from which she obtained two crops of well-grown potatoes in September and October weighing from eight to twelve ounces each: and the crops were very plentiful in proportion to the quantity planted.

We have reason to believe no method of raising early potatoes will be found more cheap and easy in management than this; the potatoes are remarkably well flavoured, and may be kept longer without prejudice after gathering, before dressed, than potatoes grown in the natural ground.

Another method has been proposed, which is thus.—Take some dry vegetable mould, cover the bottom of a large box, about two inches thick, then lay potatoes of the kind (and the largest of their kind) called ox-nobles (chiefly used for cattle) side by side, so as to cover the mould; then cover these with two inches more mould, and so on for four or five courses. The box may stand covered with dry straw in any warm cellar. If this plan be adopted in the month of November, a very large supply of beautiful young potatoes will be obtained very soon after Christmas, and the potatoes may be repeated so as to have a succession till the season produces them in the natural way.

The last mode which we shall record is to preserve some fine kidney potatoes, as long through the summer as possible, and by keeping them cool, and rubbing off the sprouts, they may be kept sufficiently fresh to vegetate till late in July, or the beginning of August; then plant them with manure in the usual way, but closer, each set within six inches of the other, and in rows twelve or fourteen inches asunder. The shavings of grass-plats are preferable to manure. These potatoes will grow very rapidly, and when the October frosts come, the young ones at the roots will be about the ordinary size of the early Lancashire ones. If at this time, as soon as the tops are withered by the frost, the beds are carefully covered with long litter or dry straw, and if the soil be not much infested by the grub, they will remain unaltered till Christmas, and may be used in the highest perfection for more than two months from that time; and even then the only alteration perceptible is in the thickness of the skin, which the cook will find it necessary to scrape off, and which a little destroys their beauty.

Having thus shewn how to procure new potatoes out of season, it may be proper to state the various methods, lately made public, of preserving the old ones; amongst which it is a very curious fact, that potatoes may be kept good all the year, by dipping them in boiling water, as the Scots preserve eggs by killing the living principle; and as the germ is so near the skin, it would not hurt the potatoe.—One minute, or two at most, would be quite sufficient. This would be of great use for ship stores. In an open worked basket a ton may be cured in an hour; after which they must be dried in a cooling oven, and laid up in sacks in a dry place, secure from the effects of frost.

An ingenious method of preserving potatoes has been practised, which is not only agreeable, but also economical. The mode is to peel the potatoes and rasp them, placing the pulp in a coarse cloth, which is squeezed in a common napkin press, until it becomes a thin cake, like thin cheese, when it is laid on a shelf to dry, and afterwards boiled or steamed as wanted.

The expressed juice, if mixed with an equal quantity of cold water, will yield a considerable portion of fine flour, very applicable to pastry and other culinary purposes.

Many different methods have been proposed for bringing back frosted potatoes to a sound state, but we have not learned that any of them has completely answered. Steeping in cold water is only a partial remedy; for the difference of temperature is considerable; and it is well known that in vegetables, as well as in animals, the putrefactive process rapidly commences by a sudden transition to heat from extreme cold. Mr. Wilfred Wilson, of Cumberland, has convinced himself, from numerous observations and enquiries, that if potatoes, how much soever frosted, be only carefully excluded from the atmospheric air, and the pit not opened until some time after the frost has entirely subsided, these valuable roots will be found not to have sustained the slightest injury, on account of their not having been exposed to a sudden change, and consequently thawing gradually. The truth of this must be obvious to every ploughman, who, in tilling the ground in the spring, often turns up potatoes, which, when boiled, prove perfectly good, though they must have been several times alternately frozen and thawed. Their preservation must certainly be owing to their having been protected from the external air by the incumbent earth.

Strawberries are amongst the most agreeable articles in private gardening; and may be made much more so, both in horticultural appearance, and in quality, by the revival of a mode of management, now almost obsolete.

This mode is to lay straw neatly arranged under the plants as soon as the fruit begins to swell. There is no doubt indeed that this custom was the real origin of their name, with us, though their appellations in foreign languages have no reference to it whatever.

The advantages of this method are considerable. It preserves an extensive crop; shades the roots from the sun; prevents the want of moisture by evaporation; keeps the fruit off the ground; and gives a most pleasing air of neatness and cleanliness which is always agreeable to the eye. Let it be remembered too that even in very dry seasons, it nearly saves the whole labour of watering; and that at the end of the season the straw makes excellent manure.

To preserve vegetables in general from frost, will always be necessary in our winters; but vegetables slightly touched by frost ought not hastily to be thrown away, as in that case they may be rendered perfectly palatable and nutritious by laying them in cold water for an hour before boiling, and putting a piece of saltpetre into the kettle when set on the fire. A piece of lime the size of an egg, put into the water in which potatoes are boiling, will likewise be found to have the effect of rendering the heaviest potatoes light and farinaceous.

Turnips, or other vegetables saved during the winter, and injured by frost, may always be recovered with ease by putting their roots into cold water when a thaw appears; and letting them remain there until they are freed from all nitrous spiculæ, which the air, by its activity, would agitate into a thaw with such violence as to lacerate the substance of the root, reducing it to a soft pulp or liquid.

A most ingenious way of preserving vegetables all the winter, particularly green peas and French beans has recently been discovered; by filling a middle sized stew-pan with young peas, for instance, into which must be put two or three table spoonfuls of sugar, and the stew-pan then set over a brisk charcoal fire. When the heat begins to act, stir up the peas two or three times; then, as soon as they begin to yield water, pour them out into a dish to drain. Spread them out on paper in an airy place, not exposed to the sun, and turn them frequently so as to dry rapidly. Guard them from moisture, and you may have them green at Christmas without expense, and very little trouble.

We have also read that spring water boiled with salt into a strong brine until it will float an egg, may be made conducive to the preservation of the tenderest vegetables; which must be laid carefully in an earthen vessel, of a tall shape, and with as small an opening as convenient for the hand. This vessel is then to be carefully stopped up, and set in a cool dry place; but the vegetables, when wanted for use, must be steeped in warm water, where they are to lie for about six hours, after which they may be boiled, tasting agreeably, and preserving a good colour.

Little remains now, except to notice some useful hints regarding the best mode of gathering vegetables in the garden, and which is really a true part of domestic economy.

As even with artificial heat, melons do not always ripen equally, the upper part being fit for eating, whilst that next to the foot stalk may be intolerably bitter, it will often be judicious not to allow them to ripen entirely in any part before gathering, but to cut them off and lay them on wicker work in a green-house, or common summer-house; or in a cooler place if the weather should be very hot, so as not to ripen or *mellow* too rapidly. In a short time it will be found that the melon will have twice the goodness and flavour that it would have acquired if permitted to remain upon the stalk.

This process depends upon a species of fermentation produced by alternate changes in temperature; but though beneficial to almost all fruits, it is a process highly destructive of the principle of vegetable health in all the other productions of the garden, which ought never to be gathered, if possible, until the moment they are wanted.

To step from the kitchen garden to the

ORCHARD,

is literally so much in point that any introduction is superfluous; indeed, the numerous publications on this subject render all observations unnecessary, beyond the insertion of such useful facts as we have been able to find recorded on good authority, in the scientific publications of the day. And even with regard to these, our attention shall be paid as much to the management of the fruit itself, as to the culture of the trees; a department more particularly claiming the attention of our fair readers, whose practical gardening seldom extends beyond the parterre or green-house.

Of wall-fruit we shall only observe in this place, that the ripening of it may be greatly facilitated by having the walls covered, previous to the trees being trained against it, with a thick coat of black paint. Mr. H. Davies, of Slough, tried the experiment with respect to a vine, and found that the weight of grapes gathered on the blackened part of the wall was 20 pounds 10 ounces; whilst the other part yielded only 7 pounds 1 ounce; being little more than a third of the other. The fruit on the blackened part of the wall was also much finer and riper, and in larger branches, than on the other part; and the wood of the vine was stronger, and more covered with leaves, on that part of the wall where the paint had been applied.

In regard to specific fruits, we merely select the gooseberry and the vine; of the former of which it is to be observed that it may be much improved by a process that will not only give it an unusual degree of richness and flavour, but also preserve it fresh on the bush until the frosts set in.

The mode is to cover the bush with a light straw thatch, a few days before perfect ripeness; so as to exclude not only the sun-beams and showers, and dew, but even the light itself.

Gooseberries will also be improved by adopting the espalier system, so as to fix every branch horizontally and at equal distances from each other; to effect which, there must be provided a quantity of hooked and forked sticks two feet long and upwards, made of the young shoots of hazle, elder, or any kind of wood that will not strike root. The *forks* are to *support* such shoots as have an inclination downwards; and those shoots must be fastened to their respective forks by soft woollen bandages; otherwise, when they have produced two or three long shoots each, in the ensuing summer, they will be blown off them, unless such newly-formed shoots be themselves secured, as they ought to be, by forks or poles, &c. When the trees have extended four feet from the stem their branches ought to be

turned up, and each of them fastened to a hoop
made of cleft hazle, ash, willow, or brambles dis-
armed of their prickles, and spliced together, if too
short, to make a circle large enough to give the
trees when finished the form of a *punch-bowl* rather
than a *goblet*; for the greater the horizontality of
the branches, the better in all respects, save that of
gathering the fruit; but that is a very minor consideration in comparison with the attendant advantages.

The vine is not merely an ornamental plant in
this country; it may also be made useful, independent of its fruit. Its leaves, if dried in the
shade, make an excellent beer. They will also
make vinegar. The prunings, on being bruised,
and put into a vat or mashing tub, with boiling
water poured over them like malt, produce a liquor
of a fine vinous quality, which, if fermented, forms
good beer; or, distilled, yields brandy.

The value of the vine may be ascertained from
the fact that a single plant, growing against the front
of the hotel at Tenbury, Worcestershire, produced
a crop of grapes calculated to be worth 60*l.* a-
year at market price.

There is a method of treating grapes in France
which might be practised with great success in
England, and would form an elegant addition to
the amusements of the green-house.

Have earthen garden pots made with a notch in
the side, and extending half across the bottom.
Lay in that notch a vine branch after the fruit has
been fully formed, bending the branch just so much
as to break it slightly, close to the bottom of the
pot. Fill the pot with good earth, which must be
judiciously and carefully watered; fix it on a stand,
and leave it to nature.

The fruit thus treated will be found to surpass

the others in size, but it ripens more slowly; in
fact it must be allowed thus to remain until the
approach of frost; when the branch must be cut,
and the pot carried into the green-house; from
whence, even in winter, ripe grapes may thus be set
upon the table, and the effect will be more curious
if the pots themselves are brought in with the fruit
growing in the midst of the dessert.

This practice has the additional advantage, that
the vine branch, in the spring, may be planted
with success as a new vine: for it will be found full
of sap, the bending or breaking of the branch, in
the first instance, having had the effect of stopping
the descent of the sap, as well as forming shoots or
radical tendrils at the base.

It has been recently ascertained that fruit trees
are much improved by peeling off the outer bark,
when it shows a tendency to exfoliation.

The advantages are, that it increases the quantity
and improves the quality of the fruit, even at a
rate of more than double; it makes barren trees
productive; it prevents some diseases and cures
others; it cures the canker; and it dislodges an
immense number of insects.

Apple and pear trees may be peeled in winter,
when the inner bark adheres most strictly to the
trunk; but cherry trees in summer.

The reason of this is, that we thus give assistance
to nature. An accurate observer will perceive that,
sooner or later in the season, or in its age, every
tree will exfoliate. It is best done in winter, because then the inmost bark adheres most strongly
to the wood; but with care, it may be done at any
time. Indeed, to young trees and small branches,
it is best in March and April, when the sap is
rising.

When apple and pear trees become apparently

barren, it is too common to consider them as hope-
less. This, however, is injudicious; for it has
been proved by actual experiment, that trees which
had remained five or six years without bearing,
have been restored to fertility by the simple operation of making an incision all round the bottom of
the trunk, right through the bark, and even deep
into the tree itself.

Even single branches have thus been restored to
fertility, whilst the rest of the tree remained barren; the branch itself alone being cut nearly
through.

The best mode of performing this operation, is to
form two circular incisions with a penknife about a
quarter of an inch asunder, and then to make a
vertical incision between the two circles, when the
bark will readily peel off. The principle on which
this is supposed to act is, that the sap ascends by
the inner bark, but descends by the outer; but the
incision stops the descent, and therefore gives that
branch a greater power of retaining the sap than it
possessed before.

With respect to *grafting*, we have to observe
that a common method is by making a transverse
section in the back of the stock, and a perpendicular slit below it; the bud is then pushed down,
to give it the position which it is to have. This
method is not always successful; it is better to reverse it, by making the vertical slit above the
transverse section, and pushing the bud upwards
into its position—a method which rarely fails of
success; because as the sap descends by the bark,
as has been ascertained, and does not ascend, the
bud thus placed above the transverse section, receives abundance, but when placed below, the sap
cannot reach it.

Here let us recommend a greater attention to the

culture of the Chesnut tree, than is at present paid by practical gardeners. It is now scarcely thought of as an orchard tree; yet will be found a very useful one—but those who wish to have this fruit in perfection, should procure grafts from such trees as produce good fruit, and graft them on young chesnut stocks; by which method they may continue the kind, and the trees will be more fruitful than those which are ungrafted.

There can be no doubt of this tree having been formerly in great abundance in several parts of England, since many old buildings are found to be principally of this timber; and there are records which mention several forests of these trees. But how it has happened, that a tree once so common, and whose timber is so valuable, should be almost extirpated in England, is not easy to account for.

Peach trees have recently been much improved by a system which may be easily applied to any species of wall or espalier fruit. No house, fire, or hot-bed, is employed, but each tree is planted in its separate frame, which is nothing more than a hot-bed frame, only that, being placed on the common ground, its sides are made proportionably higher, so as to allow the stem of the tree planted *within* it on its south, or lower side, to rise to the height of three feet five inches, from which height the branches are trained almost horizontally under the glass slides, upon a wooden frame, or trellis of laths; so that the tree lies within the glasses on its back, as it were, exposed to the influence of the sun.

The gentleman who communicated this experiment, added that his ground is a good rich garden soil, from twenty inches to two feet thick. No other crop has hitherto been attempted to be raised from the ground thus inclosed in the glasses under the trees. The trees were planted in November, at four years of age, began to bear at six, and bore very plentifully at seven, eight, and nine.

Another ingenious botanist, in a notice to the Horticultural Society, states his experience of the beneficial effects of watering fruit trees well, at the time of the setting of the fruit. " Thus," he says, " a tree which in 1814, produced a very few pears, of about half a pound each, in 1815 (by this method) produced a great number nearly double that weight. "

In regard to preserving fruit trees, it is said that tallow, whiting, and linseed oil, worked well together, and of a proper consistence, if applied to fruit and other trees where a limb has been lopped off, will effectually prevent decay ; and by occasionally using linseed oil with a brush, it will prevent all injury from weather for a very long period. This composition will also be found far superior to clay for grafting or budding; as it entirely precludes wet and cold, and is at the same time more yielding and durable, and never cracks.

We have seen an account of an experiment which is said to be infallible in producing a full crop, even in the worst fruit seasons.

The mode is, to every acre apply a load of muck straw, or orts raked from the grass fields. Lay it in heaps, five or six to the acre, agreeable to the size of the orchard To every heap put about three ounces of sulphur ; then chuse a clear day with a favourable breeze and set fire to the heaps, the smoke of which will kill all worms and insects on the trees, even though they should be lodged under the bark. Or place a fire of damp straw in one or more pans adapted to the purpose, into which scatter half a handful of powdered sulphur. Let the pans be moved about, keeping them to windward, and the smoke being blown through the trees, will cause the flies to fall by thousands; this must be repeated as long as any grubs or flies remain.

But if this cannot conveniently be applied to wall fruit, especially to Peach Trees, then sprinkle sulphur, or flower of brimstone, on the leaves and branches with a common dredging-box.

To clear moss from all fruit trees requires only the simple process of sprinkling the dust of common wood ashes on the trunks and branches, particularly in moist or damp foggy weather. It is best done after the leaves are off the trees. The American farmers are said to prevent the blight in apple trees, and to secure plentiful crops, by the simple process of rubbing tar well into the bark, about four or six inches wide round each tree, and a foot from the ground.

A gardener in Lancashire has found out a cheap and effectual method of preventing hares and rabbits from injuring fruit or other trees by eating the bark in winter. It is this:—Take hogs lard, and as much whale oil as will work it up into a thin paste or paint, with which gently rub the stems of the trees upwards at the fall of the leaf. If this application be repeated once in two years, it will prevent the depredations of those animals, without the slightest injury to the trees.

It is said that the canker in apple trees may be effectually cured by rubbing the part affected with a brush dipped in train oil; and Sir G. M'Kenzie has discovered that oil rubbed upon the stems and branches of fruit trees destroys insects and increases the fruit buds. Mr. John Linning has added to the discovery by using it successfully upon the stems of carnations, to guard them against the depredations of the ear-wig. The coarsest oil will suit; and only a small quantity is required.

An ingenious botanist has recently communicated a method of destroying the aphis on apple-trees, which he has practised for some years with complete success. As soon as the insect makes its appearance, which is in general early in the spring, by exuding a white flocculent cotton-like substance upon such of the rough knotty surfaces of the bark as have afforded it shelter during the winter, he cuts away with a pruning knife all the dead bark from the parts affected, and covers the wounds by means of a brush with a composition of oil of tar, and yellow ochre, of the consistence of cream. Such is the pungency and penetrating property of the oil of tar, that it effectually destroys both insect and ova in the most secret recesses, without injury to the tree, and for some months secures the parts from future attack. The application may be used at all seasons, and by the addition of lamp-black may be made to correspond in colour with the bark of the tree.

We have also seen a new method of destroying slugs and snails from fruit trees.—Melt the necessary quantity of tar, to which add sufficient pitch to make it dry quickly, and give it tenacity; and while melting, stir into, and completely incorporate with it, such a portion of horse-hair, cut very small, as will pervade every part without making it too thick. Apply this with a coarse painter's brush to the walls, a foot from the ground, and in a band of about three inches in width, twice or three times over; the last time it must be dabbed on, to render it as rough as possible, and to allow the ends of the hair to project. A circle must also be made with these ingredients round the stem of each tree, so that no communication be left free from it between the ground and the fruit for the slugs to crawl up. This method is perfectly effectual, attended with little trouble, and not a tenth part of the expense of the hair bands so much in use.

To a person of taste and benevolent disposition, it must be pleasing to see his orchard filled with birds, even though they should destroy as much of the buds and fruits as they are accused of. But the fact is, that instead of destroying the blossom as supposed, they actually are seeking for the worms that would cause them to perish. The bullfinches are particularly useful in this respect.

It is, however, too much the practice with gardeners to destroy, or frighten away, the feathered race from orchards, whether in blossom or in fruit; a system most injudicious, and in some degree cruel. We will not moot the point that the birds of the air have a right to share in the fruits of the earth, even when raised by man's industry; but it is interesting to note that the birds which frequent orchards, especially bullfinches, during the bloom, are not only seeking their own proper food, but benefiting the proprietor by the destruction of numberless insects —" the worms in the bud"—that lie in the yet unfolded blossom, where they had been deposited until the warmth which swells the buds acts upon them also, bringing forward a most numerous race already in the form of caterpillars, and ready to annihilate the early hopes of the year.

Let it also be particularly remembered that titmice pick off the defective buds of fruit trees, in search of insects. These little birds are considered by gardeners as peculiarly injurious, by destroying the bloom buds, and, in consequence, are persecuted by them without mercy. But, were they to examine carefully the fragments of the buds which, in this search, the birds scatter about the ground, they would observe that each had been pierced by an insect, which alone had been the object of pursuit. These insects would not only have destroyed the buds they had immediately attacked, but would have given birth to a number of others, equally injurious with themselves. The titmice, therefore, in picking off such buds as contain them, ought rather to be considered the preservers, than the destroyers of fruit.

In the early part of the spring, it is common to see small spots of froth in fruit-trees, vulgarly called " cuckoo spittle;" but which, if examined, will be found to contain an insect extremely deleterious to the tree. This should be instantly cut away, together with all the dead bark around the spot, which, with its vicinity, must be painted with a mixture of oil of tar and yellow ochre, with the addition of a little lamp black, if a darker colour is wished for, in unison with that of the tree.

By this means the insects and their eggs will be effectually killed as far as the paint reaches.

It will be found a very efficacious way of destroying caterpillars in their nests, upon trees or bushes, to boil together two pounds of potash, and two pints of water, until reduced to one-half the quantity. Strain the ley through a piece of linen, and let it settle for three or four days. Draw off the clear water, and mix it with six ounces of lamp oil, which will form a whitish liquid, into which dip a linen rag, and wash it round the various nests; when all the insects will instantly die.

To preserve apple-trees, and others, from the effects of insects, there has recently been practised the simple and efficacious method of forming a thick white-wash, of unslacked lime and soft water, which must be applied with a soft painting brush over the stem and branches of each, just as the sap begins to rise. No effect is immediately perceivable;

but in the course of the summer the tree will be-cleared of all its moss and insects, whilst its bark will acquire and preserve a healthy clear appear-ance, fresh and green. By this the growth of the tree will rather be improved than injured.

A simple, but evidently a philosophical, mode of preserving fruit-trees from the effects of frost, has for some years been practised with great success in the vicinity of Prague, and in other parts of Bo-hemia. The mode is, to surround the trunk of the tree, when in blossom, with a wisp of straw or hemp; the end of this is sunk, by means of a stone tied to it, in a vessel of spring water, at some dis-tance from the tree. One vessel will conveniently serve two trees, or even several, if the cord be long enough, and made to pass round them before its end is plunged into the water.

The water vessel must be placed in an open si-tuation, and carefully removed from the shade of the surrounding branches.

In all cases of gathering fruit for winter use, ob-serve not to touch them, until ready to drop off spontaneously; then take that which appears ripest in your hand, raise it on a level with the footstick end; if it comes away readily, lay it in your basket carefully. When a sufficient quantity is pulled, lay the fruit, whether apples or pears, in heaps, cover them with clean cloths and mats, and let them sweat to clear away the superabundant mois-ture; which operation may require three or four days.

Next, wipe them one by one with clean cloths, and lay them in glazed earthen jars, with layers of sand, an inch thick, which has been well dried in an oven. Close the jar when full, and place it in a cool airy place, but be careful to secure it from frost

Fruit may thus be kept fresh and good until the next year's growth are ready for use.

Remember the fruit trees must not be beaten for gathering the fruit; it destroys future fruit buds.

In preserving apples, pears, &c. through the winter, it is proper to note, that fern is always preferable to straw in forming the bed between the layers of fruit; for it never imparts that musty flavour which is so often produced by the latter.

In America, apples are preserved throughout the winter, merely by laying them on a floor, and covering them with a linen cloth, which secures them from both frost and damp; a woollen cloth will not have the same effect.

There is a very ingenious chemical method of placing fruit in an exhausted receiver, without even the intervention of an air-pump. The process is thus:—In the bottom of a glazed jar, well dried, place some pebbles, just to cover the surface; fill the jar with the apples, or pears, rubbed dry; cover the fruit with a piece of wood made to fit exactly, and over that lay some fresh mortar. The *rationale* of this is, that the pebbles attract the moisture of the fruit, whilst the mortar imbibes the air of the jar, and actually draws it off, leaving as perfect a vacuum as could be produced by a machine. The apples are thus preserved, not only from the pressure of the air, but also from its putrescent or fermentative qualities, and will keep good all the ensuing summer.

When apples, or other fruit, are frozen, steep them in cold water until they swell; but the necessity for this may be prevented by covering them with a thin linen cloth before the frost sets in.

To preserve chesnuts, mix them with walnuts, and they will keep sound. This may appear whimsical but is asserted to be efficacious.

To unite the agreeable with the useful being one of the main objects of this work, we proceed cheer-fully to the next head, since there is no part of domestic management more pleasing than that of the

FLOWER GARDEN,

whether in the country, or attached to a town resi-dence; and the most economical mode will be al-ways found to consist in uniting simplicity, as much as possible, with ornament. It is well known that the system of gardening has, even of late, been much improved, in regard to simplicity, whilst, as a science also, it has made rapid progress. But we write not for those who can throw gardens into parks, and parks into gardens, though even they may here find some useful hints; we offer our economical suggestions to those with whom economy is both a virtue and an act of necessity; and, who, having no room for separate summer and winter gardens, must have for their principal object the ar-rangement of their flowers, and plants, and shrubs, to suit all seasons; and so to blend their colours as to display their chief beauty when in full bloom, and to provide throughout the greatest part of the year for a succession of enamelled borders, with a sufficiency of evergreens to remain during the winter.

Even if the garden is too small to walk in, it may yet, by a little tasteful management, be made to appear much larger than it really is, when viewed from the house. For this purpose it is always pro-per that it should have a southern aspect, and that the flower plats should be mixed with turf, planting the flowers with the darkest leaves and gaudiest petals close to the windows, whilst those of lighter colour and more modest bloom shall be placed, in gradation, at the greatest distance. The effect of this will be more striking than may at first sight be imagined.

Should, however, gravel walks be preferred to turf, they may be managed so as to increase the optical deception, by making those broadest which are nearest to the apartment, narrowing them gradually by a perspective approach of the borders, which will produce all the effects of approaching lines upon paper. These walks, when once formed, and well gravelled, may always be kept in good order by watering them occasionally with a little strong brine, from a common watering-pot.

It will be found, however, that the grass plots are more susceptible of ornament than the gravel walks, especially when diversified by baskets of roses, growing in pots; the baskets to be made either of common rods or of iron, painted of different shades of green, and so varying in size as to admit of gradual diminution in progressive arrangement.

The sun-flower also, if well managed, will be found highly susceptible of this arrangement; besides which, it furnishes a valuable fodder for cattle in the leaves; when in flower, bees flock to it from all quarters to gather honey; the seed is useful in feeding sheep, pigs, and other animals, and produces a striking effect on poultry, occasioning them to-lay more eggs; and the stalks, when dried, burn well, the ashes affording a considerable quantity of alkali.

The box may also be transplanted of various sizes; but it ought to be made generally known, that the box tree is a strong poison. The box borders of several beds in a garden near Stamford, were lately thrown upon some manure in which, nine pigs were rooting, four of whom died from eating the noxious leaves, notwithstanding castor oil and other antidotes were administered.

Whilst attentive to preserve neatness, it is proper to observe, that if the decayed leaves of bulbous plants are cut off, the plants are thereby deprived of much nutriment for the ensuing year. The same applies to herbaceous plants; and here we may insert some observations and experiments of Mrs. Agnes Ibbetson, who for the last sixteen years has bestowed indefatigable attention on the examination of the form of plants, and has exposed the absurdity of the practice of burying weeds and vegetable matters in the ground, under the idea of their speedy conversion into manure. A trench, into which she had put a variety of plants, was opened, after an interval of three months, on the 1st of June; there was no alteration except in the weeds and grasses; the first had thrown out suckers, and the latter a set of roots, which ran among the earth; all the branches of trees were alive: the cabbages, carrots, &c. all in a perfect state of preservation. The next opening was in September—still all was alive and well, but the weeds had again thrown out suckers, though before cut off, and the grasses spread upwards. The branches were in the same state as before; the leaves of the cabbages began to look brown and moist, and a degree of fermentation seemed to have commenced. The third opening was in November; all the leaves had fallen from the branches, but they were still alive; the weeds had not sprung up again, but they were still existing, though, if they had been exposed to the open air, they would not have been so; the earth therefore would certainly appear to possess the power of suspending their decomposition, and rendering the process far more slow and torpid than it would be under ordinary circumstances. The cabbages, which were before in a state of fermentation, were now evidently advancing to putridity, but it was only the leaves that were undergoing this change, for the stalks though dead were still perfect. The original potatoes were also beginning to decay; but the roots were still alive, with little fibres growing to them; the carrots were likewise still alive and perfect. As to the grasses, and more especially the everlasting peas, they ran through the earth in every direction. Hence, she observes, that to return weeds and grass to the earth, after digging them up at a great expense of time and money, is but filling the ground with their roots, and that it will never be clean as long as this is done. If, on the contrary, they were brought to a waste place and burned, and their ashes collected, they would not only make excellent manure, but the earth would in a few years become perfectly clean from weeds. The same argument holds good against the ploughing in of green crops. Neither can the decomposition of vegetable matter buried in the ground with lime be depended upon.

As some of our fair readers no doubt take delight in the laboratory as well as in the flower-garden, we feel happy in giving them a hint as to a useful union of their pursuits both in chemistry and in botany; as it has recently been ascertained that water, impregnated with oxygen gas, and applied to the roots of plants, even in the feeblest state of growth, will rapidly effect a change in their health, and speedily produce a most luxuriant vegetation.

This, however, is only practicable in the summer; but in winter other methods must be pursued, amongst which the following easy remedy, to counteract the effects of frost on tender vegetables, has been communicated by a gentleman who has tried the experiment. The method he takes is, to water the vegetables on a frosty morning, before the sun shines upon them; for it is to be remembered, that it is the sun which completes their destruction, and not the frost itself.

But the greatest enemy of floral beauty is to be found in the snail or the caterpillar, against whose ravages the utmost precaution is sometimes inefficient. In many cases, where the decay of favourite flowers or tender shrubs is supposed to proceed from blight, or mildew, from unseasonable frost, want of watering, &c. it may often be found, on strict examination, that unseen insects are alone the secret cause.

When insects become very troublesome, it would be proper to frighten them away from favourite flower parterres or vegetable beds, as more consonant to humanity than destroying them in toto; but as in particular cases an instant remedy may be required, it will be found beneficial to sprinkle the plants or flowers with the following mixture:—Take a pound of American pearl ashes, or of any other alkali, to which add four pounds of slaked quick-lime, dissolving the whole in five gallons of water.

The application of this will kill earth-worms, in the ground, or caterpillars on the leaves, without any injury whatever to the vegetables or flowers themselves. But where the destruction is not so rapid as to require instantaneous remedy, a simple and certain remedy, or rather preventative, will be found in the process of whipping, strongly, such plants as can bear it, with the green leaves and branches of the elder tree; after which, for some months, insects will not attack them. Where the plants are too tender to admit of this rather violent.

remedy, the fair florist may water her favourite flowers once or twice, with a pretty strong infusion of the elder leaves.

In absolute destruction of life, however, the life which God has given for wise purposes, there is something unpleasant to a feeling mind, especially when we consider that those humble animals are only seeking that food which God has sent for all. Still we do not deny the right, at least we must acknowledge the power, which man has to destroy such animals as may be either useful or pernicious to him: but yet, when it must be done, it may be more agreeable to employ other agents; for which purpose, and indeed for actual gratification, we would recommend the encouragement of birds, particularly of the sparrow; which is extremely destructive of caterpillars. When caterpillars are particularly troublesome, and require to be destroyed by wholesale, prepare a cone of painted canvas or of strong paper, extended on hoops, and sufficiently large to cover any bush. Then sprinkle some hot lime on and under the bush; cover it with the cone, having at hand a pair of common fumigating bellows, filled with tobacco and sulphur, in equal quantities, ignited by a piece of charcoal; when the nose of the bellows is to be inserted in a hole fitted for the purpose, and a few blasts will be sufficient to suffocate all the caterpillars, which fall from the leaves, and are killed by the lime.

The dead insects may be allowed to lie on the ground, as their rapid decomposition by the lime renders them an useful manure, if in any quantities. There is certainly humanity in this mode, as the insects are rendered insensible before they are exposed to the corrosive effects of the lime; a consideration of some importance to those who believe that the smallest insect, in its mortal suffering,——

" —— feels a pang as great
" As when a giant dies."——

An ingenious, but rather whimsical botanist, many
years ago, recommended, as a ready way to get rid
of caterpillars, first to confine them to the shrub
where they had taken up their summer residence,
by anointing it, near to the ground, with tar, over
which the caterpillars would not pass. He then
proposed that pismires should be gathered, put in
a bag, and hung on the shrub; and, as they had
as great an aversion to tar as the caterpillars, they
would not then leave it for food, but would be
forced to devour their new companions.

When we consider, however, the relative sizes of
the ant and caterpillar, it necessarily follows that a
larger number of the former must be invited to the
feast than it may always be convenient or expedient
to procure, with this after inconvenience also, that,
like modern parasites, after they have eaten all to
which they were invited, they will prey upon their
host in other quarters.

The best time of destroying caterpillars, with a
reference to a future season, is in autumn; and the
best mode is, to sow a bed of mignionette, even for
that express purpose; for these insects will then
collect round the mignionette, and may be destroyed
en masse.

It sometimes happens that minute insects infest
whole parterres of rose bushes; for which there is
no remedy so efficacious as to take up the plants
carefully, cutting off the most infected branches
and suckers, brushing off such insects as may be on
the other branches, sweeping the whole into the
spot from whence the bush was taken, and pouring
boiling water upon it; after which the roses may
be replanted with safety.

Some of the finest flowers in the garden are sometimes observed to perish just as they emerge from their buds, or from their bulbs. If they are accurately examined, it will be seen that their leaves or petals are completely pierced with small holes, or often with the appearance of having been gnawn by minute insects. The damage, however, is done by the snail; which may thus be known to be in the ground, though it should not yet have been seen.

In such cases it will be proper instantly, early in the morning, or late in the evening, to take up all the sickly flowers, and to pour boiling water into their beds, carefully replanting them, after cleaning their roots from every extraneous substance, especially from the eggs of the snail, which are easily known by their pearl-like appearance.

This is the most certain method of getting rid of those destructive insects; but when the season, or other circumstances, will not permit the transplanting, and the snails, in open air, will not make their appearance, it may suffice to invert a large garden pot over the roots, when the snails will soon come out and fix themselves to its sides. To succeed better in dry weather, it will be expedient to water the plant before the pot is inverted; as the shade and moisture, together, induce the snail to consider the night as having arrived; for the ground snails do not willingly come out in the day, except after warm showers, and then either very early or very late. The slugs are more troublesome to get rid of; but they may be congregated in particular places by distributing pieces of haulm, or cabbage leaves, at certain distances, where they may at once be destroyed by pouring lime water over them; a remedy equally efficacious with strewing lime, and that too with a saving of ninety per cent., an object of consequence where the grounds are extensive, independent of its superior neatness and cleanliness.

One final point of economy we shall recommend is, to avoid, as much as possible, all artificial ornaments in small gardens, unless we wish for a floral toyshop. These things are always in bad taste, either with regard to selection or size; there is however one exception, and that not far from town, which it may be amusing to point out to our curious readers. We allude to a handsome house, with a small garden attached, not very far from Greenwich, on the lower road. In this garden there is a bridge, an alcove, shrubbery, serpentine walks, and some of the gaudiest, yet best arranged, parterres and flower knots, when in full blow, that we recollect to have seen any where round the metropolis. It is close to the road side, and requires no card of admission, as its bosky dells and gay parterres may all be seen from a barouche, or curricle, or from the humbler elevation, as we are now preaching economy, of the outside of a Greenwich stage!

Even in large gardens, ornaments are best avoided, unless appropriately chosen; for we have seen many structures of high pretension but ill suited to the genius of the places. It is true that our real ecclesiastical and military ruins are highly beautiful and impressive, but all effect is lost when they are imitated upon a small scale.

In our moist climate too, particularly in the marshy and fenny districts, grottoes and hermitages are worse than absurd—they become too often but the vestibule of the grave!

To those, however, who will have ornaments, and those so artificial as to be unlike any thing in the heavens or upon the earth, we shall beg leave to point out some cheap materials, from the use of which little else than time and patience are likely to be lost. These consist of glass-house and foundery cinders; of flints, broken pebbles, rough ores;

branches of trees and shrubs, dipped in boiling rosin, coloured with vermillion, or white lead, or lamp black, or yellow ochre.

To fix these in their places requires a strong cement, which may be cheaply formed of a mixture of four pounds of white rosin, double the quantity of bees-wax, a quantity of powdered stone, and a pound of flower of sulphur. These must be melted over a slow fire, and well kneaded together under warm water. When wanted for use, the cement must be warmed, and, if it can be done conveniently, the substance to be fixed up ought to be warmed also.

Should any of our readers wish for cheapness, taste, and elegance beyond this, we must recommend to them a rural walk from Whitechapel Turnpike towards Mile-end; where, with a little sedulous examination, they may perceive many ingenious specimens of human art, in the variegated arrangement of broken slates, glass bottles, tobacco pipes, laths, brickbats, &c. in spots of eighteen feet by six; where effects are produced by civic genius in retirement, with the aid of daffodils and perriwinkles, which would have been unthought of by a Capability Brown, or a Repton !

Economy, as well as botanical propriety, now leads us to a slight view of the

APIARY.

Bees and flowers seem to form an inseparable association in the mind. The transition, therefore, from the flower garden to the apiary is equally natural and agreeable. We do not, however, intend in this place to offer a treatise on the management of bee-hives; writers on that subject are numerous, such as Columella, Warden, Debraw, Thorley, Wildman, White, and others: but to impress on the minds of those who wish to increase their comforts, whilst varying their amusements, that the produce of bees is more profitable than the generality of persons may be inclined to imagine, and the time bestowed upon them is seldom uselessly employed. A French bishop being about to make his annual visitation, sent word to a certain curate, whose ecclesiastical benefice was extremely trifling, that he meant to dine with him, at the same time requesting that he would not put himself to any extraordinary expense. The curate promised to attend to the bishop's suggestion, but he did not keep his word, for he provided a most sumptuous entertainment. His Lordship was much surprised, but could not help censuring the conduct of the curate, observing, that it was ridiculous in a man whose circumstances were so narrow, to launch into expense, nay almost to dissipate his entire income in a single day. " Do not be uneasy on that score, my Lord," replied the curate; " for I assure you that what you now see is not the produce of my curacy, which I bestow exclusively upon the poor." " Then you have a patrimony, sir," said the bishop. " No, sir."— " You speak in riddles; how do you then do ?"— " My Lord, I have a convent of young damsels here, who do not let me want for any thing." " How! you have a convent! I did not know there was one in the neighbourhood. This is all very strange, very unaccountable, Mr. Curate." " You are jocular, my Lord."—" But come, sir, I entreat you that you would solve the enigma; I would fain see the convent."—" So you shall, my Lord, after dinner; and I promise you that your Lordship will be satisfied with my conduct." Accordingly when dinner was over, the curate con-

ducted the prelate to a large enclosure, entirely occupied by bee-hives, and pointing to the latter, observed—" This, my Lord, is the convent which
gave us our dinner; it brings me in about 1800
livres per annum, upon which I live very comfort-
ably, and with which I contrive to entertain my
guests genteely." The surprise and satisfaction of
the bishop at his discovery may readily be conceived.
The sequel of the story informs us, that afterwards,
whenever a curate made application to his Lordship for an improved living, he would only reply,
" Keep bees."

That this anecdote is not fanciful, may be veri-
fied by an experiment of little expense and certain
profit; especially if those who keep bee-hives will
be careful to let their bees have sufficient room for
their industry, in proportion to the fineness of the
season.

In favourable years, as for instance in 1809, a
single stock of bees has been found, by judicious
management in this respect, to produce 12 gallons,
or 96 pounds of honey, making, at the moderate
price of 1s. per pound, nearly a clear profit of five
pounds sterling. What a treasure to a poor family
would one such stock be, with the profits of it to
help them through a dreary winter! When it is considered likewise how cheap and innocent a luxury
may thus be extended, absolutely for nothing, to the
rosy smiling prattlers, that are always found in
clustering swarms around the cottage hearth, and
to whom a spoonful of honey on their brown bread
would be a delicious treat, surely we need not
exhort our female readers, at least, to attend to
this beautiful branch of domestic economy; particularly as they cannot contemplate the habits of the
little insects under their care, without seeing in

them their own most endearing virtues of obedience, industry, regularity, and cheerfulness set forth.

Bees are not only useful but ornamental: yet it must not be concealed, especially in a work on economy, that they are, in some instances, destructive to flower-gardens: not so much by robbing the flowers of their juices, as by the liberties they take with the favourites of the florist, who will often find the leaves of his rose-tree destroyed by these insects for the purpose of making their cells. This damage is, however, principally done by the wild bees, the common bee being the least destructive, or rather the greatest economist of the tribe; nor do all the species of the wild bee fly to flower gardens, to commit depredations, as the corn rose is, with them, a great favourite for their domestic uses.

The care attendant upon keeping bees never goes beyond the common amusement proceeding from a garden; and there is the less reason to feel alarm from them, in regard to children, inasmuch as the larger the bee, the more rough, fierce, and useless it is; wherefore the domestic bees are selected, where it can be done, small, oblong in shape, smooth, bright and shining; and, as an accurate observer may speedily notice, of a gentle mild disposition.

This appearance seems the most agreeable to the bees themselves; for the queen bee, which is always chosen by the others, may be easily distinguished by her small size and redness of colour, shining brilliantly in the sun's rays, and generally with wings only half the usual length.

Who, that is fond of contemplation, and has indulged it in rural retirement, but must recollect how much his feelings, whether of joy or sorrow, have been enlivened or softened by the hum of the bees, whilst proceeding to their morning labours, or retiring to their evening's rest!

Let your bee-hives, then, be adjuncts to your domestic rural economy, whether your residence may be rural or suburban. Place them in cheerful situations as early as the beginning of April, if the season is genial, and they will admit of three honey crops in the course of the summer. The first in May, the second in July, and the third about the commencement of September; but taking care, at this latest period, to leave sufficient food for their winter subsistence. Humanity alone will prompt to preserve them, not only in winter, but also when seeking their honey; for which purpose, a mode has been proposed, by having double hives, the one over the other, so that when the lower hive is full of honey, some is to be put into the upper, and a passage opened in the top of the lower hive, through which the insects may pass, when the lower one is to be removed. Midsummer is stated to be the best season for this change.

There is another mode, more rapid, but not quite so humane :—Late in the evening the full hive is removed from its stand, and turned on its top into an earthen crock; a new hive prepared and put over it (bottom to bottom) surrounded closely by a linen cloth, to prevent the escape of any of the bees; then, with long plants of ragweed, the bottom of the full hive is beaten fifteen or twenty minutes, as smartly and loudly as possible; after which, almost all the late inhabitants emigrate to the upper hive, which is immediately placed on the same stand from whence the other hive was taken, and these bees carefully fed with brown sugar for some days after; but as some bees unavoidably remain with their stores, who would

o

desperately sting and annoy the plunderers, unless
prevented, it therefore becomes expedient to turn
the full hive over a hole made for smothering this
remnant; but very few, after such a process, will
remain. In the operation, however, the brimstone
used discolours the combs, and affects the taste of
the honey.

It may therefore be more prudent to burn the
puff ball, which acts as a powerful narcotic; but
suffers the bees again to recover. In a word, bees
are very nimble at their work, and presently recruit
their loss.

> Full fifteen thousand bees one hive supplies,
> That try with novice-wings each year the skies:
> And what I know, incredible will seem,
> They are all the offspring of one fertile queen.
> This truth not ev'n the *Mantuan* poet knew,
> Who search'd with piercing eyes all nature thro'.
> Four days inanimate the eggs remain,
> And then begin the vital pow'r to gain;
> In a worm's shape the bee first strikes the eyes,
> And in that form, four days successive lies,
> While milky juice the embryo's food supplies.
> In the ninth day a perfect bee appears,
> And nature on it's feet the insect rears,
> Two little fluttering wings adorn each side,
> And soon it sprightly shines with glossy pride.
> These, free from envy, by their labours strive,
> Who shall enrich the most, the common hive.
>
> DIMSDALE.

Passing from the more ornamental, to the humbler domestic precincts, we approach the

POULTRY YARD,

and to the economical housewife, we here offer a few
hints, which, if she pleases, she may add to her
family receipt book.

An experiment has been tried of feeding geese with turnips, cut in small pieces like dice, but less in size, and put into a trough of water. With this food alone, the effect was, that six geese, each when lean weighing only nine pounds, actually gained twenty pounds each in about three weeks' fattening.

As common food for geese and turkies, malt is most excellent; but economy will point out the grains in preference, unless for immediate, and rapid fattening. It will be proper to boil the grains afresh.

When poultry do not fatten as rapidly as may be wished, without cooping, they have been fed with great success upon steamed potatoes, chopped small and mixed with water: the object of which was to induce them to eat, in order to procure the drink.

Other cheap articles for fattening, are oatmeal and treacle; barley meal and milk; boiled oats, and ground malt.

But to those who wish for excellent food, without regard to economy, we shall hint, that they may fatten their chickens with ground or pounded rice, scalded with milk and sweetened with sugar, and as thick as paste. Their drink must be beer, and the food given in small quantities during the day.

We are not friendly to the system of *cramming*; but those who choose, may adopt the system of the Sussex higglers, who go to a considerable expense in procuring the materials for the large gobbets forced down the throats of the unhappy animals.

These materials consist of ground oats, mixed up with suet minced small, and treacle; or else of a species of gruel composed of pot liquor, thickened with coarse oatmeal unsifted; to which milk, sugar, and pig's fat are added.

As it is of importance that hens should lay during the winter, an experiment to that effect may not be unworthy of notice. It is said that nettle-tops, gathered when going to seed, then dried and mixed up with a little broken hemp-seed and pollard in barley meal, and given in the proportion of two or three little pellets or balls daily throughout the autumn, will produce the desired effect. It is known indeed, that hens, judiciously fed, have laid upwards of two hundred eggs in a season.

It is the opinion of some, that round and short eggs produce males; but that long and sharp eggs contain the female chickens. This might, however, be very easily ascertained by placing a sufficient quantity of one shape, under a hen, and observing the result.

To guard the hen-roost against the depredations of foxes and other vermin, must depend upon local circumstances; one thing, however, we shall record, which is but little known, that tar, rubbed on the necks of young lambs or geese, will prevent the depredations of foxes among them; those wild animals having an unconquerable aversion to the smell of tar.

Though poultry have but two legs, yet rabbits with four, are sometimes introduced into the poultry-yard, as well as into the poulterers' shops in the metropolis. This is an economical plan; because they are easily bred and fed. Their best food is the shortest and sweetest hay; and their keep must be economical, when it is ascertained that, with a little care, one load of hay will serve two hundred couple of rabbits for a year.

Connected usefully with this department, is the

PIGGERY

This subject is, indeed, an humble one, but not the less deserving of economical notice. We shall not, however, detain our readers long at the sty-door; yet reminding them that pigs, like men, are fond of company at their meals, and will fatten much sooner, if kept, four or five in each sty, instead of being confined to the eating of their meal in imperial solitude. Let it be observed too, that a little antimony thrown amongst their food, twice or thrice a week, during the last weeks of their fattening, will promote that operation considerably.

Among many advantages that might result from growing Indian corn in this country, the favourable nature of it with regard to feeding pigs, may be mentioned; as a proof of which we can state, that a pig gained, by feeding on Indian corn, in the course of six weeks and three days, the enormous weight of fifteen stone.

We shall conclude with the following economical notice.

Fifty store pigs have been fed per day in the following cheap manner:—One bushel of potatoes, at 1s. 3d. have been boiled in a wash with as much meal of any description as could be bought in a common cheap year for 1s. 4d.; to which were added, 20 lbs. of clover hay at 10d. The coal to boil this wash was estimated at 3d. and attendance at 6d. forming a total of 4s. 2d. or about 1d. per head, from 3 months old up to any age. In the article of potatoes alone, this is a saving of 4-5ths in comparison with potatoes given in a raw state. Those who are most skilled in the delicacies of

" swine's flesh" will not willingly buy pigs that are fattened upon barley meal; giving the preference to those which have been fed on potatoes and milk, as possessing a much finer flavour, and likewise taking the salt more readily when cured.

It is not our wish to leave any part of domestic economy unexplored, to which we can add any useful hints deduced from modern discoveries, and not yet to be found in works written expressly upon those subjects; a motive which, we trust, will be a sufficient excuse for proceeding to the

FARM YARD.

Let not our fair readers turn with disgust from this homely subject—though, generally speaking, the province of male superintendence, and we write for both sexes—yet still may it be admitted as a point of consideration even in female domestic economy.

We shall, however, avoid any thing like a studied dissertation, contented simply to record a few passing facts, important to the economist, but which, as before observed, have not yet found their way into professed works upon the subject of agriculture—in short, such points as bear more particularly on the peculiar circumstances of the times, rather than the more elaborate investigation of scientific agricultural practice.

The first point then which we would recommend to well meaning economists, is to attempt the speedy diminution of the poors' rates, in their respective parishes, by finding as much manual occupation as possible for all sexes and ages of the industrious poor who are willing to work; and those who are not, deserve no further attention, except that which the laws apply to their specific cases of idleness and vagrancy.

If it were, indeed, proposed to bring all the kingdom under the spade husbandry, we should deprecate the plan as injudicious, or laugh at it as impossible; but still, when there is quiescent labour unemployed, it will be found a double saving to employ that labour in the spade husbandry and in the et ceteras of weeding, hoeing, &c. connected with it—nay a treble saving, since it will save poors' rates, afford a gain by the greater productiveness in proportion to the price paid, and save in the necessary keep of horses.

Several experiments, of this kind, have already been tried, so as fully to demonstrate its useful practicability; of which one will suffice, the result of the observations of a person who rents a whole parish in the West of England, and is a strictly practical and laborious farmer. Instead of horses he uses for his arable land, the three-tined fork, breast plough, and hand hoe; the spade being seldom used, except for old sward. He pronounces spade labour to be not only far better than that of the horse-plough, but even cheaper; and he invites (in the Farmers' Journal) farmers to go and examine his practice. This kind of hand labour has been done lately for a small farm as low as 24s. per acre.

In the manuring of land we may also notice a recent communication to a philosophical work, which mentions, that where lime is laid on the ground in small heaps, at a distance from water, it should slightly be covered with mould, and when rain comes, it will be reduced to as fine a powder as if water were immediately applied. Whereas, when it lies long in the small heaps, exposed to the sun and air, it tumbles down into gross particles, and does not incorporate with the soil, nor have the same effect in the decomposition of decayed vegetables as when applied in the flour. The expense of covering the small heaps with mould will not cost sixpence per acre.

In the, formerly very expensive, system of drainage, several economical observations have recently been brought before the public attention. We understand there are at this moment many thousands of acres of land in Essex, which are now draining, without straw, by digging the ditches in the usual manner, (after ploughing them) and placing at the bottom of the ditch a board, about one inch and a half in thickness on the lower edge, and two inches and a half at the upper edge; in breadth eight or nine inches, and in length about four feet, with two joints; this board fitting the ditch, the earth to be rammed upon it, and the board drawn out by a hook or short chain affixed to it. This method is practised with the utmost success at Old Sampford, and at Thaxted, in Suffolk. But where the soil does not admit of this particular mode being adopted, another may be substituted by a process by no means expensive; that is by tiles: first applied in Nottinghamshire, upon land the subsoil of which had a quick or running sand, mixed with clay, which frequently warped, or filled up the drains. The tile is first formed in a mould, and struck in the same manner as a common building tile: the length of the mould in the inside 13 inches, the width at the end ten and three quarters, made convex; at the other end six and three quarters concave. The clay being formed in this mould, was then wrapped on a round mould, the circumference of which was a quarter inch more than the width of the first mould, by which means a tile was made in the form of a frustum of a cone, with a small aperture on the side; the wide end of one tile being sufficient to admit the smaller end of another about one inch, so that when put in the drains, they form a pipe. The aperture is covered with a thin sod of turf, which keeps out the sand, and the water filters through it. In 1809, these tiles cost by contract thirty-eight shillings per thousand, being a moderate load for a waggon and four horses, and will lay about 300 yards.

To save corn, and to save time even, by always having straw ready for use, we must recommend the practice of thrashing out as early as possible, but still keeping the straw in stacks. Where that is not convenient, a very simple mode of preserving corn from vermin, when in the stack, has been practised in Ireland, with considerable success. The mode is to throw some fine sand between every two or three layings of the sheaves in making the stacks or ricks. This sand, if fine and dry, will absorb any little moisture that may be in the corn; and is so offensive to rats and mice that they will not live in it. The sand produces no inconvenience; always falling out when the corn comes under the flail.

From the corn stack we may proceed to notice a few recent economical discoveries in saving the grain when sown; an object both of direct saving and of ultimate profit: it has been ascertained in Pennsylvania, that the water in which potatoes are boiled, sprinkled over grain or plants, completely destroys all insects in every stage of existence, from the egg to the fly.

In some parts of France it is the practice to make use of tobacco, either green or in rolls, as a preservative against weevils. These animals, which are apparently liquorish, will come to the tobacco from all parts, and, as soon as they have eaten of it, they certainly die.

The mildew in wheat, now known to be produced by extremely minute insects, has been reently counteracted at a very small expence, by a mixture of the following ingredients: salt, one part—water eight parts. With this mixture, sprinkle the diseased corn. Where the corn is sown in drills, this may be done with a watering-pot; but the best and most expeditious mode is with a flat brush, such as white-washers use, having a tin collar made water-tight round the bottom, to prevent the mixture dripping down the operator's arm, and running to waste. The operator having a pail of salt and water in the one hand, and dipping the brush into the mixture with the other, makes his regular casts as when sowing corn broadcast. In this way he will readily get over ten acres in the day. About two hogsheads will do one acre: wherever the mixture touches, in three or four days the mildew will disappear; upon those parts that escape, the sprinkling must be repeated. If judiciously cast, the mixture falls in drops as uniformly as rain.

All these plans, however, proceed upon the principle of destruction; but we rather approve of Uncle Toby's conduct to the troublesome fly; and where we can, think it best " to live and let live," agreeable to the old adage. On this principle then we highly approve of a mode, recently adopted, to guard against the inconvenience produced by the turnip fly—a mode too, which, though apparently expensive on one trial, must, in a series of seasons, amount to a real saving, by the certainty which it gives of fair annual crops.

This little insect feeds on the first leaf, which is soft and smooth, and which shews itself in a very few days after sowing; but when the second or rough leaf appears, the flies either die, or remove in search of other food. Many ingenious contrivances have been invented to exterminate them, but their incalculable numbers and dexterous instinct of self-preservation always defend them. A Norfolk farmer, aware of the folly of systematically counteracting nature, sows more than double the quantity of turnip seed usually sown by others, or which could possibly come forward to a crop. At this extraordinary feast the flies are left undisturbed, and before the superfluous and otherwise useless vegetation can be consumed, the rough leaves appear, when they instantly emigrate to his neighbour's territories, with probably four or five generations of their families; where, if there be only an ordinary sowing for their support, they eat up the whole in a day, and leave the farmer nothing.

Much saving and great gain have frequently, of late, been loudly prophesied from the cultivation of various new plants, many of which have failed entirely, whilst others have turned out rather hurtful than otherwise. We shall, therefore, merely select one which has recently succeeded in experiment, and has been already described under the head of *kitchen garden*.

This is the Cæsarian Kale, a valuable and most excellent vegetable; for where the ground attached to the residence exceeds not the limits of an orchard, the Kale may there be planted amongst the potatoes, which a judicious economist will raise under his fruit trees, so as to be applicable to the feeding of a cow, from keeping of which useful animal many are deterred, even in the country, through the difficulty of procuring ground enough for summer food and winter fodder.

We write not for those who farm on a large scale; but may insert a hint on a subject that families, merely domestic, need not disdain to attend to, as a matter of saving and profit, where ground is not large enough to admit of farming for consumption, though considerable profit may be made by farming for seed. To enumerate all the useful and profitable seeds that may be raised on an acre or two, belongs properly to a work strictly agricultural; but we select, as an illustration of what may be done, from a recent philosophical work, some observations on the subject of harvesting French, Turkey, and Scarlet Beans. It has generally been supposed that they should hang on the haum, until they get dry, in order to procure good seed; which is a mistaken notion; as, in consequence, very little that has proved good has been saved of late years, the seasons having proved wet and frosty before they were thought sufficiently ripe. This difficulty may be easily obviated, by gathering the beans immediately as they begin to wither, or feel soft near the strig, or upper end of the pod, and harvesting them as the weather permits. By this practice much time will be saved, and the seed being then perfect, and free from the effects of severe weather, will vegetate sooner and stronger than any that may have been saved in the ordinary way.

The profits which may, in this instance only, result from well sowed seed in an inclement season will amply repay, that is on a fair proportion of time, expense, and labour, the economic experimentalist.

To such an experimentalist it will indeed be a source of additional gratification that his experiments, if they succeed, may be of considerable benefit to society in general, especially the poorer class. One instance in illustration of this will suffice, and we give it from the observations of an intelligent naval officer, retired upon a small farm in the West of England; and who, in order to provide better for the poor, in years of scarcity through bad harvests, tried many experiments on the parsnip and carrot root; and finds that they afford as nutritious a beverage as malt, if culti-

vated, and harvested in the following manner :—
Instead of the common method of sowing the seeds
in February and March, he proposes, for this purpose, to sow them from the beginning of June to
the middle of August ; and early in the following
summer to dig them up and harvest them, by first
splitting their roots from the crown for about three-
fourths of their length, and then hanging them on
lines, or laying them on straw, under cover in the
shade (in order to retain their volatile salts in as
high a state of perfection as possible), till they are
thoroughly dry. One acre of good ground will
produce about fifteen tons of either of these roots,
which, when divested of their tops and dried, will
weigh four tons and a half, these four tons and a
half will contain from 2,500 to 2,700 pounds of
fermentative saccharine extract. These roots, thus
harvested, are a most excellent and nutritious substitute for hay, in unfavourable seasons. In order
to use the dry roots for brewing they must be
ground, and treated in every respect as malt.

To this we will subjoin some remarks of an intelligent Leicestershire agriculturist, who raised
Indian corn in this country with considerable success, not only as to its growth, but in regard to its
economical qualities as food for cattle. Even in
our changeable climate it will grow many feet in
length ; the stems shooting upwards, from seven to
ten feet in height, with many joints casting off flag
leaves at every joint. Under these leaves, and
close to the stem, grows the corn, covered over by
many coats of sedgy leaves, and so closed in by
them to the stem, that it does not shew itself easily,
till there burst out at the end of the ear a number
of strings, that look like tufts of horse-hair ; at first
of a beautiful green and afterwards red or yellow.
The stem ends in a flower. The corn will ripen in

September; but the sun at that season not having strength enough to dry it, it must be laid upon racks, or thin open floors, in dry rooms, and frequently turned, to avoid moulding.

In the Southern States of North America, it ripens readily: but in the more northern ones, it is sometimes found expedient to leave it on the stalks until the frost sets in; which in a few days gives to the ears that dryness and hardness that fit them for harvesting, although not with that complete state of ripeness which warm climates produce.

As it is not a grain of frequent importation, some little description may be necessary. It is sufficient to say that the grains are about as big as peas, and adhere in regular rows round a white pithy substance, which forms the ear. An ear contains from two to four hundred grains, and is from six to ten inches in length. They are of various colours, blue, red, white, and yellow. The manner of gathering them is by cutting down the stems and breaking off the ears. The stems are as big as a man's wrist, and look like bamboo cane; and the pith is full of a juice that tastes as sweet as sugar. The joints are about a foot and a half distance. The encrease is upwards of five hundred fold. Upon a large scale, to save the expense of hilling, the seed may be drilled in alleys like peas; and to save digging, the ground may be ploughed and harrowed, which will answer very well. It will grow upon all kinds of land. The ears which grow upon dry sandy land are less, but harder and riper. The grain is taken from the husk by hand, and when ground upon French stones, makes an excellent flour; of which it yields much more, with less bran, than wheat does; and exceeds it for crust, pancakes, puddings, and all other uses except bread; but a sweetness peculiar to it, which in other cases makes it agreeable, is here nauseous. It is excellent for feeding poultry and hogs; and fattens both, better and sooner than peas or barley. The stems make better hedges for kitchen gardens than reeds do. It clears the ground from weeds, and makes a good season for any other kind of corn. It was the only bread-corn known in America when first discovered by the Spaniards, and is there called maize.

Even the meanest articles of nature's bounty ought not to be neglected; as with judicious care they may often be rendered both useful and profitable. The thistle, for instance, is here considered as a nuisance; which in truth it is, where land can be turned to any account: yet it is important to know that in Germany they are used as food for horses, first undergoing the process of being beaten in a sack until the prickles are destroyed; horses will then devour them greedily.

In corroboration of this we have seen some observations respecting the good effects of this food on a German cavalry regiment in the British service; the horses of which were brought from a very poor state into good condition in a short space of time.

With respect to the veterinary art in regard to farming, we leave it to the regular practitioners; but it is, nevertheless, of some importance to mention that as drought, by depriving almost all kinds of vegetables of their natural moisture, gives rise to complaints not epidemic, but endemic, which may be simply ranked among inflammatory diseases; &c.; the following treatment, the result of a long series of observation, and of the efficacy of which no doubt can be entertained, may be tried with certain success. To cattle attacked with disease, water,

whitened with barley-meal or fine bran, sharpened
by a little nitrate of potash, and slightly acidulated,
should be administered three or four times every
day; and as most of the diseases of ruminating animals have a tendency to putridity, although they live
entirely on vegetables, it is proper to put, evening
and morning, into their drink, a little vinegar, and
one glass of an infusion of aromatic plants, such as
wormwood, sage, rue, camomile, rosemary, angelica,
juniper-berries, &c. to each animal.

Care should also be taken to rub and exercise
them; but those barbarous scarifications which are
sometimes employed, should be avoided. A seton
may, however, be made in the dew-lap with black
hellebore or perriwinkle-leaf.

To the experimental farmer, even on the smallest
scale, we strongly recommend a perusal of the various works of Mr. Curwen on subjects of agriculture. To extract from these would far exceed our
limits, on this article, but with one observation we
shall close.

In consequence of a great deficiency of straw, a
year or two since, Mr. Curwen dried the stalks or
haums of his extensive crop of potatoes, and they are
stated to have made comfortable litter for the cattle:
—matter of the utmost importance in the management of the dairy, as the milk of a cow, well lodged,
will always be found much superior, both in quantity and in quality, to that of a neglected animal.
For this purpose, wherever the poor are allowed
plots of ground to raise potatoes, they ought to be
encouraged to save the haums, even when other
litter is not in scarcity. The habits of economy,
which this will encourage, are not to be overlooked
as considered with the saving.

As the *ferme orneé* has been long in fashion,
we can need no apology for uniting it with the

ORNAMENTAL GROUNDS,

as we cannot omit this department in domestic economy, were it only for the purpose of pointing out to our readers the propriety of rendering that which they adopt as an amusement, also useful to the country, and more particularly so to themselves.

Where quick growth is wanted, where the ground is circumscribed, and perhaps only leasehold, then indeed poplars, or mere shrubs of quick growth need alone be planted; but on freehold ground the case is far different.

In fact one would suppose that the advantage of extending the plantations, and of bringing into use a timber possessed of valuable properties, is obvious: it is not only the planter, but the country in general that will be benefited; as, at the same time that it reduces the extensive importation of foreign timber, which is at present necessary, it can scarcely fail of being the means of promoting industry at home, and by bringing both land and labour into use, which are at present idle, or producing nothing of real value, will contribute materially to the general welfare of the nation.

Such are the sentiments of a very ingenious essayist of the present day; to which we shall add a few, and but a very few practical hints, merely intending to prompt to further inquiry, on a subject so interesting, and ultimately so profitable.

Birch trees, we may say without any intention of hurting the feelings of our younger readers, can be applied, at an early age, to various useful purposes.

Beech trees also form the most delightful clumps, and woods for ornamental walks; especially as they do not destroy the plants below them, but actually give shade and support to many species interesting to the botanist. They also form lofty hedges, of a close texture even in winter, from their leaves remaining during great part of that season. The numerous uses for the wood render it valuable even to the branches; and the beech mast is excellent for the piggery. Nay it is said that the leaves collected in Autumn, are not only softer, but more wholesome than any other substance, except feathers, wool, or hair, for filling the bed cases of the poor.

Chesnut wood has recently been successfully applied to the purposes of dyeing and tanning; thus forming a substitute for logwood and oak bark. Leather, tanned by it, is declared by the gentlemen who made the experiments, to be superior to that tanned with oak bark; and in dyeing, its affinity for wool is said, on the same authority, to be greater than that of either galls or sumach, and consequently the colour given is more permanent. It also makes admirable ink.

But the *Larch tree* is perhaps the most profitable of any, when at the same time it cannot but be esteemed as highly ornamental.

Evelyn, and almost every writer on timber, since he published his *Silva*, has recommended planting larch; and it is truly surprising with what little effect, as it is well known to be a very durable timber, and the most profitable to the planter.

By experiments tried on larch trees, and reduced to fair calculation, it appears that those trees, on an average, increase nearly two cubic feet and an half, during every year of their growth; which, at the low rate of one shilling per foot, would be about half-a-crown per annum, for trees allowed to stand from thirty to fifty years.

The larch is also one of the quickest growing trees in this climate, whereas the slow growth of the oak, is almost proverbial. A larch tree was lately

cut down on his Grace the Duke of Athol's estate,
at Blair, which contained 252 cubic feet of timber;
the age of the tree 79 years: and larch trees of
60 years growth contain from 60 to 70 cubic feet
at a medium. From these facts it would be
easy to estimate the value of a plantation of larch
at the expiration of 60 years, as there ought to be
nearly 800 trees upon an acre at that period : and
in making this estimate, it must be recollected, that
larch does not require a rich soil, as it thrives best
on the sides of hills, and in barren and rugged
districts, where the land is of little or no value for
any other purpose.

The comparative value of larch and Scotch fir,
will not bear calculation. In 1800, a larch of fifty
years old, sold for twelve guineas; while a fir of
the same age, and in the same soil, brought fifteen
shillings. The larches are never broken by snow,
and very seldom torn up by winds, and then only
in single trees. Scotch firs are bad and shabby
growers, at about 800 feet of altitude. Larch
grows luxuriantly some hundred feet higher. Such
is the surprising fertilizing quality of the leaves or
spines of the larch, that in the course of between
twenty and thirty years, they convert the most
barren and rugged mountains, formerly not worth
ninepence per acre, into an herbage worth from ten
to fifteen shillings per acre.

Larch trees may be planted much nearer to one
another than oak; and consequently a greater number may be grown upon an acre: the successive
thinnings will soon more than repay the expenses
attending the planting, inclosing, and repairing the
fences.

It is necessary to state, that there are three species
of timber trees called larch; viz. the *pinus laria*,
or white larch; the *pinus pendula*, or black larch;

and the *pinus microcarpa*, or red larch; but the preceding observations apply to the *pinus larix*, or white larch only, which was originally brought from Italy.

It appears by experiments, carefully tried, that larch is superior to oak in stiffness, strength, and lightness; and also in the power of resisting a body in motion (called resilience), and it is inferior to Memel or Riga timber in stiffness only.

The wood of the larch is well calculated for ship timber, and would make excellent masts, as it is peculiarly fitted to withstand the effect of sudden gusts of wind; it is preferable to oak for most of the purposes of architecture and engineering. It makes excellent floors, when properly seasoned; and the best steps for stair-cases, because it wears well, and is not liable to splinter at the nosings. It has been used by the Duke of Athol for boats and mill-axles, and found to answer better than any other wood.

Among the various species of timber-trees, there are not many that are calculated for ship-building and domestic purposes: and when we are limited to those that will thrive well in this country, we may venture to say, that there are not more than two kinds that are generally useful; the others are either of short durability, or are durable under particular circumstances only, and therefore not eligible for extensive plantations, though highly valuable for particular purposes.

Larch bark is coming gradually to be used for the same purposes as oak bark, and considerable purchases of it have recently been made for tanning. In particular, it may be mentioned, that his Grace the Duke of Athol has sold one hundred tons of larch bark, at ten pounds per ton.

It appears by experiments, instituted on a large scale, for the express purpose of estimating the relative value of the bark of larch, (*larix pyramidalis*) to that of oak, that the results were as follow :—1. Of equal weights and quantities of skins, prepared in precisely similar methods, by means of oak and larch bark, the larch tanned specimens were found to be specifically heavier than those prepared by the oak bark. 2. The colour of the larch tanned leather is a light fawn, while that of the oak tanned is of a deep brown. In respect of durability, the great test of the utility of leather, specimens of both kinds were submitted to actual experiments in shoe soles, and found to be equally lasting.

If it were necessary to shew the advantages that may result from a little attention to the care and preparation of ornamental grounds, we could readily do so, by a reference to the exertions of an amiable clergyman, recently deceased, which might serve as an useful example to many of his brethren. This was the late Rev. William Smith, rector of Kingswinford, near Dudley, but in early life rector of Bideford, where his praiseworthy conduct is still gratefully remembered. At that place, the parsonage is situated on an eminence, at a considerable distance from the church, and commands a most extensive prospect; but it was, till that time, only a mean dwelling, surrounded by stone quarries, and altogether presenting a scene rather repulsive than attractive; and what was worse, from its elevation and proximity to the ocean, it seemed to bid defiance to improvement. Notwithstanding all this, such was the energy of the new possessor, and so correct was his judgment, that he overcame every difficulty; and, in comparatively a short time, converted a bleak and cheerless desart into a little paradise. By introducing a vast number of hardy shrubs, to spots where they were likely to resist the rough blast and the sea air, he contrived to provide an ample shelter for those of a more tender character; and by cutting out walks through the irregular grounds, and skirting them with a variety of the most simple but pleasing plants, common to that neighbourhood, he gave a picturesque beauty to what had been hitherto a wild and disgusting waste.

With one or two slight observations we shall now conclude.

It has been said that sheep are the best gardeners; and it is true that sheep-feeding will keep the grass-walks and lawns as smooth and even as the scythe; with the advantage, too, that nothing is allowed to go to waste, as is the case with the short cut grass. But where the flower parterres are too beautiful to be exposed to sheep, the scythe must be used, and its produce may be disposed off to very great advantage; provided care is taken to plant all the produce of the kitchen garden in regular rows or drills, between which, trenches may be dug from time to time, and filled up with the short grass, over which the earth ought again to be thrown.

Thus, in the course of a few weeks, a large garden may be managed so as to contain between its rows a considerable supply of new vegetable manure of the best quality; and which will be in full activity even on the hoeing and earthing up of that season; imparting rapid vegetation, and an improved flavour to the various plants and productions.

The preservation of paling is always an object of economy. One mode of preserving iron is simple and efficacious. Boil eight pounds of hog's fat, cut very small, in a glazed pot or pipkin, with three or four spoonfuls of water; when well melted, strain it through coarse linen or cerecloth, then set it on a slow fire, with four ounces of camphor broken small, allowing it to boil gently. Take it off, and whilst hot, mix with it as much black-lead as will give it colour and consistence, and lay it on hot. This will not only preserve the iron in the atmosphere, but also whatever portion may be in the ground.

For the preservation of rails and pales, another process, equally cheap and simple, may be pursued.

Take three parts of slaked lime, two parts of wood-ashes, and one of fine sand. Sift the whole, and add as much linseed oil as is necessary to bring it to the consistence of thick paint. The more intimately it is beaten and mixed, in the preparation, the more serviceable it will be; and only two coats will be required: the first laid on of a thin consistence, so as more readily to enter into all the irregularities of surface in the wood, and the other of the thickest consistence; when the whole will be impermeable to water, and equally capable of resisting the action of the sun or weather; becoming, in fact, more hardened or durable from exposure.

Intimately connected with this department, where fortune favours the practical economist, is the

CONSERVATORY,

which, with a little judgment, may be made useful as well as amusing. Indeed, we cannot too often repeat that, the elegancies of domestic life are as compatible with domestic economy, as with the most extended fortune.

'Tis not so much the wealth that can purchase, as the taste that can arrange, and the prudence that can regulate, which justify many things not absolutely necessary, and apparently expensive. In fact, when the pecuniary means of an individual, or of a family, are so far beyond the limits of penury, or of supplying the absolute necessaries of life, that a little time is left at leisure, and a little money is floating in the pocket, not so small as to be husbanded for the expenditure of the morrow, nor so large as to become an object of thrifty saving and preservation—in short, in that state which is vulgarly called "burning a hole in the pocket," then is it an essential point of future economy, as well as of present usefulness, to give the expenditure of those small sums such a bias as will still preserve them in some actual shape; forming a basis for future expenditure of the same kind, yet not so imperative as to render future expense absolutely necessary, nor fulfilling the old proverb "that one expense makes many."

A system of this kind, so managed as not to interfere with a due attention to prudent accumulation, becomes indeed a preservative against useless or vicious expenses. He that has a little money, which he *will* lay out, rather perhaps from want of a wish to keep it, than from any strong momentary impulse, may, notwithstanding, meet with temptations to expenditure of a nature from which nothing will remain except regret, chagrin, perhaps remorse; and will soon find this habit grow upon him, his prudence and forethought diminishing as his habit increases : whilst he who wisely commences his *useless* or extra expenditure, (an expenditure which every individual has more or less,) with objects of rational amusement, though not of absolute immediate utility, will find his prudence and forethought improve with his progressive expenditure; with this very important difference,

that, in the first instance, his cash is gone, and
" like the baseless fabric of a vision, left not a
wreck behind ;" whilst, in the latter, he will have
something to shew for his money—and the grand
secret is to render that something at least *ornamental*, even though it claims not the epithet of *useful*.

As our aim, however, is Economy, let us not be
misunderstood, as advocating frivolous or imprudent
expenditure—like canal projectors, our wish is to
retain the otherwise waste waters in a proper reservoir; not only because they may at some future
period be useful, but in order to prevent their unlimited overflow from damaging the adjacent lands.
We advocate not the expenditure of a single penny
that *can* and *will* be saved for accumulation. We
are aware that no man, however great his fortune,
can *feel himself* rich, unless his expenditure is within
that which he may otherwise prudently expend;
and we know that the poorest individual *will feel* a
sense of riches and independence, the moment that
he has so balanced his necessary expenditure, as to
save a trifle, however small, out of his certain means.

We cannot illustrate this particular feeling better
than by an old, homely, gossipping story of a man
who kept his accounts so accurately as to balance
them at Christmas even to a shilling. On one occasion, upon a careful calculation, he found that, after
every allowance, his expenditure had exceeded his
income to the amount of twelve pence sterling!
This was to him a matter of serious regret. He
looked round his fireside and noticed a recent addition to it on the mother's knee, which made him look
rather grave ; but, turning up his eyes towards
Heaven, he happened fortunately to cast them up
the chimney, where he espied a flitch of bacon that
had unwittingly been omitted in his inventory of
stock in hand, a sight which instantly drew a balance

in his favour; and, like the famous Dunmow flitch of old, if not the reward, was at least the harbinger of domestic peace and content!

But, apropos! we had lost sight of the *Conservatory*, though not of the principles on which we wish to recommend the adoption of such an elegant domestic arrangement to such as, on these principles, can afford it—for its erection and general management, we must, indeed, refer to the various works that have appeared upon the subject; our object is merely to offer a few hints, which, if adhered to, will enable economy to associate with apparent expensive gratification.

To begin then with Conservatories on the smallest scale, these may be used solely for the temporary protection of spring flowers that naturally blow from February to May; but are too often exposed to blighting weather, and to harsh winds that nip them in the bud, whilst in the humblest conservatory they will expand with vigour.

This refers to mere shelter; but when a house is warmed by air flues, or where a flue can be conveniently carried from the parlour or kitchen fire-place to the little conservatory, then it may be made conducive to an earlier display of the productions of nature.

Conservatories may be fitted on such a plan as to be merely temporary; but it will certainly be much better, where occupancy is likely to be permanent, to commence on such a scale and on such a plan that future enlargement shall be practicable at the smallest expence.

This must indeed depend upon local circumstances, which taste and ingenuity will know how to regulate; one rule however we recommend, whenever practicable, to make the conservatory adjacent to the usual morning sitting-room, with an imme-

diate communication. A slight glazed shed, run
up in this manner from a parlour-window, will
relieve much of the trouble and attention required
for the management and preservation of bough-pots;
and may be rendered conducive to elegant gratification, even though it should only give shelter to
flowers already plucked from the parent stalk.
Under the head of *Dressing-Room*, this branch of the
subject has already been particularly noticed; we
shall content ourselves in this place by giving publicity to a simple process, by which the lovers of
flowers will be enabled to prolong the enjoyment of
their short-lived beauty for a considerable period.
For this purpose, it is merely necessary to place the
faded flowers in scalding water, deep enough to cover
about one-third of the length of the stem; by the
time the water has become cool the flowers will be
found erect and fresh; then cut off the shrivelled
end of the stems, and put them in cold water.

In some situations, conservatories become a har-
bour for flies and other troublesome insects, which
are not only a general nuisance, but also particularly destructive of every species of flowers.

It is an old saying, indeed, " that all trades must
live;" and so must we say of all animals, even insects; which, notwithstanding their destructiveness,
are always beneficial. We therefore would rather
advocate, and point out, as far as we can, an economy of life upon uncle Toby's principle, that
there is room enough in the world for all of us;
teaching not to destroy, but merely to remove whatever is particularly troublesome, whenever absolute
and actual necessity do not justify the cessation of
existence.

Various recipes have been given by various
authors for waging mortal war upon insects of all
kinds; but those, who prefer serving them with an

ejectment, will have recourse to the more lenient method of concentrating tobacco smoke for a few minutes in their Conservatory, and then opening the sashes to permit them to escape from a vapour always unpleasant to them, and fatal indeed if applied in excess.

A cheap method of forming conservatories will suffice as a conclusion to these short hints; and here we shall recommend a mode for which a patent has recently been obtained, and which deserves adoption.

The patentee's method, which he denominates perforated shield-glazing, consists in uniting panes of crown or common glass, previously cut out in the shape of shields on coats of arms, which he causes to lap over one another in the manner of fish scales, in frames of metal or wood. Instead of common putty he unites the panes with a cement, on which the action of air, water, and frost has but little if any effect; leaving an aperture at the base of the shield, so that the condensed steam or water may pass off, which in the common manner of glazing falls upon the plants to their great injury. By this shape and method of shield-glazing the lap-over of the glass becomes an inclined line; and the cement, being furrowed out on the under side, forms a channel for the condensed water to escape between the laps of the glass, without freezing, as is the case in the common method of glazing, which is very destructive to the glass, and occasions a very heavy annual expense for repairs.

From the conservatory to the

HOT-HOUSE

is but a step, even in general practice. Let not our readers start to find this head introduced in a

treatise professedly economical. On the new principles of the application of artificial heat, a green-
house may be rendered a hot-house at an expense
scarcely worth mentioning; and, if not upon a
very large scale, not only a green-house, but even
hot-beds may be kept at a proper degree of warmth
solely by that surplus of culinary heat, which is lost
or expended uselessly in old kitchen fire grates,
with the trifling additional expense of keeping a
small fire burning through the night.

The plan is to construct steam pits for the purpose of forcing all hot bed plants, from the cucumber to the pine apple. These are to be filled with
earth instead of tan, and to be heated by passing a
perforation steam pipe through a reservoir of water,
occupying the whole space below the pit. The
water, thus heated, communicates its heat to the
earth above, through perforated planks, raising it
to a high temperature, and actually retaining its
own heat for some days without fire.

. The application of this practice to the green-
house and hot-house, is too simple to require explanation beyond a mere hint.

Where expense is not absolutely an object, it
has been recently proposed to make such improvements in hot-houses as will meet every idea of
beauty, variety, or elegance of form; and satisfy
the most sanguine expectations in respect to durability, and the admission of light. The funda-
mental source of both these improvements is a
solid iron sash bar of great strength and elegance,
and which admits of being bent in every direction
without diminishing, but rather increasing its
strength.

It is contended that the leading advantages which
a solid wrought iron sash-bar or astragal possesses

not only over wooden ones, but over every other species of bars hitherto used, either for windows, sky-lights, or hot-houses, are manifold.

They admit of being bent in every direction without diminishing their strength; hence in hot-houses they offer every possible variety and beauty of shape.

They may be made of any required magnitude; and this without the use of rafters, but merely by the position and curve of the bar, or in some cases by an increase in its dimensions.

They admit of more light. The best constructed wooden hot-house roofs, render one-third of the roof opaque; the best metallic sashes and iron rafters from one-fourth to one-sixth; but these not more than one-tenth, the panes of glass being supposed of the same size in the three cases.

They are of greater durability, and occasion less breakage of glass. Iron bars composed of two parts, as fillets inserted in a grooved head or astragal, are liable to be corroded by moisture when they separate, and thus break the glass. Copper, tin, and iron, and all compound bars in that way, soon have their parts separated by oxidization in the grooves of junction. But these are solid, and therefore not liable to the same process of destruction. They can merely rust on the surface, when the coating of tin or paint decays.

With all these advantages they are less expensive than copper or any other iron or metallic bar whatever; in some cases coming cheaper than wood, and in general cases not exceeding the price of a hot-house roof formed of rafters and bars of that material.

It is urged by the inventor, that we may render glass roofs expressive of ideas of a higher and more appropriate kind, than those which are suggested by mere sheds, or a glazed arcade.

He says, imagine, instead of a row of glazed sheds, a row of detached sections of spherical bodies of an almost perfect transparence—the genial climate and highly coloured productions within, obtaining, during the whole day, the unobstructed influence of the sun's rays, and the construction of the edifice combining the greatest strength and durability—what will be the expression?—Instead of the usual conservatories attached to mansions, imagine a lofty arched roof wholly transparent; and joined to it, according to the magnitude and style of the mansion, globular projections, elevated circular towers, surmounted by Eastern domes of glass, or other beautiful or characteristic forms, all transparent and of permanent duration. Will not this substitution of new forms and almost perfect transparence be an improvement, gratifying both to the man of taste and the horticulturist?

It is true, that these ideas apply only to extensive establishments; but, if they are correct, it shews that an increase of elegance is by no means incompatible with increased economy: and on this principle we notice another observation, where it is asked—ought not such scenes as exhibit the various fruits and flowers of the torrid zone, and support the gaiety and beauty of spring and summer amidst the frigid scenes of winter to be appended to the mansion, or at least appropriated to the more elegant parts of a residence? It is true, numerous attempts have been made to do this in those architectural conservatories so frequently joined to mansions; and to render them tolerable for this purpose, the *shed-like* appearance has been disguised by stone piers and parapet walls. But the construction of

such buildings is radically bad; for in proportion
as they are dignified by architectural forms, in the
same ratio will the plants, to be inclosed, suffer from
the want of the light excluded by the masonry.
The state of plants which have passed the winter
in such conservatories proves this.

But it must also be remembered, that this proposed improvement is capable of being introduced
upon the most economical plan, as independent of
the curvilinear designs in which the above advantages are only to be obtained to their fullest extent,
these bars are applicable, with advantages superior
to all other bars, to every description of common
hot-house or hot-bed sashes; which may either be
entirely formed of this article, or wooden frames
may be fitted in with it at less expence than with
any other material equally durable.

To render the hot-house even more useful than
in its general purposes, the

AVIARY

may easily be connected with it; for though we
certainly are no friends to slavery, even of birds,
yet, as the passion for domesticating these little
creatures exists so universally, we feel anxious, like
the moderate advocates for the Slave Trade aboli-
tion, to improve the lot of the confined, if we
cannot impart to them the perfect freedom of
nature.

For this purpose, whenever pecuniary means and
space will admit of it, we recommend that bird-
cages shall be superseded by an AVIARY, not only
to contain specimens of each kind, but also both
the sexes in each class, whether Goldfinches, Lin-
nets, Thrushes, or Canary Birds. Birds, that will
not breed in cages, may do so in a less confined

state; and even if they do not, yet there is still a charm in society of which we ought not needlessly to deprive them. It is true, indeed, that the sexes of most of the several species of singing birds do not appear to adopt particular association, except in the genial months of Spring and early Summer; but as we are certain that in some species of the feathered race, as the Nightingale, the Dove, and the Pigeon, the sexual attachment is constant, so is it possible that in the other species there may be a more continued attachment than we are aware of. At one season of the year we know there is a personal choice; and that feeling may operate throughout the year, though in a less degree, and unnoticed by ornithologists.

Canary birds, in particular, breed three or four times a year; and the females of that class, as well as some others, will sometimes commence the formation of a second nest before the first brood are fledged.

An Aviary ought always to be turfed, if possible; and there ought to be a ready access to lime; especially for Canary birds. It ought also to be supplied repeatedly with chick-weed, groundsell, and various other wild herbs, that are green and pleasant, either in leaf, or in flower, or in seed; and the garden must supply lettuces, rape-seed, &c.

To enable them to build their nests, let there always be a supply of hay, or soft dried grass, with cotton, wool, the refuse of silk, hair, &c. Hang these up in little nets in various parts of the Aviary, or immediately outside of the wires, so that the birds may gather them as an employment; and then there will be no waste, whilst the little prisoners will be amused and occupied, in the way most congenial to their natural feelings.

Where the Aviary can be placed in a conservatory or green-house, it will add much to the comfort of the birds, inasmuch as it will take off something of the appearance of confinement, especially if the plants are trained to twine in and about the wires: or it may be fixed so as to contain growing plants and shrubs, on the natural turf, with glass frames so fitted as to cover the wires, when necessary, and to screen the little captives from the inclemency of the weather.

Those who wish to enjoy the melody of their little prisoners, in the room they are in the habit of occupying, may easily do so by opening a communication through one of the windows into a large cage or compartment, which may occupy a certain space of the interior. In winter, particularly, this will be an improvement, as the birds will then be enabled to partake of the artificial warmth of the apartment, whilst the utmost cleanliness may still be preserved by a little judicious arrangement.

Having thus gone over the general ground of the usual domestic precincts, we may now extend our walk, and take a view of such

IMPROVEMENTS

as are facile for the practical economist.

To enter at large upon the general system of improvements in country residences, and upon landed estates, is not exactly, indeed, within the province of a work of this kind; nor could it well be addressed to any but a small portion of our readers. But there are, nevertheless, some points that refer so particularly to the domestic economy of even small country establishments, that we should deviate from our plan, were we to omit them entirely.

The exterior and interior of the mansion, the

gardens, orchard, &c. being fully noticed in other
sections, we come now to the enclosures, beginning
with the *Iron railing*, which surrounds, or fronts
so many rural residences of metropolitan vicinity.

To preserve these in a handsome state, and at a
cheap rate, it will be sufficient in spring-time to
give them a coating of pitch and tar, in equal quantities, melted and thickened with common soot.
This coating suffered to dry, and then well rubbed,
will keep them in good order during the year;
and, from its not scaling off so readily as paint,
will at all times act as a more powerful preservative against the effects of weather.

In more extensive grounds, the *Paling* becomes
an object of some consideration. To preserve
this effectually, and cheaply, take any quantity of
air-slaked lime, adding two thirds wood ashes, and
one part of fine sand. Mix them well, and sift
them; and add as much linseed oil as will bring
them to the consistency of paint. To grind them
on a slab like paint will be best; but a common
mixing, if carefully done, will suffice. If any specific colour is wished for, some cheap ochre may
be added; and two coats, for the first season, will
be found sufficient, adding a fresh coat every
spring .

When *Hedges* can be well attended to, they
always look better, in small grounds, than paling;
but they require more time to be efficient. In
some instances, indeed, in the vicinity of town, we
have seen old hedges grubbed up, and paling substituted; but a little care would have rendered
this expense unnecessary. Even in twelve months
an old hedge may be made useful, if care is taken
to put down stakes at five or six feet distance;
encouraging the branches to shoot horizontally, but
not to cut the heads off, simply cutting away the

old wood, thereby giving more room, air, and, in general, more vegetable nourishment, to the younger branches.

It is sometimes difficult, indeed, to preserve these hedge-stakes from nocturnal depredators; but a whimsical means, once tried with success, may be used to prevent these petty thefts.

A gentleman, suffering much from this nightly pilfering, took up all his hedge-stakes, and bored holes in them, which he filled up with gunpowder, pegging up the holes firmly, and then replacing the stakes. As the thefts merely took place for culinary purposes, the consequences were found so destructive to the domestic economy of the pilferers, that, in a short time, the remedy was found completely efficacious.

Even on a small scale of improvement, *Planting* will be found not unprofitable; but where the grounds are so small, that every portion of verdure is valuable, it will be best not to plant too many trees to overshadow the grass, particularly *ashes*, as that species of tree not only impoverishes the ground, by its wide spreading roots, but also injures both the grass and the hedge, by the droppings from its branches.

Where ground is so very moist as to be comparatively useless, without draining, and that too at a cost much beyond any possible profit or convenience, a great saving of present and of future expense, together with a considerable future profit, may be derived from planting it at once with willows or oziers; which may be planted very close, and, in a very few years, by their annual cuttings, will be found to pay a very handsome rent.

This may be put in practice in very small portions of land; but on a more extensive scale, *alder* will be found lucrative in planting upon waste grounds, as it is, when full-grown, in great request for various purposes in machinery, and also for water-pipes, though perhaps less so now, since the introduction of those of cast iron. Its bark also will pay well, as it is much used for dying cotton black.

We have heard of a gentleman, whose lands were more extensive than fertile, whose practice it was to plant 1500 trees, on the birth of every daughter, upon his waste grounds, which were, on an average, worth one pound each on her coming of age ; thus enabling him to give her a fortune of 1000*l.* without any extraordinary economy on his part, the regular thinning of the trees, at proper seasons, with barking, &c. paying off all the current expenses, besides yielding him a small rent for the land.

This, however, was when 1000*l* was thought a larger sum for a daughter's fortune than at present; but we shall here state some experiments of a later date, that sufficiently manifest how much planting of trees, even upon small portions of land, is connected with domestic economy.

In the year 1758, ninety-two fir trees were planted upon a piece of ground, about three-quarters of an acre in extent. The land was waste, and poor ; no extra expense was incurred, and no further attention was paid to the young trees. In 1813, they were cut down, and yielded ninety tons of timber, then worth 4*l.* per ton, giving a round sum of 360*l.* which was equal to a rent of 6*l.* 10*s.* during the intervening 55 years.

Can a more convincing proof be given of the facility with which a man may save a fortune for his grand-children ? It is indeed, long to look forward; but who is there that does not look so forward? Who is there that does not extend his family hopes much beyond that period?

In Yorkshire, very recently, 5000 oaks were cut down, which yielded the sum of 100,000*l.*; and, as recently, in Somersetshire, the timber of an estate of 2000 acres, was refused to an offer of 50,000*l.* Even in Scotland, a piece of ground, not worth 30*s.* per acre, for agricultural purposes, was planted with sycamores, and at the end of sixty years the trees fetched such a sum as paid 14*l.* per acre per annum during that long period.

There are ways, however, of making land, apparently fit for nothing else but planting, yield even an immediate profit, by a very simple process; for it has been ascertained, that a pound of turnip-seed sown (after harvest) upon an acre of light, sandy, and even gravelly land, which had been worn out by overploughing, and ploughed in after two months growth, leaves, roots, &c. had as fertilizing an effect as could have been produced by 25 loads of manure upon that quantity of land. The practice, we believe, has not been uncommon in some parts of Surrey.

Many families are deterred from settling in retired parts of the country, from the inconvenient intercourse with the great post roads; and, in general, nothing can be done in the way of improvement, except under the exertions of some spirited individual, who is, unhappily, often checked in his plans by the difficulty of procuring good and cheap materials, for the purpose of making or mending the lines of communication.

Therefore, and speaking in general, as few things contribute more to the pleasure and prosperity of the country than good roads, we shall here make public the great advantage which may be derived from making the roads with bricks. This is of great consequence to be known, in low tracts of clay and loam, where stones and other materials cannot be obtained: but these can be most strongly recommended from trial on a private road; they never cut through, and they resist every thing. The road was partly made with old broken bricks, and was always firmer in that part, than that which was made of stone. Bricks are allowed to be burned for the use of roads duty-free; only observing to make them of such a shape that they cannot be used for any other purpose. If they were made much thinner than usual, they would be still harder and better. Should fuel also be scarce, as well as stones, even this difficulty may be removed, by planting a few acres, in each parish, with willow, alder, and the Canada poplar: these would yield most abundant crops of faggot-wood every third year, and would answer extremely well to the landlord and the tenant;—but ash would be still better to plant for this purpose.

Where roads have already been made, but are become almost impassable in winter, in consequence of there being nothing but a loose friable gravel to repair them with, a very simple mode of repair presents itself. We must take advantage of dry weather in May to rail off one-half of the road, and having carefully scraped off the whole of the dirt down to the hard road, then cover it with stones, broken very small; six or eight inches thick. Over these let the strongest stone-lime mortar be poured in a fluid state, and the stones covered in every part four inches deep with it, laying the surface properly rounding, and as even and smooth as possible. The mortar should be made with the coarsest sand, or rather pulverized stones or bricks. Let nothing pass over the road till it is completely dry

throughout, then let the other half of the road be
finished in the same way. This once properly
done, would be done almost for ever.

It is also worthy of notice, as it has been ascertained by experiment, that three loads of riddled
gravel will be more efficacious in repairing roads
than six loads of unriddled; and, of consequence,
a saving of one-half in cartage must instantly ensue.

It will be a most important consideration for all
landholders, whether on a large or small scale, so
to manage their improvements, as to give employment to their own immediate poor. The saving
in poors' rates will speedily recompense them for
this judicious care; on this subject, however, we
shall treat more at large under a separate head,
and therefore now leave the point for future discussion.

SECTION VII.

GENERAL OBSERVATIONS.

DOMESTIC ACCIDENTS — *Fires—Foul Air — Wells —
Cellars — Drowning — Suffocation — Insects, &c.*
TRAVELLING—*Short Hints.* POOR—*Economy—Industry—How to be encouraged—Useful and efficacious modes of Employment, &c. &c. &c.*

DOMESTIC ACCIDENTS.

THE " Economy of Human Life," as it may
literally be called, presses upon our attention some
little notice of *Domestic Accidents,* and of the best
means to counteract them; rather, however, to collect into one focus all the practical and novel floating information upon the subject, and thus bring it
usefully before general readers, than to examine
elaborately its extensive principles.

If the projectors of non-inflammable houses had
succeeded in their plans, these cautions would indeed have formed a work of unnecessary reference;
but we fear there is little practicability in the various
modes proposed, not of guarding against or check-

ing fires, but of using materials which shall not
burn when exposed to accidental ignition.

It is a difficult thing to get over inveterate habit,
even in the commonest concerns of life; but it is also
a subject worthy of remark that in countries, whose
climate requires most artificial domestic heat, the
mode of erecting habitations is more dangerous
than in warmer climates. In the north of Europe,
a great proportion of the houses are composed entirely of wood. In England even, there are inflammable materials used which might be well dis-
pensed with, without finding proper substitutes
more expensive. But in Italy, Spain. &c. where a
fire in the family apartment is unthought of, and
where even the kitchen fire seldom exceeds a little
charcoal in an earthen pan, there we find staircases of stone, door and window frames of the same
material, the floors laid with brick or tile, the
walls unincumbered with wainscotting, and the furniture so scanty, that it might be all burnt in one
room, without rendering insurance necessary.

It is true that, in England, the adoption of such a
mode of domestic comfort, or rather of discomfort,
will meet with few advocates; yet where non-inflammable materials can be used with propriety, a
saving will ensue, without reference to absolute
destructive accidents. Stone staircases, for instance,
might be more generally adopted, even in second
and third rate houses; and, though our chamber
floors must still be of wood, and perhaps the larger
beams, yet it would not only be practicable but
economical to introduce one iron beam into each
floor, with several smaller for rafters; an arrangement which would not only protract the falling in
of floors, thus giving more time to the inmates to
escape, but would also be a preservative against

accidents where the dry rot has destroyed the strength of the timbers.

It may be noticed also that some species of timber are not so susceptible of ignition as others. Poplar, for instance, does not burn readily; and, though it may not grow to a very useful size in this country, might be imported with facility from the northern ports of Italy.

In trying experiments upon a small scale, it has been ascertained that wood, if soaked in a strong solution of alum, will not ignite readily; and, when ignited, it emits no flame. This is an observation of some importance, when we contemplate the quantity of fir timber introduced into modern erections, as if building fire-ships instead of habitable dwellings. There is a wide distinction between wood, so saturated with alum as only to acquire a red heat that merely affects objects in immediate contact, and fir deal, so saturated with turpentine that its blaze will extend across our widest streets.

In the absence, however, of absolute existing preservatives, the best safeguard is caution; next to which are the ready means of arresting a fire in its progress, and finally of escaping when all further exertion becomes useless.

As to the means of arresting fire in its progress, it may be useful to observe that, when it merely breaks out in a chimney, there is no cause for extravagant alarm, especially if there is no wood work immediately connected with it. In such a case merely stopping up the vent, taking care to do so with substances not easily inflammable; or applying even inflammable substances in such a way that they will answer the purpose intended without catching fire, will generally be found, if conducted with patience, to answer every necessary purpose; but if doors and windows are thrown open, whilst the inmates run about wringing their hands, or merely calling out for that assistance which they themselves ought coolly to afford, then, indeed, it will be fortunate if the house is insured, and the sooner those, who are in, get out of it, the better.

Perhaps one of the best artifical modes of securing presence of mind upon these occasions, is to have previously ascertained the safest and readiest means of escape, when escape becomes absolutely necessary; added to which, we may adopt the invariable practice of having the window seats of all upper rooms fitted up as boxes, to contain either a rope-ladder, or even a knotted rope. Nay it might be judicious to have a knotted rope, and also a ladder, fitted to the same window; by which means, whilst females descend by the ladder, one of their male friends might descend by the rope at the same time, thereby affording them both courage and assistance.

But where these means are not at hand; and fire ladders cannot be brought in sufficient time, it has been very judiciously suggested, in order to guard against accidents in jumping from windows, that a large feather bed or hair mattress should accompany every fire engine: or two or more mattresses might be so contrived as to be made into one in the space of a minute by two expert persons. Hair deserves a preference for this purpose to other materials, both on account of its elasticity and durability; for such a mattress, if provided with a stout linen cover and kept dry, would last for fifty years.

Indeed, when a fire happens in a town, if the neighbours should have presence of mind sufficient to supply mattresses or beds for this purpose, or common carpets, much inconvenience and even danger might be avoided.

, We may add, that when fires happen in livery stables, or in domestic offices in the country, cattle are too often lost through the silly alarm and hurry of the people concerned. It ought, therefore, always to be remembered, that if a horse does not see the fire, he will not be more unwilling to leave the stable then, than at any other time. In fact, generally speaking, a horse accustomed to be led out for pasture, without saddle, bridle, or harness, will not oppose any difficulty; but if others hesitate, from the novelty of the thing, throw a saddle or some part of their usual geer on them, and the difficulty ceases.

We have spoken of fires as arising from overheated chimnies; but they may happen from many other points of carelessness, at first sight apparently unimportant.

Fires will happen from pokers being left in the grate until red hot, when the burning of the fuel, by a diminution of resistance against their gravity, permits them to fall out; when they too often roll from off the edge of the fender upon the carpet The poker ought always, when used in this manner, to be laid across the top of the grate, or to be placed sloping in front, so as that it shall not become red hot while serving as a conductor of radiant heat to the immediately surrounding atmosphere thereby rendering it lighter and producing a current by the cold air rushing in. But the safest way of all is to have a guard, or shoulder, so fitted to the poker as to catch on the edges of the fender whenever it happens.

It is a well known fact that globular glass water bottles, placed in windows, have acted as burning glasses; and it ought to be known by all workmen, who require strong light, that the flasks they use to concentrate the light of the candle upon their work, are very powerful burning glasses. One of them will readily set fire to any inflammable substance which is placed so as to receive the sun's rays, after they have passed through it, at the point called the focus, that is, at about the distance of one and a half, or two inches from the surface opposite to that on which the sun shines. It is therefore advisable, to be careful where they are placed in the day time, as serious consequences might result from one of them standing in the sun; which a circumstance, that occurred lately, experimentally proves. A considerable quantity of smoke and a powerful smell of burning gave the alarm of fire; when, after searching some time, it was discovered that a cloth, which was wrapped round the neck of a flask that stood in the window of an unfrequented room, was in a flame, and such was the degree of combustion, that it was with difficulty the mansion was saved from destruction.

Domestic accidents often arise from descending into wells, nay even into cellars, unless some artificial mode of ventilation has been adopted. As prevention, in such cases, is better than cure, it may be prudent, in every doubtful case, to throw a ball of combustible matter into the well, if dry, or to suspend a blazing ball upon an iron rod, allowing it to descend by means of a longer line: or boiling water may be poured down; which, if in sufficient quantity, will so rarify the foul air at the bottom, as to cause it to ascend and make room for that of the atmosphere. It will be proper, however, for the operator to guard against the rising vapour, otherwise partial suffocation may ensue.

When entering a cellar badly ventilated, it will be proper to advance a candle upon the end of a long rod previously. If the candle continues to burn brightly, there is no danger: but, if the flame sickens, or expires, no person ought to enter until artificial ventilation has taken place; which may readily be done by means of a pair of common bellows fitted with a long tin or leather tube, which will speedily supply atmospherical air; for even when the bad or foul air is the heaviest, yet the action of blowing will give the wholesome fluid a degree of energy that will act as a lever, and force the foul air from its resting place.

The danger of *Drowning* can scarcely be reckoned amongst domestic accidents; but yet accidents of that kind have so often produced domestic sorrow, that one or two hints deserve notice here, in addition to the means promulgated by the Humane Society. It happens, unfortunately indeed, that persons, who cannot swim, falling into water, are too apt to lose their presence of mind; but if they can command their recollection, and have a hat on their head, it may be made to answer all the purposes of a cork jacket, simply by laying it on the water on its crown, or on its brim if more convenient, and holding it in an even position by the two sides: but if the individual thus exposed can keep himself afloat long enough to pass a handkerchief over the hat, thus enabling him to hold it by one hand, he will then find a resistance against sinking fully equal to the pressure of ten or a dozen pounds weight, which is more than the surplus of a man's weight in sea water, even when his clothes are fully saturated.

When accidents of this kind do happen, we ought not to despair too soon of the possibility of restoring life. We must persevere even after hope is gone: for many most extraordinary instances of recovery might here be recorded. Even when death appears the result of disease, the practice of

stripping off the bed-clothes and laying out, as it is
called, ought not to be too speedily adopted; especially with children after convulsions. A recent
very ingenious writer, observes, that " the means
proper to be pursued in cases where it is doubted if
death has taken place, are extremely simple. The
body should lie in bed undisturbed, and occasionally, if the lips and mouth appear parched, they
should be moistened with wine and water. If the
weather be hot or sultry, the curtains of the bed
ought to be drawn aside, and the room freely ventilated. In cold weather a pan of coals should be
at intervals drawn over the bed, so as to keep up a
gentle warmth ; by doing this, we aid the powers of
nature to restore the patient, if the body be alive;
or, if death has taken place, we more speedily bring
on putrefaction, relieving the friends from a state
of dreadful anxiety. As soon as a livid greenish
hue is observed about the face or breast, and the
limbs, which were once rigid, become again pliant,
we may be certain the fatal catastrophe has taken
place."

As nothing ought to be left untried in cases of
suffocation, whether from drowning or foul air, or
convulsions, we shall venture to introduce here some
observations rather of a more scientific nature than
the general purpose of this little work ; but we
shall carefully avoid all technicality beyond what is
absolutely necessary for coming at the useful result.
A chemical philosopher, of some known eminence,
being desirous of witnessing the progressive effects
of carbonic oxide when freely respired, with a view
to comparative analogy in reference to nitrous oxide,
lately made an experiment, which had nearly proved
fatal to him. Having carefully prepared a considerable quantity of the gas, he first noticed some
points of resemblance between it and the nitrous

oxide, particularly the remarkable sweetish taste; and having first exhausted his lungs of common air as completely as possible, next made three or four inspirations of the gas, and immediately fell upon the floor senseless, and indeed apparently lifeless, pulsation being nearly extinct. Various means were employed for his recovery, but in vain, by several medical gentlemen who were present; at length the introduction of oxygen gas by compression into the lungs was suggested and tried. A rapid return of animation ensued, accompanied, however, by convulsive agitations, excessive headache, and quick irregular pulsation. For some time after mental recovery, total blindness, extreme sickness, and vertigo, with alternations of heat and shivering cold, were painfully experienced, and were succeeded by an unconquerable propensity to sleep, which was broken and feverish. An emetic of tartarised antimony removed these alarming symptoms, and the only unpleasant effects felt the following day were those occasioned by the fall. Though this alarming accident prevented the observation of the phenomena which was the object of the experiment, yet, from its results, we may fairly deduce that oxygen gas would prove highly efficacious in cases of suspended animation produced by carbonic acid, choke-damps, and other suffocating gases; and we trust that no one will now be suffered to go down to the grave, after all other means have failed, without trying the application of oxygen gas, which, in the metropolis particularly, may be prepared by a skilful chemist in sufficient time to give it a fair trial, whenever the accident is instantly taken in hand. Its effects, even after half an hour's immersion in water, ought not to be despaired of.

As accidents often happen from substances not intentionally swallowed, some notice must here be taken of them. The swallowing of pins by children is often attended with very dangerous consequences, especially when there are no ready means at home of attempting a cure. It is important therefore to mention that an individual, very recently, who was informed of a neighbour having swallowed a pin, administered four grains of tartar emetic in warm water, and afterwards prevailed upon the patient to drink the white from six eggs, which coagulated upon the stomach before the tartar operated, enveloped the pin, and brought it up.—There is also a well authenticated instance upon record, of a person, who swallowed 24 pins, being made to throw up the whole by the above method. The same may be used with success for fish and other sharp bones.

We may also record, that whenever any of the preparations of opium, henbane, nightshade, hemlock, tobacco, fox-glove or stramonium, or any poisonous fungus mistaken for mushrooms, or spirituous liquors in excess, or any other unknown matters, have been swallowed, exciting sickness without pain of the stomach, or producing giddiness, drowsiness, or sleep, it will be proper to give instantly one table-spoonful of flour of mustard in water, and repeat it in copious draughts of warm water, constantly, until vomiting takes place. If the person becomes so insensible as not to be easily roused, give the mustard in vinegar, instead of water, and rub and shake the body actively and incessantly.

Caution, however, must be used with regard to the vinegar, as a judicious chemist has laid it down as a system of rules, to be observed in these cases, that vegetable acids always hasten death when introduced into the stomach with narcotics; that acidulated water is very useful in counteracting the effects of narcotics, after they have been rejected by vomiting: thus animals, which would infallibly have died within an hour, have been saved for 24 or 36 hours by the administration of doses of water acidulated by a little vinegar; that a strong infusion of coffee is an antidote to narcotics; that the decoction of coffee is much less efficacious than the infusion; that camphor is not a counterpoison to narcotics, though it diminishes their effects when administered in small doses; that water and mucilaginous preparations, instead of being beneficial, accelerate death, because they promote the absorption of the poison; that bleeding is never injurious, but frequently sufficient to restore plethoric animals, which would nevertheless die in two or three days without proper attention, and that it is always best to open the jugular vein; that chlorine acts nearly in the same manner as vegetable acids.

It has been observed, upon good authority, that when mineral poisons, technically called oxide, whether of copper or arsenic, are taken inwardly, one table spoonful of powdered charcoal is a complete antidote, mixed with either honey, butter or treacle, taken immediately: within two hours administer either an emetic or a cathartic; in this case the effect of the poison is prevented.

Note also, that when oil of vitriol has been swallowed, water alone must by no means be used, on account of the excessive heat produced by the mixture; but it may be taken thickened with chalk, magnesia, or soap; or oil may be freely administered. When it has been spilt on the skin or clothes, tear off the clothes and wipe the skin, to free it as much as possible from the acid, before washing with water.

But when spirits of salt, or aquafortis, have been swallowed, or spilt upon the skin, immediately

drink, or wash the part with large quantities of
water; and, as soon as they can be procured, add
soap or potash, or chalk, to the water.

Finally, whenever a preparation of arsenic,
mercury, or of any metal, or when any unknown
substance or matter, has been swallowed, and there
have speedily ensued heat of the mouth and throat,
violent pain of the stomach, retching and vomiting, immediately drink plenty of warm water, with
common soap scraped or dissolved in it. Two or
three quarts of warm water, with from three or
four ounces to half a pound of soap, will not be
too much.

A wasp or bee, inadvertently swallowed, may
be killed before it can do any absolute harm, by
instantly taking a tea-spoonful of common salt and
suffering it to dissolve. It not only kills the insect,
but cures the sting. Indeed salt, at all times, will
operate as a cure for external stings; but it is proper that the sting itself, if left in the wound, should
first be extracted. Then apply, *ad libitum*,
sweet oil, or *eau de luce*, or pounded mallows, or
onions, which are all equally efficacious, though the
salt may be the readiest remedy.

We shall close this essay on Domestic Accidents
by one hint that may sometimes be worth remem-
bering, provided the Domestic Economy is not
regulated upon the principle of Mr. Shandy's parlour door-hinge!

In retired rural situations, a temporary inconvenience is sometimes experienced from want of repairs, that cannot instantly be attended to. Amongst
others we may reckon the breaking of window sash-
lines, as a minor domestic evil: but a simple and
most ingenious contrivance may be adopted in lieu,
which will render them at all times unnecessary.

Bore three or four holes into each side of the

ascending sash, into which insert common bottle corks, leaving a projection of about one sixteenth of an inch beyond the surface; when it will be found that the elastic pressure of the cork is always sufficient to keep the window up, without opposing any resistance to its being pulled down.

TRAVELLING.

In this wandering age, when ladies explore Pyramids, and gentlemen propose to visit the North Pole upon dandy accelerators it may not be uninteresting to know how six months' provisions can be packed up in a ridicule, or a cream-pot replenished in Spitzbergen.

The first of these objects, it appears, may now be easily accomplished; as an indefatigable experimentalist asserts that, after various attempts, he has succeeded in forming a vegetable compound, by which persons engaged in exploring hot and desart regions, may be saved from perishing by hunger and thirst. The ingredients are few, reducible to a small bulk, and not liable, in a state of composition, to spoil by keeping. With a pint of jelly, made from starch with boiling water, mix two ounces of gum arabic and half a drachm of catechu, both previously reduced to powder; and to the whole then add one drachm of crystallized citric acid, also pulverized. Spread the compound upon a clean board or paper, and gradually dry it in an oven of a gentle heat, till it becomes hard and brittle, when it may be broken into pieces of a proper size for being carried in the pocket. Dr. Pearson calculates that two ounces of this compound will sustain life for 24 hours, but supposes that during the exertion of travelling, four ounces may be required; so that 2lbs. would last a person, totally destitute of every other sort of aliment, eight days, by which time he would probably arrive at some place where other food might be procured.

It is possible, however, after such a feast in duodecimo, that the philosophic tourist may wish for something to drink; and we find that an ingenious French chemist, after an examination of the means which are, or may be adopted, for the preservation of fresh water at sea, gives the preference to the following: $1\frac{1}{2}$ parts of oxide of manganese in powder are mixed with 250 parts of water, and agitated every 15 days. In this way water has been preserved unchanged for seven years.

We have not yet, indeed, discovered a mode by which a butt of water can be abridged into the size of a canteen, and therefore adventurous tourists to the banks of the Nile may, in the dry season especially, find nothing but turbid water to wash down their culinary *multum in parvo*. To remedy even that defect, chemistry steps in with its aid, and the bad taste and unpleasant odour of Egyptian springs, may now be corrected by mixing a small portion of magnesia, and submitting the water to manual agitation.

Generally speaking, when water begins to grow putrid, it may be sufficiently purged by throwing in a handful of salt, and, if salt is wanting, sea-water. For this reason, therefore, the seamen at Venice, when bound on a long voyage, take their supply of water from St. Nicholas's well; which, by being near the sea, is impregnated with salt, and on that account continues long pure and wholesome, the brackish taste being scarce, after a few days, perceptible. We read of the like in the Scriptures to have been done by the Prophet Elisha; who, in Jericho of Palestine, by throwing salt into a fountain, made the waters potable, which before ware, brackish and putrid. If the water begins to engender maggots, they are killed by throwing in lime. Any of the ingredients used for the clarifying of wine, may be applicable towards the purifying, and preserving of water.

For exploratory breakfasts, whether to Baffin's Bay, or to the source of the Nile, preserve eggs by packing in small casks, or tin cases, and fill up with melted mutton suet.

Preserve cream by adding half its quantity of powdered white sugar, and boiling it.

POOR.

So much has already been said upon this interesting subject, in voluminous tracts, that it may well be supposed there is little of novelty to offer upon it: but, as to curtail the poors' rates must now be an immense saving in domestic expenses, we shall endeavour to collect every practical hint, and every practicable fact, that has transpired on that head, within the last few years, and which has not yet been embodied into any of the prevailing systems.

In doing this, we trust that we shall be, in some measure, the means of suggesting to various individuals opportunities of doing good, which might otherwise have escaped their observation, teaching them to cultivate charity as a useful political science, and not a mere instinct or impulse of the moment; thus enabling them to experience all the pleasure which benevolence never fails to impart, and without the pain of witnessing those evils which indiscriminate bounty too often occasions.

In fact, we wish, whilst prompting to active and judicious benevolence, to guard our readers against any thing like indiscriminate charity, either indi-

vidually or in the aggregate, except on particular
and pressing occasions. We wish to shew them
that real charity consists more in the prevention of
distress, than in its relief; inasmuch as every
pound expended in the one case, does twice as
much good as in the other. For truly has it been
said, that the immense sums which have been raised
for the relief of the poor, when they are exhausted,
leave them in no better situation than that in
which they were before; and no traces are left to
evince the good that has been done. Had such
money been expended in works of utility or em-
bellishment, either for the benefit of the public, or
of the persons who raised the money, it would have
afforded equal relief. to the labourer, and the improvement executed would have transmitted to
posterity a memorial of the public spirit which
carried it into effect, and at the same time afforded
assistance to the distressed. We mean not, in these
observations, to suggest any thing against those
laudable exertions by which age and infirmity are
relieved; but only to offer hints on the improvidence
which, we conceive, is evinced in supporting health
and vigour in idleness, with so great a hazard of
contaminating the morals and debasing the character of our honest peasantry.

In this point of view, and to establish our principle, we shall first select a few important and well
authenticated facts; some at home, and others of
foreign experiment.

In the first place, it is worthy of record, that a
very few years back the farmers of Dauncey, in
Wilts, let to the poor labourers of their parish,
who had large families, three acres of land, at two
pounds per acre; and soon afterwards the late
Lord Peterborough gratuitously built a barn for
them, where they could thrash their corn; the

consequence was, that those men had their names immediately struck off the parish book; have brought up their families to industry and honesty, and all of them now cheerfully pay to the aged and infirm of the said parish their regular rates. The farmers declare that the parish have saved hundreds by this plan. The gentlemen and farmers of Great Comerford, in the same county, are now pursuing a similar plan, by letting the same number of acres to the poor with large families and paying their taxes. Each farmer allows according to the extent of his farm.

From Warwickshire we can present a proof that the culture of land by hand labour, is a most suitable employment for parochial poor, afforded by the testimony of an intelligent gentleman, at Birmingham. He says—" He was an overseer of the poor in the years 1817 and 1818; that there were 800 adult poor in the workhouse, for whom there was no employment; that about thirty acres of land belonged to the town; that these were let to different tenants; but that four acres were obtained, on which they planted cabbages and potatoes, and obtained a sufficient supply for 600 persons in the house, from July to September. In March, 1818, he took seven and a half acres more, and cultivated two acres in flax. The soil was hard and sterile, but being dug by the spade, and the turf buried without manure, it soon had a most promising appearance."

In Leicestershire, also, in the village of Thrussington, inclosed about twenty-four years since, the Earl of Essex is a considerable proprietor. At the time of inclosure, the noble earl had four cottages and twenty-six acres of land laid out, which were let to four labouring men at the commissioners' value; these four men have amply compensated

for the noble Earl's liberality, in bringing up thirty-
two children, without any assistance from the
parish ; most of whom are in service, and of excellent character in their situations. If the great
land-owners would follow this noble Earl's example,
the poor-rates throughout the country, it is now felt,
would be considerably reduced, and industry and
sobriety laudably encouraged.

From Germany we shall present only one instance, but it is a custom worthy of imitation ; and
the good effects of which are already apparent.

In the duchy of Gotha there are many villages
which obtain a rent of 200 or 800 dollars, or more,
for their fruit trees planted on the road-side, and
on the commons. Every new married couple is
bound to plant two young fruit trees. The rent is
applied to parochial purposes, (at present to payment of the debts incurred during the late wars.)
In order to preserve the plantations from injury,
the inhabitants of the parish are all made answer-
able : each of whom is thus on the watch over the
other ; and if any one is caught in the act of com-
mitting any injury, all the damage done in the
same year, the authors of which cannot be discovered, is attributed to him, and he is compelled
to atone for it, according to its extent, either by
fine, or by corporal punishment.

In England we are very careless of the comforts of
our poorer brethren ; for though, with the indolent
pride of wealth, we give them our money for their
actual support, yet we never take the trouble to
consider of how much more service it might be to
them, by a more judicious expenditure of the same
sums. A gentleman at Colchester makes it a rule,
whenever he builds a cottage, to plant a vine against
its walls, and two or three apple or pear trees in
its garden, and thus he confers a greater benefit on

his tenant, by giving him an innocent source of gratification to his children, and an excitement to a little extra industry on his own part, than if he had let him a comfortless, mean-looking hovel, at half the rent.

Encouragement to industry is an object which ought always to be kept in view, alike by the benevolent contemplatist and the prudent calculator; and under this head, we cannot help noticing, with pleasure, a plan recently proposed, which united in itself that encouragement, together with a principle of economy, and of absolute active charity, striking at the very root of that feeling, or rather want of feeling, which prompts the labouring poor to depend too much upon the poors' rates for their safeguard against the accidents of life, or the consequences of their own idleness, and want of forethought.

An amiable clergyman, in Buckinghamshire, proposed, in conjunction with two or three other benevolent persons in his parish, so far on the plan of the saving banks, to receive the earnings or savings of such persons as were regular in attendance on divine service, and to repay the entire amount at the end of the year, together with a premium of one-third or fourth of the whole, by way of remuneration to them for their industry and frugality. Suppose a poor man lays by 6d. every week, from the 1st of January to the 31st of December, the total amount will be 26s: if to this an addition of one-fourth be made by any benevolent person who undertakes to do so, here is 1l. 12s. coming to the poor man at a time of the year when he most requires it; money which he may lay out in the purchase of firing or warm clothing, or articles of provision; money in part the produce of his own industry which he has saved in small sums with hardly any inconvenience to himself, and part the donation of his benevolent superior. This plan has since been followed with success in a small parish; where, though many grown persons were not induced to adopt it, the children of the parish-school did so with few exceptions, and thankfully received the amount of their savings, with whatever donation their benefactor was pleased to bestow.

Fourteen Sunday banks of this description have been instituted in different parishes in Hertfordshire; and may be considered as auxiliaries to the county saving banks, in which the depositors frequently deposit afterwards the principal part of their weekly accumulations.

It is indeed a practical truth, that employment and instruction are the only true helps and benefits for the vigorous poor.

If, therefore, upon a general system, tradesmen who cannot afford to purchase materials should be furnished with a small apartment, which the sale of their work may subsquently replace; or if ablebodied mendicants could obtain slips of waste ground to bring into tillage with potatoes, the poors' rates would diminish by means congenial to the moral sense and honest pride of human nature.

It has, therefore, been suggested, that if overseers of the poor were empowered to take land and let it out to poor families to cultivate, and supply them with seed, potatoes, carrots, and cabbage plants, the produce would be found a most seasonable supply to such families, and would tend very much to ease the poors' rates of such parishes. As there is much waste land in the kingdom, there can be no doubt but that many Lords of Manors would sanction such a plan.

That it would answer has been fully proved by the experiment of an intelligent manufacturer in the west of England, who adopted something of this kind with his own workmen in the country some years past, and found it fully answer the desired effect. He let a quarter of an acre to each family; and supplied them with seed to stock it. Each quarter of an acre produced about twenty-five sacks of potatoes yearly, beside other vegetables; each family consumed from ten to twelve sacks of potatoes annually, the remainder was applied to fatting pigs, &c.

It is an important and established fact, as stated by the late worthy Secretary to the Board of Agriculture, that in the counties of Rutland and Lincoln, the practice is, to attach land to cottages, sufficient to support that number of cows which the cottager is able to purchase; they are tenants to the chief landlords, and sub-tenants to farmers, yet these latter are very generally steady friends to the system: well they may be so, for the poors' rates are next to nothing, when compared with such as are found in parishes wherein this admirable system is not established. In the late minute enquiries made by the Board of Agriculture, into the state of the labouring poor throughout the kingdom, many persons were written to who reside in the districts where this system is common; and it was found by their replies, that the practice stands the test of the present distress, as well as it supported the opposite difficulties of extreme scarcity. It is much to be regretted, that so admirable an example is not copied in every part of the kingdom. In those counties where no such practice is met with, it is very rare indeed to meet with a labourer who has saved any money; their reliance is entirely on the parish, and their present earnings dissipated at the ale-house: not so in Lincolnshire; the man who wishes to marry, saves his money to buy cows;

and girls who design to have husbands, take the
same measures to secure them.   Sobriety, industry,
and economy are thus secured ; and children are
trained from their infancy to the culture of a garden, and to attending cattle, instead of starving with
unemployed spinning-wheels.   No object can better
deserve the attention of men of considerable landed
property : for, if some change of management, deci-
sive in its nature, does not take place, poors' rates
will continue to increase, till they will absorb the
wholel anded revenue of the kingdom.

That indefatigable philanthropist thus now speaks
from the grave ; we trust that his sentiments will
not be lost upon our readers.

The venerable Bishop of Chester also most
strongly recommends a mode once adopted by himself, among the married labourers at Wallingham,
near Cambridge, at the time he was rector of that
parish.   His lordship divided a certain quantity of
glebe lands into allotments of half and single acres;
and each labourer, with a family, was allowed to
rent one of these allotments, at the rate of three
guineas per acre a year.   Upon this land, with the
assistance of a little common grazing, they were,
in most instances, soon able to keep a cow and a
pig ; to raise more than sufficient vegetables for
their families ; to add materially to their comfort in
many minor respects ; and they were shortly
enabled to contribute to the parish funds, instead
of being consumers of them. " At the same time,"
adds his Lordship, " the men were kept from the
ale-house, their leisure time being more happily
occupied in cultivating their little spot of ground ·
the rent was always punctually paid, and the land
as well, if not better, cultivated, than any in the
parish."

It is universally allowed, that want of profitable

employment is the cause of the present distress of the poor; but the question naturally arises, What are the subordinate causes whence this great cause is produced? To answer this question in part, we cannot be blind to the fact that the increase of the number of large farms has rendered it possible to cultivate the same quantity of land with a smaller proportion of hands; and the consequent decrease of the number of small farms has made it more difficult for the poor man to subsist his family; for the great farmer will not accommodate him with a small quantity of meat, a little milk, or other trifling necessary, which the small farmer, attentive to the smallest profits, is willing to do.

Some part of the evil might, however, be alleviated, if spade husbandry were more attempted, where practicable. It appears that the Society for Bettering the Condition of the Poor, have received very conclusive calculations of the advantages to be derived from it. Among others, Mr. Taller, of Gateshead, near Newcastle (a gentleman to whom they were referred for information, by the venerable President of the Board of Agriculture,) has communicated a variety of important facts on this head. He gives an instance of lands cultivated by the spade, and the wheat *planted* in dibbles, producing the enormous return of *seventeen* quarters of wheat to the acre! The average produce in the ordinary mode of cultivation, is not more than *four* quarters; so that the extra expense is more than repaid fourfold; the expense of *digging* an acre of ordinary land, at nursery price, he states to be 33s.; and this, he adds, is an operation worth two ploughings; and besides, by planting the wheat, there is a great saving in seed. In the usual mode of broad-cast, it requires two bushels to the acre; but in planting, one peck is sufficient. Mr. T. also states, that by spade husbandry, he has made an

acre of land produce the almost incredible quantity
of. 800 bushels! and he gives it as his opinion, that
the more general use of the spade would have the
most beneficial effect, not only upon the agricultural labourers themselves, but on their employers
also; for although the farmer might not be able to
find labourers to cultivate large quantities of land
in this way, he might at least cultivate sufficient to
employ his quota of the labourers of his parish,
and so at onc eexonerate the poors' rates, and be himself amply repaid.

This seems to establish the utility of the practice
beyond all doubt; but where nothing better can be
done we would even recommend almost unproductive labour, rather than encourage absolute idleness; and, upon this head, we cannot but admire
the laudable plan not long since adopted at Frome
for the relief of the industrious poor. So many as
were out of employ, on application to the parish
officers, were instantly engaged in quarrying stones
by the load, at which they earned eight or ten shillings per week; the stones were then taken to a
depôt, and disposed of for the purposes of building,
and repairing the roads.

It must indeed be admitted that where the poor
are thrown out of employment from stagnation in
any particular branch of business, it can be of only
small avail to employ them in manufacturing goods
of a species with which the market is already over-
stocked; but with a little examination we might
discover modes of manufacturing specific articles
for which we are at present indebted to foreign
countries, a practice that would be clear of the
foregoing objection.

In our maritime districts one simple and easy
mode of employment, and of profitable employment
also, presents itself.

A patent was granted, in 1780 (of which the term is now expired), for a new invented British barilla, the method of making which is as follows:— To any quantity of wood ashes, add an equal quantity of the ashes of ferns, whins, thistles, rushes, or bean or pea-straw; sift them through a fine sieve, and add to them an equal quantity of soapers' waste ashes; all these being thoroughly mixed together, there is to be added one twelfth of fine quick-lime: these different materials are to be put into an iron pan, and boiled two days and two nights, with a sufficient quantity of sea water, which is to be renewed from time to time; the mass is then put into a reverberating furnace, and fused for about an hour, which, when cooled, is the British barilla.

Of the numerous plans which have been proposed for the alleviation of the distressed state of the poor, those appear to be far preferable, in which the pauper is obliged to earn his subsistence in some way or other; by which means his natural habits of industry and economy are kept alive; he is prevented from associating with persons of an idle and profligate disposition, as he would very probably do for no other purpose than that of killing the time which lay heavy on his hands, in a state of idleness so unnatural to him. In many parishes in the country, the poor who could not be fully employed have been supported altogether from the rates, generally in proportion to the size of their family. Certainly no greater reward could be held out for idleness, than to pay a man for doing nothing, equally with another whose day is passed in hard labour.

Here then is at once a supply of labour so easy and plain as to be practicable for the most uninformed, even for women and children, in many of its details; so cheap as to require little capital, and with the advantage of supplying us with that which at present we are forced to purchase from foreigners. This is surely worth the experiment.

Let it be remembered too that money raised for the relief of the poor has frequently been expended in a profuse manner; thereby encouraging them to depend on the parish for support, and rendering them thoughtless of providing for themselves.

In contradistinction to this we shall offer some practical hints of what has been done to make the poor support themselves, independent of the poors' rates. The first we shall select took place very recently in Surrey, where some public spirited inhabitants of the parish of Dorking, at the head of whom was the late lamented Earl of Rothes, associated for the purpose of trying whether the labouring classes might not be induced to place their future relief on a more independent foundation than parish charity, by saving a portion of the fruits of their industry. The success of this experiment surpassed the most sanguine expectations. The scale of contributions was proportioned to the number of each family dependent on the head of it for support: the lowest, for a single person, 6s. a year; and highest, where there were five or more in family 24s. a year. There were 263 subscribers in the class that might require relief: representing in the aggregate of the families above 1000 individuals, nearly one-third of the entire population of the parish, and above one-half of the labouring class: not one of these was deficient in the weekly payments, which enabled the committee, aided by the liberal subscriptions of the more opulent classes, to afford relief to the subscribers according to their several necessities during thirteen weeks of a bad winter, by distributing 2,982 quartern loaves, 906 pounds of meat, 742 bushels of coals, and 1,978 faggots. This kept upwards of 80 families from seeking parish relief, and afforded essential temporary comfort to the whole 1000, without any feeling of degradation, or a known murmur or complaint.

The Penny Society, established in Mansfield in 1815, has in one year been enabled to relieve 102 persons; thirty-two poor women having received a bed-gown, flannel-petticoat, shift, and a pair of stockings each; the same number of poor men, a hat, a shirt, and a pair of stockings; and twenty poor persons a blanket each. The clothes were made up by the ladies, and the whole carried on without any expense.

Through the benevolent exertions of some ladies of Winchester, a subscription was set on foot of *one penny weekly;* and from 300 subscribers, and a few donations, 150 persons were relieved with coals, blankets, and warm clothing during the winter months. This donation was received with great gratitude, and many poor people voluntarily offered to subscribe on their own account.

An institution, denominated a *Penny Club*, has been formed at Cheltenham; the intent of which is to teach the parents and children a habit of economy, by shewing them how much may be done by small savings. Each scholar contributes a penny weekly: to this small sum are added the subscriptions and donations of honorary members, in the parish and elsewhere, which are divided once a year, and expended in such articles of clothing as the children stand most in need of.

There is, at Howden, a working society of young ladies, who meet every Thursday evening during the winter half-year, for the benevolent purpose of making clothing for the children of the poor in Howden, of materials procured by subscription

among themselves and others who admire their
labours of charity ; and during the last season they
have furnished to the poor, gratis, nearly 400 articles of clothing.

Young ladies, thus amiably disposed, will considerably add to the benefit of their exertions by
kindly devoting a few hours occasionally, not only
to working for the poor, but also in teaching them
to work for themselves; as many females who have
been brought up in factories, and manufactories of
different kinds, from their infancy, are very deficient
in the arts of sewing, cutting out, contriving and
mending : insomuch that when they marry, which
they usually do very young, they are soon at a loss
how to cloathe their families, and let their children
flaunt it in the cast-off garments which may be bestowed upon them, without any proper alterations,
so that they look among their little companions
like the daw in borrowed plumes; or like that
member of the same family, whose office it is to be
perched up among the corn, to scare the rest of
the feathered race from coming near it. A school
opened for young women once or twice a week, to
teach them their domestic duties, would produce the
happiest effects under the superintendence of some
benevolent lady, who might add to her instructions
a few plain directions as to the making of broth,
and preparing their humble fare in the most frugal,
and yet the most palatable and nourishing manner.
Mrs. Melroe's Economical Cookery will be found
a great help to a design of this kind, and a most
useful present to the cottager's wife at a very trifling
expense, as the work itself consists of merely a few
pages, and contains no account of dishes beyond
the power of the industrious labouring man to
procure.

To these instances of judicious general philan-

throphy, we shall add but two of individual benevolence, though we have numerous specimens before us.

The Earl of Dartmouth, whose example ought
to be held up to the imitation of the opulent, recently spent the winter at his seat, personally visit-
ing and relieving his poor neighbours. His chari-
ties during that time were very extensive; his
draper's bill for bed-clothes alone amounted to
£500. A hundred quarts of soup were also daily
distributed by his cooks: and these favours were
heightened by a kindness of manner which rendered
them doubly acceptable to the poorest.

Sir John Sebright, not long since, adopted an
excellent plan in the village of Flamstead, where
he resides. He has apportioned certain plots of
waste ground to the poor, for gardens, and he gives
various premiums to those who cultivate them, so
as to secure the best crops.

In addition to these active exertions, we feel
anxious to give increased publicity to another useful hint.

The poor have in many instances formed asso-
ciations or benefit clubs among themselves, for the
relief of the members when sick; but in no instance, we believe, have they yet made provision
for the deserving members who have been long subscribers, when they begin to experience the infirmi-
ties of nature; yet how desirable that a virtuous
and industrious peasant should in the decline of
life experience some of those comforts which he
then so much requires, without being obliged to
exert himself as he did in the days of his youth!
This can be effected only by an active co-operation
of the rich with their poorer brethren, and we
would suggest, that in order to create a fund for
the aged, as well as to supply occasional calls, such

as sickness, every poor person who is a member should have some friend who would subscribe a large sum, suppose 5l. or 10l. which should be immediately put out at interest for a period of twenty years, at the end of which time the accumulated interest thence accruing might afford a supply for the relief of the poorer member when sinking into years and decrepitude.*

We shall merely add that a very original and striking suggestion has lately appeared respecting the formation of *National Circulating Libraries*, for the use of the lower orders. Having given them the capacity for reading, it seems but right that we should now furnish them with the most useful and amusing books which are fitted to their situations. To this end it has been proposed, that in each large and populous town a cheap circulating library should be established entirely for their use and convenience, consisting of short and plain tracts, and books on most subjects, especially on those which are connected with the improvement of the labouring orders. Of course, neither controversial divinity, nor political pamphlets, should be admitted. The books being short, and consisting chiefly of tracts, there would be no great expense in the first formation of this library; and it might afterwards be supported by its own subscriptions. This measure would be productive of great advantages to the people at large; it would gradually draw them off from that exclusive attention to

---

* Whilst this sheet is in the press, we observe in the daily papers the important announcement, that the parish of Greenwich, by dint of judicious regulations, and by a careful expenditure, have, during the past year, 1820, reduced their poors' rates from £16,000 to £9,250! This is completely a practical illustration of the plans and hints here recorded.

politics which so often engenders party violence; it would carry forward the public mind in the path of useful knowledge, and would be the strongest practicable remedy which could be adopted in a free country to counteract the licentiousness of the press.

Ideas often presented to the understanding will affect the heart, and influence the conduct; and books where morality assumes the gay aspect of amusement may engage young persons at home, when without those pleasing resources they might abuse intervals of leisure in the haunts of vice.

THE END.

LONDON:

SHACKELL AND ARROWSMITH, JOHNSON'S-COURT.

INDEX.

a

WORKS

LATELY PUBLISHED BY

HENRY COLBURN AND CO.

CONDUIT STREET.

---

1. The **ART** of **EMPLOYING TIME** to the greatest Advantage—the true Source of Happiness, 1 vol, post 8vo, 9s. 6d.

    Time is the only property of which we should be avaricious. The art of employing it is but the art of being happy.

2. **HISTORY** of **CULTIVATED VEGETABLES**, comprising their Botanical, Medicinal, Edible and Chemical Qualities, Natural History, and relation to Art, Science, and Commerce. By HENRY PHILLIPS, Author of the Pomarium Britannicum, or History of Fruits known in Great Britain, 2 vols, 8vo.

    Also by the same Author,

3. The **HISTORY** of **FRUITS** known in **GREAT BRITAIN**, Second Edition, in 1 vol, 8vo, 10s. 6d, boards.

    " We know of no class of readers which is not much obliged to Mr Phillips for this very useful and very entertaining publication. It is one of those popular works, which combining in a happy degree the pleasing with the instructive, teach us science as an amusement, and promote information and improvement by lively anecdote and curious story. From the most learned horticulturist, to the least anxious epicure that bites an apple, this volume deserves a friendly reception; and we are sure that it only needs to be known to become a favourite. For extent of information, utility, and most of the other good qualities, which can be desired in a production of its kind, it is really deserving of the warmest eulogy." *Literary Gazette.*

4. The **FLORIST'S MANUAL**, or Hints for the Construction of a Gay Flower Garden ; with Observations on the best method of preventing the depredations of insects, &c.; to which is added, a Catalogue of Plants, with their colours, as they appear in each season. By the Autheress of 'Botanical Dialogues,' and ' Sketches of the Physiology of Vegetable Life,' with two engraved plans, price 4s. 6d. boards.

---

14. PRIVATE EDUCATION; or, a Practical Plan
for the Studies of YOUNG LADIES, with an Address to Parents,
Private Governesses, and their Pupils. By ELIZABETH
APPLETON. 2nd edition, 1 vol. 7s. 6d.

" This work is judiciously adapted to become a useful manual in the hands
of persons who are desirous of securing for their tender charge all the advantages of elegant literature, and the accomplishments of polished manners,
without putting to capricious hazard those pure and firm principles which
can alone render them useful in this world, and happy in the next."

15. The HERMIT in LONDON; or, Sketches of
ENGLISH MANNERS. New Edition, 3 vols. small 8vo.
Price 21s.

16. The HERMIT in the COUNTRY. By the same
Author. 3 vols. 18s.

" Quite weary grown
Of all the follies of the town,
And seeing in all public places
The same vain fops, and painted faces."

THE NEW MONTHLY MAGAZINE,
And Literary Journal, for the year, 1821.

Containing Poems and Lectures on Poetry, by THOMAS CAMP-
BELL, ESQ.—The Journal of Jonathan Kentucky.—Doblado's
Letters from Spain.—Walks in the Garden, and upwards of 200
other Original Articles, in Prose and Verse, on subjects of Literature, Philosophy, Morals, Manners, &c. may now be had Complete, with Titles, Indexes, &c. in 3 vols, 8vo. price £2. 2s.
boards; and those who desire to possess this Work from its commencement, are requested to send their orders without delay, to
their respective Booksellers or Newsmen. It may also be regularly transmitted abroad, by applying to the General Post Office,
or to any local Postmaster.

296
J

Lightning Source UK Ltd.
Milton Keynes UK
UKHW020801081118
331957UK00010B/1055/P